HALF A MILLION STRONG

The New American Canon: The Iowa Series in
Contemporary Literature and Culture

SAMUEL COHEN, SERIES EDITOR

HALF A MILLION STRONG

Crowds and Power from Woodstock to Coachella

GINA ARNOLD

UNIVERSITY OF IOWA PRESS, IOWA CITY

University of Iowa Press, Iowa City 52242
Copyright © 2018 by the University of Iowa Press
www.uipress.uiowa.edu
Printed in the United States of America

Design by Lindsay Starr

The University of Iowa Press is a member of Green Press
Initiative and is committed to preserving natural resources.

Printed on acid-free paper

Library of Congress Cataloging-in-Publication Data
Names: Arnold, Gina, author.
Title: Half a million strong : crowds and power from
    Woodstock to Coachella / by Gina Arnold.
Description: Iowa City : University of Iowa Press, 2018. |
    Series: The new American canon: the Iowa series
    in contemporary literature and culture | Includes
    bibliographical references and index. |
Identifiers: LCCN 2018014099 (print)
    LCCN 2018015994 (ebook)
    ISBN 978-1-60938-609-2
    ISBN 978-1-60938-608-5 (pbk. : alk. paper)
Subjects: LCSH: Music festivals—Social aspects—United
    States—History. | Music festivals—United States—History.
Classification: LCC ML3917.U6 (ebook)
LCC ML3917.U6 A76 2018 (print)
    DDC 781.64078/73—dc23
    LC record available at https://lccn.loc.gov/2018014099

Contents

vii   ACKNOWLEDGMENTS

1   Introduction

9   Chapter 1: Millions Like Us

19   Chapter 2: Our Friends Electric

35   Chapter 3: California Dreamin'

57   Chapter 4: Networks R Us: The US Festival, 1982–1983

81   Chapter 5: The Chevy and the Levee

107   Chapter 6: Girls Gone Wild

123   Chapter 7: A Peculiar Euphoria: Raves, Crowds, and Freedom

141   Chapter 8: Hardly Strictly Utopian, Hardly Strictly Bluegrass

163   Conclusion: Small Is Beautiful

179   NOTES

185   BIBLIOGRAPHY

197   INDEX

Acknowledgments

The only true crowd is the one that precedes us.
—ELIAS CANETTI

WHEN I STARTED GRADUATE SCHOOL at Stanford University in 2003, an idea for a dissertation topic eluded me. I'd messed around with ideas about the fiction of nonfiction, news in fiction, and what might now be called "fake news" in fiction, but the whole concept of writing a book-length essay was anathema to me. At one point, someone told me, "It will come to you all of a sudden, sometime in your third year," and that is exactly what happened. It arrived, midway through my third year, fully formed, like a ripe pear of sorts, in one perfect thought bubble above my head, during a German Studies class that was taught by a visiting professor named Andreas Dorschel. The class had exactly two people in it, myself and a girl named Kate, and we were reading exactly two books, *Masse und Macht* by Elias Canetti and *Group Psychology and the Analysis of the Ego* by Sigmund Freud. Every meeting, Kate and I and Professor Dorschel would comb over some theme in both texts, and then Kate and I would bike to yoga together afterward. One day, a particularly noxious passage stood out to me, notable in part because of its gendered language and the bizarre image it conjured up, one that was both different from yet strangely similar to many of the grunge shows I'd attended the previous decade.

> We only have to think of a troop of women and girls, all of them in love in an enthusiastically sentimental way, who crowd round a singer or pianist after his performance. It would certainly be easy for each of them to be jealous of the rest; but, in face of their numbers and the consequent impossibility of their reaching the aim of their love, they renounce it, and, instead of pulling out one another's hair, they act as a united group, do homage to the hero of the occasion with their common actions, and would probably be glad to have a share of his flowing locks. (Freud, *Group Psychology* 87)

Ping! "Rock Crowds and Power." It came to me unbidden, and what was more, the minute I thought of it, I knew exactly what I wanted to do: theorize about the many rock festival crowds that I had participated in as a rock critic throughout the 1990s, uninterrupted by the aesthetic problems that plagued me as a journalist. Rather than weigh up the pros and cons of various rock acts, or rock 'n' roll itself, I thought it would be nice to take a step back from the world that I came from and think about why it existed in the first place. What was its appeal? What was its purpose? What was at stake? According to Freud, joining crowds is a libidinal urge. According to Canetti, it is a biological imperative. According to me, it is neither. By the end of yoga that day, I knew what I hoped would be in each chapter, more or less, and from then until today, my concept hasn't really changed much, except for the fact that rock festivals have, if anything, become bigger and better attended and are much more of a universal youth experience for Americans than they were in 2006.

The bulk of this book was conceived of and written as part of that dissertation, and it's fair to say that it certainly would not have been possible without the help and encouragement of the following people, first and foremost, my dissertation advisor and committee members, Andrea Lunsford, Ursula Heise, and Fred Turner. Also at Stanford, Franco Moretti, Jeffrey Schnapp, and Hayden White, as well as Henry Lowood, who pointed me toward the Apple Archives. I am indebted also to Monica Moore, Paula Moya, Shantal Marshall, and the program in Critical Studies of Race and Ethnicity, the latter of which helped to fund my final two years at Stanford. I'd also like to give my most heartfelt thanks to Sam Cohen for his championship of this manuscript at the University of Iowa Press, as well as to my peer reviewers, Greil Marcus and Kevin Dettmar.

Everyone who was interviewed or quoted herein was of course of the greatest of help, as were the many people whose interest in my work predated my time at Stanford and who furthered my career as a rock journalist roaming the *actual* fields of rock crowds and power. On that front, I'd like to give a special shout-out to Stuart Ross, Ted Gardner, and Mark Geiger, who shepherded me across America with Lollapalooza several years running, a formative experience that shaped most of my thoughts herein. My thanks also to Dawn Holliday and the late Warren Hellman, and, in another vein entirely, to George McKay, who has been wholly supportive of this project even in years when it fell fallow.

There are a ton of other people who contributed in ways small and large to this work, and I give them too my heartfelt thanks, but most of all, I want to thank my brother, Corry Arnold, who remained interested and enthusiastic throughout this decade-long project and who gave me many of the original ideas that sustained me throughout its writing. We always joke that he is my crack team of experts, and indeed he is. This book is dedicated to him.

HALF A MILLION STRONG

Introduction

I**T'S A FINE SUMMER DAY** sometime in the latter part of the twentieth century, and you are standing in a field smack dab in the middle of America—a beautiful field, a rural idyll, far from the ravages of civilization. It is the kind of field where novelists and filmmakers set their best scenes, where Tom Sawyer hides from Becky Thatcher and Shane gallops off into the sunset.

This field is a little different today, though. There are no bulls in this field. No cowpats, no flowers, no locusts, no amber waves of grain. Instead, the earthen floor has become a cesspool of loamy garbage. Also, the field is far from empty. All around you are other people, and they are wearing hardly any clothing because it is very, very hot. Let me repeat that. *It is very, very hot.* You're packed in tightly together with them, elbows locked to your body. It smells like teen spirit: sweet sweat, mown grass, suntan oil, and weed, an odor that will forever after remind you of this moment in your youth. The taste in your mouth is the stale beer you drank an hour and a half ago and now wish that you hadn't because you have to pee so badly. As for sound? It sounds like the skies are splitting open with noise—not exactly music, but a medley of different audibles, echoes, rhythms, fuzz, guitars, melody, and underlying it all, the low-buzzy monotone voices of the people behind you who are having an argument about where they parked their car and who is going to drive home and where to find their friends when this is all over. "This" is a music festival. In the angry distance there is a stage, so far off that the people on it look like tiny ants dancing about under a large, brightly colored set that's vaguely shaped like a dragon, or a castle, or a forest, shooting fire at you.

And for all that, it feels like utopia. Later tonight, you'll be stumbling around some other nearby field with your ears ringing, looking for your own car alongside the neighbors you will never see or recognize again; you're horribly sunburnt and tired and feeling like your eyeballs are stuck to the inside of your skull. Nevertheless, you will go home and tell everyone what a great time you had, and you won't even be lying. It will be true. Having been at that concert will have changed you, and that's not the only thing that will have changed. After today the very landscape will have changed its tone. Before today, this was the kind of field that, on other days and in other circumstances, was called "the middle of nowhere." But today and forever after it will be somewhere. From now on, people will drive by the exit you took on the freeway to get here and look out at this field with faraway eyes, remembering today. Forever after, there will be an imaginary geo-tag on this site, marking it for historical purposes as a place where *something important happened.*

A rock festival experience like this one is a rare shared memory for many an American. If you were a relatively young person between 1965 and now, you have probably, together with your peers, listened to music performed in a field somewhere very like the one described above and felt this form of collective transcendence. Before 1965, amplification technology just wasn't good enough for it to have happened in exactly this way. After the 2000s, smartphones, Wi-Fi, and social networks may well have changed the crowd experience into something more dispersed and less intense: something different. But for a forty-year stretch or so, the rock-festival crowd experience was a way that American teenagers forged for themselves a shared past, and in so doing, wrote themselves into history.

Initially, I called this book *Rock Crowds and Power*, after Nobel Prize–winning author Elias Canetti's book *Crowds and Power* (1960). My book has subsequently morphed into a snapshot of a time and a place—or rather, many times and many places—that are to my mind emblematic of the rock-festival era. It is not a complete history of the rock festival (for that, please turn to the internet). It is not even a very thorough history. In truth, it is not really about rock festivals, but about the crowds that attend them. In these pages, I posit that rock festivals were one of the late twentieth century's most characteristic formations, dependent on the era's communications advances, saturated with new uses of new technologies, and yet imbued with that most postwar affordance, pure pop pleasure. Especially in the 1970s and 1980s, rock crowds were an undocumented, unacknowledged form of "soft power." As Joseph Nye, the inventor of that term, said in 2012, "the best propaganda is *not* propaganda." At their best, rock festivals were giant advertisements for Western values, flagship enterprises pushing the pleasure of personal liberty.

Of course, anyone who has spent time within them knows that rock crowds are about *some* kind of power. But who is deploying it, and to what end? Considered as a social experience unique to the late twentieth century, rock festivals have shaped how many baby boomers think about their place in the world: for those too young to have experienced a world war, too suburban to have been in a riot, and too middle class to have raged against societal inequities, attending a rock festival is sometimes the only way they have, or think they have, directly participated in history. Also, rock crowds differ from mobs and armies (that is, masses of people threatening violence) in that people feel safe in them even when they aren't.[1] In fact, the rock festival crowd is often a place, and maybe the only place, where people feel a sense of community with strangers and where they are able to briefly retrieve what industrial society has taken away: that is, a sense of interpersonal intimacy that's been lost to the internet, to the triumph of commodity forms, to the ever-increasing gigantism of every single thing in modern life.

In short, there is something indefinably positive, something sexy and proud about a rock crowd that defies logic. The real conditions of a rock festival's material existence are not pretty. But the imagined ones are beautiful beyond compare. Rock festivals might even be what Hakim Bey has called a "temporary autonomous zone"— that is, an area where official control has temporarily been ceded to a nongovernmental, nonofficial, nonhierarchical force: to the people, as it were. Or they might be the opposite. Either way, attending rock festivals may well have been the touchstone experience of American youth in the second half of the twentieth century.

One reason why I think this way is because I was a rock critic for many years, and my beat was Lollapalooza, a touring festival launched in 1991. From 1991 to 1995, I worked long summer days covering scene upon scene in the fields of Michigan, Ohio, Missouri, Kentucky, Tennessee, Louisiana, Texas, Arizona, and my home state of California. Years later I realized that, with the exception of working musicians and stagehands, I had probably attended more rock festivals than most people on the planet. And then, having reached a place (a PhD program at Stanford University) where it was my task to observe, research, and critique something very, very closely, the topic of rock festivals began to present itself in another light. Having spent all those years writing about what was occurring on the stages of America—Metallica's fireworks! Mötley Crüe's spinning drum set! U2's giant lemon and its failure to launch!—it felt liberating to look in the other direction, out at the crowd. The crowd, after all, is where most of us reside.

Any story about rock festivals is in part a story about technological development; it is about sound in the age of mechanical reproduction. Prior to the invention of the phonograph record, music clearly had a different role in society than it does today. Since, of course, it had to be experienced live, music was mostly played in private settings or in concert halls where sound could carry better. Once music was recorded, commodified, and then widely disseminated via radio, records, film, and television, its live performance became but an echo, in several senses of the word. A live performance was an echo of the recording, rather than the other way around. And the live performance also had *more* echo, as it was now amplified.

For a short time, rock festivals helped to reverse this equation. Jazz aficionados always understood the power of the live recording, but in the 1960s and 1970s, many rock bands released live albums that captured the special qualities of rock shows in situ, in part because increasingly sophisticated recording technology allowed for better-sounding LPs. The LPs then attracted more potential festivalgoers, seduced by the sound of liveness into stepping back in time.

But rock festivals were much more than the technology that made them possible. It is important to define what I mean by the term "rock festival" in these pages, since there are all kinds of definitions and examples of the phrase. The word "festival" often applies to any kind of multiact event. Sometimes, for example, it is a loosely grouped set of shows at clubs around a single city—like Toronto's North By Northeast, or Austin's South By Southwest. At other times, it can refer to some bands playing together at a small club under the aegis of one kind of sound or genre or theme: the International Pop Underground Convention in Olympia, Washington, in 1991, for example, or Yoyo A Go Go in the same city, or the recurring Noise Pop Festival in San Francisco, or Burgerama and Burger Boogaloo in Los Angeles and Oakland.

These are all important kinds of rock festivals, but in this book, I use the term "rock festival" to refer to a large outdoor gathering of many different rock acts, performing in a centralized location, usually, but not always, on a piece of land that has been repurposed for the day. This land could be a farm, a municipal park, a racecourse, or an airfield. It could be a sports stadium, an amphitheater, or a shed. Whatever the location, it is a place that is normally used for something else and that can hold more than forty thousand people.

What I am *not* referring to in this book is a performance by a single, headlining act, such as the Grateful Dead or Phish, that has modeled its touring and performing style to appeal to fans by putting their shows into these kinds of venues in festival-like settings. Such shows certainly have parallels to the type of rock festivals I am referring to herein, but because their audiences are largely drawn to the single act's musical oeuvre, the crowds they draw are different from those I'm interested in here.

When most people think of rock festivals, they think of Woodstock first. Although not the largest festival of its era—that honor belongs to a festival called Watkins Glen—it is the one that has had by far the most cultural resonance, appearing not only in contemporary accounts but down through the decades as a symbol of 1960s counter-culture, progressive politics, and a liberal American utopia. Wood-stock took place over the weekend of August 15 through 18, 1969, and was very much a product of its times. After Woodstock, the rock fes-tival as a concept flourished in Europe, begetting Glastonbury, Sziget, and a host of others, but in America, the idea languished somewhat until the mid-1990s, when the touring festival called Lollapalooza brought the idea back to American shores.[2] In 1999, the Coachella Valley Music and Arts Festival was held at the Empire Polo Clubs in Indio, California. After taking one year off, it reappeared in 2001 and has subsequently become a massive, yearly draw for hundreds of thousands of festivalgoers across two weekends every April. The festival is now a multimillion-dollar undertaking at which celebri-ties, fashion icons, and rock stars gather to disseminate their brands in ways that are informed more by late capitalism than by musical or countercultural ideology. The year 2002 saw the inauguration of a festival called Bonnaroo in middle Tennessee: it too has become a long-standing focal point of rock festival culture. Although Bonnaroo brings together a slightly different demographic than does Coachella, it too has solidified the twenty-first-century notion of attending a rock festival as a rite of passage; it is an event that is in itself more impor-tant than any particular band that plays at it.

But why? Rock festivals like Lollapalooza, Coachella, and Bonna-roo are often dirty, inconvenient, crowded, noisy, and dangerous and difficult to negotiate. Why, why, *why* then, do so many people the world over not only attend them, even paying vast amounts of money for the privilege of doing so, but also find solace in their midst? Baudelaire, in *Paris Spleen*, describes being an anonymous member of a crowd as creating a "mysterious drunkenness" offering "feverish delights" (Baudelaire, "Crowds"). Clearly, something about being in a festival audience brings concertgoers a similar satisfaction and con-tentment, but it is an elusive feeling at best, and one that is hard to capture on paper.

Some people believe that rock festivals offer an experience of com-munal unity, a renewal of an ancient human collective feeling in an era of industrialized, commercialized alienation. The means, ironi-cally, is industrialized music, but music that is experienced live, in material conditions that make that liveness as vivid as possible. While this is not an untenable theory, this book argues otherwise, suggesting instead that the communal unity that is both sought after and sold at such festivals is only a very well-rendered illusion. Each and every rock festival promises salvation, but that's all it is, a promise made to be broken, over and over again.

It would be easy to begin a story about rock festivals, rock crowds, and their ramifications in the mid-1960s with the Monterey Pop Festival, the Trips Festival, or the Newport Folk Festival. I prefer to start the story a bit earlier, in my home city of San Francisco, where in the mid-1960s, the concept of the free rock festival was invented and then refined by a small group of musicians and promoters in the confines of Golden Gate Park. Fifty-six years prior to that invention, a different kind of free concert, an ur-festival, if you will, had been performed in downtown San Francisco.

CHAPTER 1

Millions Like Us

ONE COLD CHRISTMAS EVE IN 1910, the citizens of San Francisco gathered in the streets to hear the world-famous soprano Luisa Tetrazzini sing from a platform built on the steps of the office of the *San Francisco Chronicle*. For half an hour the opera star, backed by an orchestra and a fifty-person chorus, held a crowd estimated at 250,000 spellbound with her unamplified voice, which the newspaper described as "sweet, clear and pure in all its artless beauty." "If you closed your eyes," wrote Samuel Dickson, "you would have thought yourself alone in the world with that beautiful voice. I was two blocks away and every note was crystal clear, every word distinct" (Nolte, "Luisa Tetrazzini's Gift").

In later years, Tetrazzini's name would enter the English language due to her liking for a particularly creamy turkey casserole recipe. But in 1910 she was the equivalent of a rock star. Her performance was billed as a gift to the citizens of San Francisco, but although one might be tempted to think of it as akin to the time in 1987 when U2 played for free at the Vaillancourt Fountain in San Francisco, it was more like the time in 2014 when they gave their music away for free on the iPhone 6.

In both those cases, the artists in question had an economic agenda that transcended merely entertaining their fans. U2 was promoting its records (*Rattle and Hum*, 1988, and *Songs of Innocence*, 2014). In the Tetrazzini case, the concert—beautiful, pleasurable, valuable, and well-meant though it may have been—was at least in one part a veiled threat. Tetrazzini was in a contract dispute with a New York concert promoter who was not meeting her salary demands. When the promoter, a Mr. Hammerstein, wouldn't release her from her contract, she threatened to "sing in the streets" instead. In other words, if he didn't pay up, she would give away for free what he had hoped to sell: her voice.

Eventually, Tetrazzini's contractual issues were resolved, and she sang (for profit) for a month at the Dreamland Ballroom in San Francisco, but she still made good on her promise. Thus, her free concert carries with it the useful knowledge that every free concert has an ulterior motive. Also, Tetrazzini's concert proves that even a hundred years ago musicians were already struggling to assert their rights of ownership over their art. As Stewart Brand once said, "Information wants to be free. It also wants to be expensive" ("Point the Institution" 49). The same thing can be said about popular music. Regarding information, Brand went on to note, "that tension will not go away" (49). In the case of popular music in the age of the internet, that tension is practically the whole story.

Because Tetrazzini's concert drew a reported 250,000 people, because her concert took place in San Francisco, the locus of 1960s free music festivals, and because it was held on Christmas Eve, it seems like a properly sentimental starting point to begin a book about rock festivals. After it was over, the *Chronicle* described the crowd as "a monumental microcosm of humanity itself . . . boot blacks rubbed elbows with bankers and painted creatures with fat and wholesome mothers of families" (Wickham, "Melody" 27). To many music lovers, it is this microcosmic element of humanity—as well as the ability and the desire to rub elbows with it—that makes the experience of seeing live music in the midst of a large crowd uniquely satisfying. Music festivals are places where we override many of our prejudices about mankind and that allow us to think we are accessing a larger social world. At the start of the twentieth century, such a gathering was rare, but thanks to subsequent developments in amplification, the next 100 years would abound with such gatherings. These festivals would be bigger. They would be louder. And they would become distribution centers for certain forms of power.

Although free and festival-like in nature, Tetrazzini's concert really had little in common with the kind of gatherings that would come to characterize the gigantic free concerts of the latter half of the twentieth century. To begin, it was not amplified, since amplification technology did not exist.[1] Thus, it is a reminder that the type of concert that today we call a rock concert is a truly modern invention. Prior to the invention and widespread adoption of the gramophone (invented 1877, adopted circa 1910) and the radio (invented circa 1895, adopted circa 1920), music was *always* experienced live, and often for free. Indeed, symphonic music was a common feature at boardwalks, parks, town band shells, and other community gathering places across America and Europe. Since the adoption of radio and records as a means of hearing music at any time and in any place, this is no longer true, but the desire to hear music performed live remains constant. People still seek out the live music experience, and they still want to gather in giant numbers and rub up against one another, often at great trouble and expense.

One reason may be simply because music sounds better when performed live. Moreover, being in the actual physical presence of an artist has a psychological value. But most importantly, I think, it's fair to say that people who love music have a deep desire to be in close proximity to others enjoying the same music. At the very best concerts, the music and the artist and the experience all merge to make an event that is something quite different from simply hearing a live performance of music. Listening to music is one thing. Listening to it *together* is a whole other experience, one that can change a simple act of appreciation into a political action. As an example, when speaking about the experience of living as a West Indian immigrant in London in the early 1970s, Paul Gilroy described the experience of community bonding over listening to Jamaican-inflected pop music styles such as ska and reggae in a crowd setting in London. He wrote that in so doing—in listening to this music alongside others from his diasporic community—members of the crowd became not so much lost as lucky. An unusually eloquent militant and musically rich culture oriented us and gave us the welcome right to employ it in order to defend ourselves, identify our interests and change our circumstances. We were buoyed up by a worldwide movement for democratic change and energized by the intensity of a very special period in the cultural life of our diaspora. ("Between the Blues" 378)

Gilroy's experience, which he calls "listening together," though specific to a time and place, perfectly captures what happened in the late twentieth century at countless other specific locations. Woodstock stands as the easiest of these gatherings to parse: attendees were able to display their allegiance to a new set of values and lifestyles in a manner that accrued emphasis and feeling; as a group, the audience appeared to become an ideological force. At Woodstock, the phrase "you had to be there" gained currency, and throughout the ensuing years, large musical gatherings have attempted again and again to serve this purpose, although the values, lifestyles, and ideologies have changed radically. In Tetrazzini's time, an outdoor concert of that type was a foreshadowing. By the end of the twentieth century, it would be a commonplace.

One of the things foreshadowed by that the crowd on the steps of the *Chronicle* building that Christmas season of 1910 was simply a fact about people—or rather, about population. The future was going to contain more of them, and they would be placed in closer proximity, in smaller spaces. In 1910, the population of California was 2.3 million; by the 1960s, it was five times that number. By then, there was a great deal of talk about overpopulation and the so-called "population explosion," thanks to the popularity of Paul Ehrlich's book *The Population Bomb*, a best seller when it was released in 1968. As a California native, I can personally recall that in those days, people often used to say things like, "By the year 2000, every human being will only have one square foot to stand on." It was a prediction that, as a small child, I used to contemplate with horror as well as disbelief, particularly when I was in an airplane passing over the vast empty plains of Nevada, Arizona, and later, many other parts of the planet. It seemed impossible.

Happily, the famine and overcrowding of the planet that was anticipated by Ehrlich did not take place (at least not to the catastrophic extent he predicted). Yet it is easy to see how the hypothesis came about, since crowding and overcrowdedness have been a feature of twentieth- and twenty-first-century life. In 1895, before the twentieth century even began, Gustave Le Bon predicted that the twentieth century would be the "era of crowds" (*The Crowd*, xv), and that prediction has proven to be accurate. For most Americans, being a part of an enormous crowd is a fairly commonplace event. Whether in shopping malls before Christmas, in sports arenas during ball games, on subway platforms on New Year's Eve, or in the city streets after the World Series, pushing one's way, shoulder to shoulder, through narrow areas in the company of countless other people is not a particularly unique or distressing experience. Some people in dense cities do it every day.

But as all of those who have experienced one know, the rock festival crowd is different. In 2014, Nielsen reported, 32 million Americans bought tickets to at least one music festival, and America is not even the prime market for music festivals; that would be Europe (www .nielsen.com). Today, attending such a festival—Outside Lands, Coachella, Bonnaroo, Lollapalooza, Wonderland, All Tomorrow's Parties, or Magnaball at Watkins Glen—is an almost mandatory experience for people aged eighteen to thirty-four, and one that cuts across geographic and class status lines. Joseph Campbell once described the experience of seeing a rock concert in the company of its fans as "a wonderful fervent loss of self in the larger self of a homogeneous community," and his experience echoes and is multiplied by what happens in these festival crowds.

At a rock festival, the crowd has entered into a space—the festival grounds—willingly and in search of a particular crowd experience, one that differs significantly from joining, say, a crowd crossing 42nd Street in Manhattan during rush hour, joining a celebration or protest, or merely attempting to get to the front of a bothersome ticket line. Rather, rock festivals are where the masses now choose to participate in public life. Beginning with Newport and Woodstock and the Isle of Wight, and continuing on through the ensuing decades at locations like Glastonbury, Live Aid, Woodstock '99, Rock in Rio, Coachella, and Burning Man, certain festivals have imprinted themselves

on the media as being events of great cultural relevance and importance. Hence, in the crowd's mind, these spaces are where participants may believe they are *participating in history itself*.

Of course, the real cultural relevance of these festivals is both less
and more than they sell themselves as. It's more, because they have
informed the personal experience of literally millions upon millions
of people on the earth today. It's less, because although today's rock
festivals are routinely capable of gathering vast crowds together on a
scale undreamed of by Hitler, Stalin, or Martin Luther King Jr., these
crowds are entirely lacking in cohesive political will. In fact, those
human bodies who participated in demonstrations in Tiananmen
Square and Tahrir Square (to name just two crowded crowd events)
have participated much more fully in public life. Taking risks, working toward civic change, and announcing one's beliefs and values in
the face of opposition are actions that deserve to be acknowledged as
true civic behavior. Truly, the ultimate point of crowds and crowding
ought to be to make some kind of meaningful ideological or symbolic
gesture, and this is a role that, as I will argue in the following pages,
rock festivals, although often willing and able, have been incapable
of following through.

And yet, despite the absence of political, ideological, or religious
cohesion, large rock festivals *do* fulfill a particular psychological function in the minds of many members of the audience. They may be political placebos, simulacra of civic duty, or even the "circus" part of the
ancient Roman figure of speech about bread and circuses. But since
the early 1960s, they have vexed their purposes by serving as marketing tools for particular ideologies, ranging from Woodstock's association with the antiwar movement to Burning Man's encomiums about
the gift economy and leaving no trace. Rock festivals are sites where
certain aspects of current history are transformed by their audiences
into contemporary fact. And they are places where new technologies
are put on display in order to better market them to the masses. What
they are not are incubators for ideological or political action. They are
not sites of resistance. They might conceivably be places of disaster,
but they cannot be utopias, and they never were. Rock festivals may
represent a certain type of power. But rock *crowds* do not.

Festivals have not always been the agoras that they are today.

When entering them was relatively accessible, they were what they purported to be: showcases for musicians to perform their art, attracting fans. But today's most popular rock festivals have conflicting aims. They not only wish to showcase music, they also wish to become significant—that is, they wish to attach some meaning to their brand. One way they do that is by using extremely persuasive narratives about culture to attract ever larger, ever richer crowds, narratives that will make the gathering seem to attendees to be more than just a concert. Ideally, the narrative, whether political, ideological, or religious, should make the gathering seem more meaningful, but the narrative's logic is often betrayed by the terms of the festival itself.

An example of a festival rhetoric that both attracts audiences and defies serious political purpose is the narrative of ecology. Rock festivals, by creating a hybrid of natural and urban settings, point toward the disjunction between them. Festivalgoers crave the former and flee the latter, but the irony is that festivals explicitly address issues of ecology and planetary health while simultaneously creating spaces that mimic the ill-effects of overpopulation. Hence, rock festivals on repurposed land—for example, Max Yasgur's farm in Bethel, New York, for the first Woodstock; the Griffiss Air Base for Woodstock '99; and the semirural stretch of Manchester, Tennessee, that now houses the enormous Bonnaroo festival every year—become temporary tent cities, mimicking the slums of the Third World. As just a small example, according to the *Guardian*, the Glastonbury Festival in 2015 generated an estimated 1,650 tons of waste—including 5,000 abandoned tents, 6,500 sleeping bags, 400 gazebos, 54 tons of cans and plastic bottles, 41 tons of cardboard, 66 tons of scrap metal, 3,500 air mattresses, 2,200 chairs, and 950 rolled mats, which it took a team of eight hundred people six weeks to clear up (York, "Glastonbury's Rubbish").

And yet, despite the despoliation that these festivals bring to these landscapes, an overarching narrative about nature—as the setting for freedom and of the natural world as an overridingly excellent feature of America itself—is one that governs much of the rhetoric of rock festivals. There is actually a historically contingent reason for this: in 1964, the same year that the Civil Rights Act ended violent struggles for racial equality, and just prior to the contentious 1965 Newport

Folk Festival, the Wilderness Act was passed by Congress. Its passage marked the legal beginnings of a movement of concern over environmental issues, a dialogue that had been increasing in volume and strength since World War II and that now entered into the mainstream consciousness. At a time when social problems involving race and class were ripping apart political discourse, preserving wilderness in America was a topic about which most people could agree.

At the same time, there is a fundamental disjuncture between rock festivals and discourse on ecology, since rock festivals also visibly ruin the land on which they take place. Taking part in a rock festival does not involve immersing oneself in Walden-like solitude but in its opposite: crowding. It is as if large rock festivals like Woodstock or Bonnaroo actually *act out* overpopulation; and in so doing, they create a different category of space, one neither fearsome nor destructive. Weirdly, large rock festivals allow people to experience all the discomforts of global material deterioration, from overflowing toilets to dust storms. What people then do with that experience does not necessarily reflect an understanding of this disjunction, but there's always that possibility.

Possibly the most unique thing about the rock festival crowd is that, unlike crowds before it, it is usually seen as peaceful, righteous, and essentially passive. Yet prior to Woodstock, crowds were generally depicted as sinister, ugly manifestations of the urban conditions brought about by capitalism's rapid move toward industrialization. In the new millennium, crowds are more often depicted as a force for good, in both fiction and nonfiction. James Surowiecki's *Wisdom of Crowds* (2004), for example, defends the crowd mentality as an important (and often accurate) market force: the concepts of crowdsourcing, crowd funding, and the crowd as a hive mind are especially twenty-first-century ideas. The power of crowds in its most positive incarnation can be seen in the final moments of the children's film *Finding Nemo* (2003). In it, the tiny clownfish Nemo exhorts hundreds of thousands of sardines caught up in an industrial fishing net to work together to break free, thus freeing his friend Dory from the evil corporate forces of an industrial fishing conglomerate while simultaneously foiling those forces in their efforts to rape the ecosystem of its natural bounty and proving to his father, Marlon, that he is all grown up. It's an ingenious and sentimental version of a crowd event that emphasizes the power of the individual while simultaneously arguing that crowds have the power to elude the death-clutch of corporate forces.

Finding Nemo's rosy depiction of crowds and individuals is a perfect allegory for the new crowd paradigm, a paradigm that was in part ushered in by the era and invention of the rock festival and the crowd experience it created. By the 1990s, rock concerts had trained consumers to cram together (much like Nemo's sardines) to cheer for various artists, experiencing a certain kind of crowded, communal camaraderie and pleasure. In a rock crowd, power is distributed in new ways. Rock stars who lead crowds in frenzied sing-alongs may seem like giant clownfish, exhorting shoals of fans to swim up to the surface and break free of their corporate shackles, but there is strong evidence that even the most charismatic of leaders—for example, Mick Jagger at Altamont in 1969—are incapable of turning a crowd's purpose in the manner of Nemo: when confronted with violence in front of the stage, Jagger makes ineffectual gestures and continues to sing. (Earlier, the Jefferson Airplane's Marty Balin, who makes a less halfhearted attempt to quell the violence, is punched in the face and retires.) Thus, the rock festival crowd represents something unique, neither a ritualized roiling mass of humanity in search of a religious experience nor an angry, psychotic mob. Most rock crowds are actually quite passive. But this does not mean that they are not malleable, even dangerously so.

Jacques Attali once wrote that music is a herald, "for change is inscribed in noise faster than it transforms society" (*Noise* 5). This has surely been true of some genres—jazz and rap, for instance, which have taught America how to listen to their racialized narratives, although perhaps not country or metal, which are inherently and, equally importantly, conservative—but it is even truer of music festivals. At their best, rock festivals can be harbingers of societal and aesthetic trends and fashions, the lived experience of a new generation, briefly put into practice. Not all music festivals rise to this height, and most fall far short of it. But if there weren't a promise of utopia embedded in every such gathering, I doubt very much they would get the attendance that they do.

CHAPTER 2

Our Friends Electric

L ATE ON A SUMMER EVENING in the last part of the last century, a massive summer rainstorm drenched an Akron-area concert bowl during a stop on a tour called Lollapalooza. As thunder and lightning battered the concertgoers and the band Ministry churned up an equally riotous noise of a song called "Jesus Built My Hotrod," the crowd took to wrenching the metal folding chairs that were bolted to the earth and hurling them like sleds down the hillside the venue occupied. Before long, the lawn area had become a mudslide down which audience members were traveling on their stomachs, landing in a heap of flesh and hair at the bottom, tangled up like giant humanoid snakes. When the concert came to its premature end, Chris Cornell, the lead singer of the band Soundgarden, surveyed the bespattered scene. "You guys look like somebody's army," he said ruefully. "The question is, whose army are you going to be?" (Arnold, *Route 666*).[1]

That was in 1992. Since then, it has become clear that those kids were nobody's army. As a group, the eighteen-to-thirty-four-year-old white males who made up a large part of that crowd and others much like it have floated through the ensuing decade more like a gaseous

emanation than a cohesive demographic force. Although that particular demographic had been gathered, sought, and studied for generations—especially as the subject of various military drafts—the kids
at Lollapalooza were clearly very different from the ones who went
to Woodstock twenty-three years earlier. Although demographically
they may have seemed similar, spiritually they had little or nothing in
common with the utopian dreamers who were their forebears. Ministry, the band that had just inspired them to violence, was misnamed
in this case. These kids had no calling. Those at Woodstock, we are
told, did. Something had changed drastically in the twenty-three-year
interim; something had been obliterated.

By no means, however, should it be suggested that the history of
rock festivals begins with Woodstock—or ends with Lollapalooza.
Woodstock was not by any means the first outdoor rock festival,
though it was certainly the largest of its kind at that time. What dis-
tinguished it from many other concerts of that time and place—at
least to the general public, who had yet to experience the rock festival
phenomenon on home ground—was that it was held on repurposed
land, a dairy farm requisitioned for the purpose after the city council of the originally selected site in Wallkill, New York, reneged on its
permission.[2] Prior to the era of rock festivals, outdoor music was most
often performed within the confines of parks and spaces officially
designated as places of entertainment. Some, like Freedomland, the
eighty-five-acre theme park in the Bronx with grounds laid out in the
shape of the United States, had admission fees. Others, like the Jones
Beach Band Shell, established in 1929, did not.[3] Still, there is a crucial
difference between concerts held in these "official" spaces of entertainment and the proposed Woodstock concert. Concerts held in officially sanctioned spaces—stadiums, band shells, auditoriums, clubs,
and the like—create officially sanctioned reactions from patrons. By
contrast, concerts held in repurposed spaces provide at least the illusion that the audience's reaction is unpredictable.

The difference between these two types of audience has been captured on film. For example, the Canadian film board documentary
Lonely Boy (1963), which depicts an outdoor concert performed by
Paul Anka in 1962, in what I would call the prefestival era, at the
now defunct Bronx amusement park Freedomland, provides a record

of sanctioned mob behavior. The audience in the film does what it's expected to do, yet there is a tantalizing promise of something else embedded in the scene. Filmed in black and white and slow motion, the documentary surveys the Freedomland scene before Anka's concert with a clinical, yet strangely loving gaze, raking the bodies of ten thousand girls as they await Anka's entrance. Held back by beefy New York cops, they squirm, squeeze, faint, wriggle, and scream. Sexual bliss is written on their sweaty, ecstatic faces; when Anka invites one of them on stage so he can sing to her, she can barely stand up.

Today's college kids laugh when they see women fainting at the sight of Paul Anka, who is not an attractive guy by our standards and who is singing what we'd now consider to be extremely silly and straitlaced pop songs ("Diana" and "Put Your Head on My Shoulder"). But the scene—captured in eloquent slow-motion detail—seems to teeter on the edge of one era, as the history of rock is about to topple over into another. It just predates similar rock crowd scenes incurred later by the Beatles, the Rolling Stones, and the Jackson 5. It predates Woodstock, Lollapalooza, Live Aid, and Live Earth, but it also bears some similarity both to them and to preceding ecstatic crowd moments, most of them religiously inspired revivals and gatherings just prior to the death of JFK, the British invasion, the Apollo missions, the antiwar movement, and the ensuing cultural cacophony.

Lonely Boy may well depict the actual balancing point between popular music in its older incarnation, as entertainment, and what popular music was about to become, that is, an expression of something much more culturally significant. Indeed, Paul Anka's concert that night is a weird hybrid, conjoining the traditional role of male crooner with the wild abandonment of audiences at rock 'n' roll shows. Anka himself performs ritualistically, even stiffly, swinging his mike, reaching out to stroke a girl's cheek, and dropping to his knees, all in ways that are clearly rote, and even balletic. Simultaneously, the girls we see in the audience are performing in unison in ways that seem equally choreographed, while the cops, bored and torpid, play their parts as well. The behaviors on display at this concert, though nominally "wild and abandoned," are as feigned as the cultural studies theorist Theodor Adorno would wish: the hollow gestures of an audience in thrall to consumerism and nostalgia. And yet, the show also foreshadows many of the changes that will take place in the quick-shifting music scene of the mid-1960s. Most obviously, perhaps, it is a reminder that outdoor rock festivals like Woodstock had a number of open-air precursors, including folk festivals, board-walks, county fairgrounds, and amusement parks like the short-lived Freedomland.

Generally, however, prior to 1964, popular music (like Anka's) was mostly performed in clubs or concert halls, while music played out-doors was usually performed by orchestras and bands in city park band shells or on piers. Freedomland's demise—it went bankrupt in 1964—does suggest some of the contingencies that resulted in the re-formation of outdoor music as "community sponsored" Be-Ins and rock festivals. According to Tom Vanderbilt's book *Survival City*, Freedomland, which was in grave financial trouble for most of its four-year existence, initially presented mainstream popular acts (like Anka, Pat Boone, and Benny Goodman), but when its coffers began to run dry, it tried to woo a younger and more urban crowd by book-ing up-and-coming (read: cheaper; also read: African American) rock and soul acts, mostly from the newly inaugurated Motown label in Detroit. In 1964, visitors could see Smokey Robinson, the Tempta-tions, and Little Stevie Wonder at Freedomland for thirty-five cents. The crowds at those shows were probably no less ecstatic than Anka's, but they were urban rather than suburban; that is, black rather than white. This was clearly a problem for the park—one which later rock festivals were able to redress in various ways (for example, by hold-ing such concerts in rural settings, which were hardly accessible with-out automobiles). But the essential strategy here of replacing main-stream white acts with cutting-edge black ones sums up the next four decades of economic success for the record labels. It was also the strategy of festivals like Monterey Pop and Woodstock, both of which featured cutting-edge music by black musicians alongside music by white artists. Thus, by the time Freedomland went bankrupt in 1964, it had (accidentally) reconfigured race and performance in American pop music and predicted the change from middle-of-the-road pop to edgy urban rock.

By 1964, something else had changed as well. No one, however moved, crowded the arena at nearby Jones Beach and fainted at the sound of "Tip Toe through the Tulips" or "Indian Love Lyrics," but at Anka's show, the crowding, pushing, and shoving were symptomatic of a different kind of music appreciation, the kind born of rock 'n' roll, and fostered by its presence on television, particularly on two of the most popular long-running shows of the 1950s, *American Bandstand* (1952–89) and the *Ed Sullivan Show* (1949–71). On these shows, viewers could see crowds of fans reacting ecstatically—in the true religious sense of the word—to performances by Elvis Presley (first broadcast in September 1956) and Buddy Holly (December 1, 1957). Thus, by 1962, the year that *Lonely Boy* was shot, audiences had been treated to almost ten years' worth of displays of "appropriate crowd behavior" at pop concerts via television shows like these.

Freedomland's closure in 1964 is significant, for that year was the beginning of major civil rights legislation and of the Wilderness Act, two events that would significantly affect the cultural movements that were brewing in the zeitgeist. It was the year that Bob Dylan's third album came out, presciently titled *The Times They Are a-Changin'*. Indeed, many people would later argue that the era of the rock festival began with the Newport Folk Festival of July 1965, which presented an enormous challenge to folk music fans who were loath to exchange what they saw as the authenticity of folk music for the popular aesthetic of electric rock music. That festival also presents itself as another flashpoint in outdoor performance—and the place where audience behavior, spurred in part by bubbling tensions between folk and rock, changed. Prior to Newport 1965, folk audiences behaved very differently from Paul Anka audiences: they sat sedately and appreciated the music. After Newport, the two kinds of concerts began to merge into one. It is a moment many people claim as significant to the history of rock, for it was here that Bob Dylan, then a popular folk artist, "went electric," supposedly ushering in a new era for both popular music and its fans as the medium became increasingly tied to social, political, and cultural narratives.

From the media detritus floating around at this moment, one might be excused for thinking that Dylan's electrification was some kind of groundbreaking moment in the history of media technology. But, of course, electrified acts had been around for some time. Indeed, that very same week of July, an electrified act called the Beatles gave one of their last public performances, to fifty-five thousand fans, most of them teenagers, at Shea Stadium in Queens, New York. By contrast, the Newport Folk Festival, which took place several states away at the historic Fort Adams State Park in Rhode Island, drew only between ten thousand and twenty thousand people, many of whom were listeners to jazz, folk, and classical music.

The two concerts present an interesting contrast. One, the more popular, was large and urban and filled with hysterical teenagers. The other was set in a rural location and catered to staid older members of the cultural elite. Both featured headliners who were extremely beloved by their audiences. The first concert was in the inner city, in a neighborhood we now think of as dangerous; the second one was in a rural idyll. Yet, if we are to believe what we read, on the night in question, it was the second concert that was filled with rage and violence. Contemporary accounts of Newport 1965 make it sound like an Insane Clown Posse gig, or maybe Altamont or Woodstock '99, without the rapes and murder. The Beatles show was probably the more typical of the times, but it was the narratives that began at Newport, when Dylan "went electric," that went on to shape how the rock festival would configure itself in the future.[4] At the Newport Folk Festival of 1965, the rock crowd as an entity, with its own voice and its own personality, began to take shape, and it presented a narrative that didn't look or sound anything like the usual story of fandom, with its shriek-ridden soundtrack and accompanying photos of tear-streaked girls' faces.

Today, opposition to the idea of a folk artist playing electric seems both close-minded and shrill. But in fact, there would have been good reason for thoughtful people to distrust any kind of enthusiastic mass audience response or celebration. The year 1965, after all, was less than one generation after the Nuremberg Rallies, so memorably recorded in the Leni Riefenstahl film *Triumph of the Will*. The sight of mass enthusiasts for Nazi ideology gathered together in a stadium, listening to words spoken through amplifiers, certainly had sinister associations. Moreover, the rise of Hitler's regime, as McLuhan notes, was due in part to the technology of amplification, which created both the public-address system and the radio, which he (prophetically) calls "the tribal drum" (*Understanding Media* 259). The effect of such a system, he says, is that of "a kind of nervous information system" (260), a description that certainly encompasses the spatial plane of the rock concert.[5] If radio had the ability to offer, in McLuhan's words, "a world of unspoken communication between writer-speaker and listener" (261), then how much more powerful would it be to gather writer-speaker and listener together in real space, permitting their communion and the exchange of information?

In the coming months and years after Newport, this real space of audience communion would transform itself into the full-blown phenomenon known as the rock festival. Newport took place in July 1965. Just fourteen months later, on October 6, 1966, the Grateful Dead and Big Brother played for free at the Panhandle in San Francisco. Similar events followed: January 14, 1967, Human Be-In, Golden Gate Park; June 13–17, 1967, Monterey Pop Festival, Monterey County Fairgrounds; August 28–29, 1968, Sky River Rock Festival and Lighter Than Air Fair, Sultan, Washington; and August 13, 15, and 17, 1969, Woodstock, Bethel, New York.

All of these festivals drew strong opposition from local civic leaders. All of them are now legendary in their locales. And all of them are considered foundational events in the creation and maintenance of a visible counterculture that was antiwar but pro crowds and power. But Newport is the logical start of any story about the era of the rock festival because it was there, on July 25, 1965, that the looming shadow of the rock crowd as an entity, with its own voice and its own narrative, began. After Newport, saying someone had "gone electric" became a clichéd way of thinking about popular music, politics, and culture, a discursive tactic that may have signified cultural anxiety around new modes of information transmission and the distortions that such modes seemed to arouse in viewers and listeners.

———

Dylan's "going electric"—that is, playing three songs from his album *Highway 61 Revisited* live on stage accompanied by electric guitars—is now considered one of the premier cultural events not just in rock history, but of the entire 1960s. *Rolling Stone* called it "the most notorious live moment in rock," and although that may be an exaggeration—to someone of my generation, a better choice for *notoriety* is the less symbolic but far more tragic immolation of ninety-six concertgoers in a Rhode Island nightclub because of pyrotechnics set off by the heavy metal band Great White in 2003—the fallout from the New-port Folk Festival undoubtedly had massive cultural resonance.

Today, it is still disputed whether audience members booed Dylan because of the poor sound quality or because they disliked his change from folk to rock. Joe Boyd, who was the soundman that night, has located some of the images that became, as he puts it, "rock festi-val clichés" in the coming years—"young girls dancing in flimsy tops made transparent by the rain; mud staining the faces of ecstatically grinning kids" (*White Bicycles* 102)—and claims these actually had their genesis at this festival (rather than at Woodstock). Boyd points out as well that the 1965 festival was awash with controversies. It was here, he writes in his memoir *White Bicycles*, that the tension between rock music and folk music played out in much the same way that the tension between Cold War ideology and socialist idealism was explod-ing in the zeitgeist in many other arenas as well.

Boyd says that many of the festival's attendees had come straight from the Deep South, where they had been working for integration in marches and on buses, and he understands the tensions in Newport over acoustic versus electric music to be of a piece with these larger struggles. Folk music was political and resistant in nature, and its suc-cess on the pop charts (just beginning in 1965 with songs like "Mr. Tambourine Man") represented a sort of victory for its champions. "The Newport Folk Festivals of 1963 and 1964," Boyd writes, "repre-sented redemption, the pinnacle of the journey back from the wilder-ness of the 1950s" (*White Bicycles* 78).

By contrast, Boyd says, Dylan's new music (that is, the music on the just-released album *Bringing It All Back Home* and the soon-to-be-released *Highway 61 Revisited*) was *not* about politics (or not explicitly so). So when Dylan opened that night with the song "Maggie's Farm," backed by the Paul Butterfield (electric) Blues Band, the audience was simply unprepared for it. Boyd writes:

> By today's standards, the volume wasn't particularly high, but in 1965 it was probably the loudest thing anyone in the audience had ever heard. A buzz of shock and amazement ran through the crowd. When the song finished, there was a roar that contained many sounds. Certainly boos were included, but they weren't in

a majority. There were shouts of delight and triumph and also of derision and outrage. . . . There are many accounts of what happened next. Dylan left the stage with a shrug as the crowd roared. Having heard only three songs, they wanted "moooooooooore," and some, certainly, were booing. They had been taken by surprise by the volume and the aggression of the music. Some loved it, some hated it, most were amazed, astonished and energized by it. It was something we take for granted now, but utterly novel then: non-linear lyrics, an attitude of total contempt for expectation and established values, accompanied by screaming blues guitar and a powerful rhythm section, played at ear-splitting volume by young kids. The Beatles were still singing love songs in 1965 while the Stones played a sexy brand of blues-rooted pop. This was different. (*White Bicycles* 105)

As Boyd's passage illustrates, that night the *folk* festival became a *rock* festival, bearing with it many of the attributes of the folk music audience, particularly its footprint as the realm of an elite, white enclave of taste-making, music-loving individuals. Even when it distributed the "low art" fare of rock 'n' roll, the Newport Festival had much in common with high-culture festivals like the Sanremo Music Festival in Italy and the Bayreuth Opera Festival in Germany; now, rock festivals would go forward in that same image.

That the Newport Folk Festival stood at some kind of cultural crossroads can be inferred by the frequency with which the phrase "goes electric" is used as a byword. "Goes electric" describes events with transformational impact and those without it: "The World Cup Goes Electric," for example, would be a feasible headline for an article about televised soccer games. A quick search on Google indicates that car companies have been using the phrase with deplorable frequency to describe their new hybrids; in short, it has now become shorthand for cultural transformation. Greil Marcus has argued that the album *Highway 61 Revisited* sonically anticipated later, more radical, events of the 1960s: Jacques Attali concurs, when he suggests that "an outburst of uncensored violence" (*Noise* 7) may have been first hinted at in the way that Dylan's performance at Newport was discursively circulated in the media in the months to come.

That rock concerts *do* contain violent elements is no secret now:

the aforementioned Great White concert is a horrifying example, and there are others, such as the deaths of eleven music fans in a crush at a Who concert in Cincinnati in 1979, nine at the Roskilde Festival in 2000, and twenty-one at the Duisburg Love Parade in 2010.[6] In 1965, prior to the invention of the rock festival as we know it, such events would have been unthinkable. But the anger generated in the audience at the Newport Folk Festival over a simple and really fairly predictable technological change foreshadowed future crowd conflicts and controversies, and this foreshadowing may be what underlies the well-documented debate about what actually happened there. It certainly is what underlies the idea that festivals can be sites of cultural change.

Today one can view the performance in question on YouTube, but this does not make it any easier to parse what was going on in the audience. No booing is apparent on film, but this is only because sound technology at the time was so primitive. In the filmed version, the sound is taken from the soundboard—that is, it's the sound that Dylan himself heard through his stage monitors, not what the audience heard through the amplifiers (or in the space around them). So the question still remains: was Dylan booed? And if he was, was it because his fans didn't want him to electrify his music, or were those jeers simply an expression of frustration that the sound quality was poor?

According to Greil Marcus, whose book *Like a Rolling Stone: Bob Dylan at the Crossroads* dissects the landmark album that Dylan recorded in 1965, there are even wider-ranging theories as to what the boos signified, including the possibility that Dylan's management cooked up the controversy for publicity. Some have even argued that the booing has been exaggerated over the years in order to bolster the idea that Dylan's performance represented a cultural break with the past: Marcus, for instance, ties the event to the Watts riots (which occurred three weeks later), arguing that the song expressed and synthesized the volatile atmosphere of the times. "It was an event," he writes, referring to the rise of Dylan's single "Like a Rolling Stone" to the top of the charts that August. "It defined the summer, but like the Watts Riots, the performance also interrupted it" (*Like a Rolling Stone* 150). Perhaps it is this *interruption* of communication that has made the Newport Folk Festival endure so long in the popular memory. Prior to Newport, no rock concert was "interrupted" in the sense that Marcus means: each one flowed smoothly from beginning to end, from the hands and mouth of performer, into the expectant ear of the listener. The interruption here implies an interruption of *meaning*, not of sound, and it is this gap in meaning that has allowed the story of "Dylan Going Electric" to snowball to the extent that it has.

Whatever the reality, it's safe to say that the first sonic encounter with Dylan's electrified music at the Newport Folk Festival of 1965 was difficult to decipher, and one possibility is that the debate surrounding Dylan's appearance at the festival was not about Dylan and his music but about what *the experience of going to rock concerts* was going to be like in the future. The Newport Folk Festival heralded a change in the way music fans perceived themselves as like-minded communities. In other words, the events at Newport in 1965 explicitly foreshadowed a future relationship between rock crowds and power.

Anyway, that's how I like to think about it. The truth is, even at Newport, Dylan's electrification there could hardly have come as a shock to anyone except the most retro-minded folkies, since Dylan's hit single, "Like a Rolling Stone," already in wide release in July, contained electric instrumentation. Nor was his playing electric live onstage at all groundbreaking: electric instruments with amplification had become the standard in rock 'n' roll, rhythm and blues, and country music by the late 1950s, for the practical reason that amplification allowed musicians to play bigger places. Ray Charles was playing electric piano on "What'd I Say" in the 1950s, and the pedal steel guitar was hardly new, so in a literal sense, Dylan "going electric" was more a matter of the artist's being realistic about how modern instrumentation actually worked in practice than it was a gesture of repudiation, commodification, or arrogance.

If Dylan's playing electric guitar wasn't the shocker that it now seems in retrospect, what was it? Most cultural theorists agree that Dylan's onstage change represented to his hard-core fans a repudiation of the old tactics of folk music. The gesture has also been widely interpreted as part of the disappointing process of commodification that haunts post-industrial society—the process that, when allied with artistic projects, is often referred to as "selling out." But although there were elements of both these concepts embedded in Dylan's electric move, the extreme anxiety that has colored the event and allowed it to permeate contemporary social history suggests that something else was going on as well.[7] John Cordwell, whose infamous call "Judas!" at Dylan's 1966 concert in Manchester has long been considered one of the most famous heckles in rock history, says that his shout at the UK concert (ten months after Newport) was prompted not by surprise at the electrification but by surprise at the *amplification*—that is, by disappointment that the sound was so bad. "I think most of all I was angry that Dylan . . . not that he'd played electric, but that he'd played electric with a really poor sound system," he told Andy Kershaw in 2005 (Kershaw, "Bob Dylan").

> It was not like it is on the record [the official album]. It was a wall of mush. That, and it seemed like a cavalier performance, a throwaway performance compared with the intensity of the acoustic set earlier on. There were rumblings all around me and the people I was with were making noises and looking at each other. It was a build-up. . . . It's strange. But certainly that wasn't the Dylan I focused on. Maybe I was just living in the past. And I couldn't hear the lyrics in the second half of the concert [the electric set with the band]. I think that's what angered me. (Kershaw, "Bob Dylan")

Surely anyone who has attended a modern rock concert since then has felt this same annoyance—and never more than at a rock festival, where the sound, rather than bouncing off the walls, muddles itself with every other noise on the fairground and then wafts up into the air, where it may, if you're lucky, meet you in another life.

———

One sure sign that the reception of Dylan's appearance at the Newport Folk Festival was more in the nature of a metaphor than a moment is that it may not in fact even have taken place—at least, not as it is now described. Although today it does appear to be the "most storied event in the history of modern popular music" (Marcus, *Like a Rolling Stone* 155), Dylan's "electric" move was barely recorded in the mainstream press when it happened. For example, contrary to many current accounts that place the negative reaction to Dylan as central to the event itself, the *New York Times*, which devoted quite extensive coverage to the 1965 Newport Folk Festival, only referred to it in *one* sentence in a retrospective article that ran a week later. In it, the writer Robert Shelton (who would ironically later make a career out of his association with the moment in question) says only that Dylan played "unpersuasively" on electric instruments and that one person in the audience jeered ("Beneath the Festival's Razzle-Dazzle").[8]

One can't help but wonder how this blasé description of a lone negative voice in a crowd of seventeen thousand could have turned into an entire discourse about the 1960s that situates the event as pivotal to the era and to a rock crowd's self-conception as having political and cultural resonance. Clearly, as is the case with many symbolic events, Dylan's "going electric" was more meaningful to those who *weren't* there than to those who were, for it was only from the perspective of those outside the concert gates that Dylan's noisy, electric show became a symbol of the distortion of information that seemed to be going on at the time. Indeed, the farther one gets from that concert location, the more it becomes a metaphor for the distortion of political messages caused by candidates debating on prime-time television or the violent images transmitted in televised news coverage of events in Selma and Vietnam. In 1965, all of these relatively new forms of media transmission were transforming how people received information, and the transformation could not have been wholly comfortable.[9]

In a similar fashion, the messages Dylan was sending via lyrics like "I got forty red white and blue shoe strings and a thousand telephones that don't ring" (from the song "Highway 61 Revisited") were cryptic and indecipherable, a new code that only a few people—those who were part of the cultural elite—were able to "read."[10] That, among other things, was maybe what was frightening the public, in a fashion echoed today by legions of listeners spooked by the limitless reach of internet memes, fake news sites, and other new forms of social distortion. As Marshall McLuhan had recently pointed out, mediums "shape the scale and form of human association and action" (*Understanding Media* 9). By electrifying his instruments, Dylan was indicating that he was willing to change scale; that is, he was willing to disseminate his supercharged messages into an extremely large forum. Today, social media have enlarged the scale of disinformation.

Another reason why Dylan's going electric may have had more

lasting cultural importance than, say, the Minneapolis band Hüsker Dü signing to Warner Brothers in 1984 (another incident booed by the so-called "serious" fans) was because of its spectral hint that his audiences would soon become mobs. The booing of Dylan at Newport suggests a recognition that rock crowds did not always have to be entirely celebratory—and that they might not even be entirely under control. The year 1965 predates the really violent gatherings, like the 1968 riots at the Democratic Convention in Chicago or the 1969 concert at Altamont, that would occur later in the decade, but Newport heralded them. From this perspective, Dylan's going electric could be read as a seizure of power, while the distortion that the amplified sound of the concert inflicted on his music—now cited by Pete Seeger and others as the source of their antagonism—only served to magnify the danger, and perhaps the audacity, of his move.

As a critic who came of age much later in the century, I like to think about what it must have felt like to be at Newport. Was it like the time I saw Einstürzende Neubauten in a parking garage in San Francisco or Mark Pauline in an empty lot in Hunter's Point? Was it like seeing GG Allin or the Butthole Surfers? Those acts really dismantled my expectations of what noises could come out of electric guitars and what was permissible on stage. I cowered during one, and experienced another—the entire Buttholes show—with my eyes shut tight so as not to have to watch a filmed sex change operation that was being cast on the screen behind them. But I don't know. Maybe it was more like first seeing Huggy Bear or the Sleaford Mods or something very, very lo-fi on the K record label, something that repudiates the rigid confines of music as we know it. As Susan Sontag had written a few years earlier, "Perhaps there are certain ages which do not need truth as much as they need a deepening of the sense of reality, a widening of the imagination. . . . An idea which is a distortion may have a greater intellectual thrust than the truth; it may better serve the needs of the spirit, which vary. The truth is balance, but the opposite of truth, which is unbalance, may not be a lie" ("Simone Weil" 50).

Today, it is harder and harder to believe that the booing at Newport was significant in the sense that it became significant to later writers and theorists. To contemporary audiences, it appears to have had no more resonance than the occasional shout-out at any local concert hall. A more plausible explanation is that, in the six months or so after the festival, the *idea* of the booing at Newport began a narrative about rock stardom and betrayal and commodification and crowds that helped explain a much larger anxiety. As Dylan himself once said, the booing wasn't about anything they were hearing. So what may be most significant about Newport isn't that Dylan went electric: it's that the audience went electric as well.

In *The Making of a Counter Culture*, Theodore Roszak describes the 1960s counterculture as a project intent on remodeling individual perception and disassociating it from what he terms "the technocracy." Roszak speculates that young people in the 1960s who were unable to come to terms with the strictures of life under the military-industrial complex turned to personal liberation in order to escape, and according to Roszak, this same transition could be seen in Bob Dylan's career. "Then quite suddenly, rather as if Bob Dylan had decided that the conventional Woody Guthrie ballad could not reach deep enough, the songs turned surrealistic and psychedelic. All at once Dylan is somewhere beneath the rationalizing cerebrum of social discourse, probing the nightmare deeps, trying to get to the roots of conduct and opinion," he writes (65).

At this distance, the idea that the roots of *conduct* and *opinion* in America would be found in the words of a rock singer seems to be sadly utopian (as well as naive), but at its foundation, it is a very sane assessment. After all, the *control of conduct and opinion* is exactly what was at stake in the battle between technocracy and counterculture. Rock concerts like Dylan's filled a void, joining together many disparate elements of society, and it was here that this cultural battle might be made visible. As Roszak notes, by 1966, "the neat distinctions between dissenting activism and bohemianism are growing progressively less clear" (*Counter Culture* 66).

So perhaps this lack of clarity was exactly what was so scary about Dylan's later concerts: the sense that what was once a community had become a crowd. Indeed, this inevitable transition from community to crowd is one that has always bothered rock fans and even rock artists: one is reminded of Kurt Cobain, who, upon attaining widespread popularity with a fan base whose members didn't reflect his own socioeconomic and political status, felt aggrieved that his records were in the same collections as records by bands he hated.[11] As Cobain well knew, by this time—the early 1990s—rock concerts had long become a kind of cultural shorthand for attendees, the fastest and easiest way to (temporarily) join in a certain shared consciousness. His fear was that this consciousness was a false one, and he was far from wrong.

In any event, the Newport Folk Festival of 1965 was the place where the spell was laid. The significance of Dylan's performance there is not that it showed the world the importance of Dylan but that it showed the world the importance of rock gatherings. No longer would the fields where rock 'n' roll drew its myriad fans together seem like silly pop dance parties for teenyboppers. Newport demonstrated that rock gatherings could and would be places where other meanings, other metaphors, and other messages could be acted out and then widely circulated. It heralded the approach of something somewhat terrifying: the shadow of an enormous crowd facing a far-off stage and listening together. Very, very, intently.

CHAPTER 3

California Dreamin'

N EWPORT WAS 1965. In the next two years, 1966 and 1967, the rock festival became codified, as rock bands and their hippie fans began organizing free "Be-Ins" in local parks. Be-Ins were a bit like outdoor concerts at piers and promenades, but they featured rock bands rather than symphony orchestras, and Be-Ins begat festivals. San Francisco, and particularly Golden Gate Park, was of course a nexus for this type of gathering, but it was hardly the only place where free music festivals were promoted. Seattle, Vancouver, and Portland all had them, as did many other major cities. It was in this period prior to Woodstock that the rhetoric of the rock festival as some kind of rural utopia was invented and encoded in the DNA of the form. When, at the end of the decade, three popular documentary films disseminated that vision to the world, the era of rock festivals was officially open.

Throughout the 1960s, developments in amplification, television, and handheld camera equipment with sound capability were responsible for the new ways that events like these were disseminated to the public.[1] Yet the denial of technology as a universal good was one of the fundamental underpinnings of both the counterculture and, to a lesser degree, rock festivals themselves. Instead, nature as an anticorporate signifier would become one of the main rhetorical strategies of Woodstock, helping to solidify young, suburban America's constant longing for antisuburban—that is, urban and rural—landscapes. Tantalizingly, the festival seems to provide a space that is neither . . . and both. An aerial depiction of the temporary city created for Bonnaroo, a yearly gathering held in subrural Tennessee, shows the rock festival spread out for miles, and what it brings to the region is not a celebration of nature, but temporary urbanity. Festivals like these are generally located somewhere near a main highway in close proximity to both rural and urban areas.

Today, the two largest festivals in America, Bonnaroo and Coachella, provide good examples of this type of locale: like Woodstock, which lies ninety miles north of New York City but just off the New York State Thruway, they are within an hour's drive to major metropolises, in places that are neither city nor wilderness. Such festivals—such imagined communities, if you will—may posit themselves as utopias, but in truth they resemble something far more temporary. A member of a rock festival crowd has rejected the city itself in exchange for the false city of the festival, a temporary home promising him or her different kinds of freedoms.

It is the freedom of the nursery, however: bounded and liminal.

——

Woodstock is more famous, but the most acclaimed hippie festival of the latter part of the 1960s was the Monterey Pop Festival, which would be the model for many mass festivals to come, particularly after it was disseminated via D. A. Pennebaker's highly acclaimed film *Monterey Pop* (1968). In addition to establishing rock festivals as both fun and culturally meaningful, the success of the two-day concert, which featured historic performances by Jimi Hendrix and the Who, gave a huge measure of economic legitimacy to rock festivals and at the same time opened up the world of the rock festival to money-seeking promoters—promoters like Michael Lang, who would attempt to profit from Woodstock two years later. By 1969, the rock festival form was a regular feature of summer entertainment plans.

Held twenty-four months after Newport, the Monterey Pop Festi-

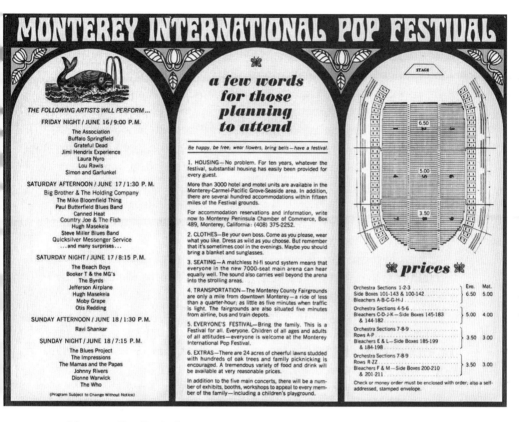

Monterey Pop Festival program, 1968.

val was in many ways the first truly commercially viable music festival as we now think of them. It lasted three days and showcased thirty-six incredibly diverse acts, ranging from bland pop types like the Association ("Windy") to rhythm-and-blues legend Otis Redding. It also featured the national debuts and seminal performances by then-unknowns like the Who, Jimi Hendrix, and Janis Joplin. More importantly, however, the festival drew together a like-minded audience of rock fans — "the Love Crowd," they were dubbed by the *Village Voice* — who would soon join forces with what was already being called the American counterculture. This counterculture had serious underpinnings, both artistic (Ken Kesey, Tom Wolfe) and political (through the antiwar movement and SDS), but the members of the so-called Love

Crowd weren't necessarily literary or political. Their visible presence at festivals like Monterey Pop was important, because it swelled the number of people who seemed to belong to the counterculture.

Lou Adler was the event's original promoter (with John Phillips, of the Mamas and the Papas). Adler was then a record-label owner who, in addition to promoting the Monterey Pop Festival, would later own the Roxy Theater in Los Angeles and become known for producing *The Rocky Horror Picture Show, Up in Smoke,* and various artists, including Jan and Dean, Sam Cooke, Carole King, and Cheech and Chong (among others). As of this writing, he is still in charge of administering the charitable funds that the Monterey Pop Festival video, album, and music continue to generate, and he says now that at the time, he was eager to get involved.

"It's a blueprint for all subsequent music festivals," Adler told me several years ago. "And it did establish rock as a force to be reckoned with," he adds (Arnold, "Pop Perfect"). Adler recalls the conversation that spurred on the idea of the festival in the first place. "It was a conversation we had at Mama Cass's house a few months before the event," he says. "It was me, John Phillips, Cass Elliot and Paul McCartney, and we were all talking about the fact that rock & roll — or what we called rock & roll then — was not considered an art form, like jazz and the blues. When it was first invented, in the 1950s, it was supposed to be this dumb thing that would be gone by the end of the summer, and here it was still thriving. So we were talking about ways to legitimize it, and one idea we had was to have a charitable event with all these different acts."

Soon after, Adler and Phillips were approached by some promoters who had wanted to do a one-day pop concert on the Monterey Fairgrounds, the site of the Monterey Jazz Festival. Adler and Phillips immediately saw this as an opportunity. "John and I had both heard that in the late '30s, the series Jazz at the Philharmonic had validated jazz to people. So we thought putting rock music at the site of the already established Monterey Jazz Festival would validate rock."

And validate it did. As Adler recalls, somehow, the three-day concert, held June 16 through June 18, 1967, seemed to take place under a lucky star. Everything that could go right, did — from the weather (gorgeous) to the music (incandescent) to the positive publicity.

"To this day," Adler says, "artists say it was one of the best events of its kind they were ever at. It really elevated promoters' outlooks on how to treat artists, and it made record companies conscious that the artist had power. After Monterey, they really gave them more freedom to choose their album cover art, their producers, their songs. . . . It had a lot of ancillary effects on the industry" (Arnold, "Pop Perfect").

One of the festival's main effects, he notes, was on concert promoting. "Artists were used to performing with a microphone and two small speakers," Adler recalls. "We wanted them to have the best sound, the best facility, the best food backstage. . . . We wanted it to be a utopia."

Adler's memories are reinforced by artists who played the festival. For example, the former Jefferson Airplane bassist and Monterey Pop Festival participant Jack Casady recalls that, since at that time there were really very few festivals, this one stood out all the more. "It wasn't like we went there with expectations," Casady says. "We weren't on tour all the time; we'd only been together a year and a half. Any gig was a good gig for us" (Arnold, "Pop Perfect"). The Monterey Pop Festival was a breakthrough event for the Jefferson Airplane, which became nationally known thanks to its performance there, but what Casady recalls best is the music itself, especially the sets by Redding and Ravi Shankar.

"It was just a great opportunity to see all these great artists we'd never seen," Casady says. "It wasn't really a free-form event, everyone had really short sets, but as a musical event it was just great. It provided everyone with a new environment to see all these different, eclectic acts that you might not listen to at home."

Adler agrees. "The music was on such a high level—the diversity of the artists, their excellence . . . and I don't really think that's ever been repeated on quite the same scale." In later years, says Adler, he and his partner John Phillips considered promoting another pop festival, but, he says, the times had already changed. "The citizens of Monterey weren't real happy about bringing it back; and prices had changed," he recalled in 2002. "The cost of the police, of liability insurance and everything—the whole atmosphere was different" (Arnold, "Pop Perfect").

But that was later. At the time, the Monterey Pop Festival had a huge impact on the public's perception of the rock scene and its fans. "The media coverage was worldwide," Adler says, "and that had never happened before. You can send out all the press releases you want, and if it's not in the media's psyche, then forget it. We had Derek Taylor, the Beatles' publicist, doing press, and we knew we had a lot of requests for media credentials, but it was still a shock, on the morning of the festival, to wake up and see all these TV crews from all over the world."

Of course, one reason why the festival was such a big success was its fortuitous timing. "Everyone was flocking to San Francisco at that time," Adler recalls. "The Haight-Ashbury was all over the news. It wasn't like people drove down from San Francisco to Monterey for the festival; they drove there from Cleveland and New York and wherever."

The filmmaker D. A. Pennebaker, who had shot the Dylan documentary *Don't Look Back* several years earlier, was hired to film the festival, and he concurs. "I had just seen the movie *Endless Summer*," he explained to me several years ago, "and it was totally apparent to me it wasn't about surfing, but about California. At that time, *everyone* wanted to go to California, so I thought about [the offer to make the film] for about two minutes and then said 'Yes.'" "It was," Pennebaker continues, "an extraordinary moment in American culture. There was a new sense of freedom in the air and that was reflected in the music, in the drugs, in everything. You could feel it coming like a hurricane" (Arnold, "Pop Perfect").

Pennebaker pauses to reflect. "What happened at Monterey," he says, "was, I found myself in the middle of this cyclonic thing, filming people of great magnitude and talent. I just couldn't miss. We just had to turn on the cameras."

Today, "just turning on the cameras" sounds like a simple proposition, but it was less so then, since film cameras were extremely large and bulky, and sound apparatus had to travel separately. Indeed, the whole idea of this kind of work was a relatively new concept in the 1960s, and it had been pioneered by Pennebaker's former employer Robert Drew in a type of documentary-making that was later called "direct cinema." (The film *Lonely Boy*, mentioned earlier, was part of this movement.) This was a filmmaking style that used very little voice-over or narration, relying instead on then-new portable micro-phone/video technology to capture dialogue as it happened. Drew had made several television documentaries using this technique, including *Primary* (1960), about the Wisconsin presidential primary, and *Crisis: Behind a Presidential Commitment*, which chronicled Attorney General Robert F. Kennedy's intervention in the dispute over the segregation of Alabama schools. (Pennebaker was a cameraman on both of these projects and went on to do his own films in the same fashion, notably the 1967 documentary *Don't Look Back*, which followed Bob Dylan's 1966 tour in the United Kingdom.)

The direct cinema style, Pennebaker says, was an especially good fit for filming festivals, and it turned out to be a good thing the cameras were there, since the money recouped from the film rights was all that made the festival economically viable. After the concert, Adler suddenly found that someone had run off with all the profits, leaving Pennebaker and the others $75,000 in the hole. They had already offered ABC television the right of first refusal for a TV special, but according to Adler, "We showed the head of ABC footage of Jimi Hendrix assaulting his guitar sexually, and he said, 'Take the footage!'" This left them free to use it however they wanted.

Pennebaker doesn't remember trying to shock ABC deliberately, however. "I suppose we could have fabricated a [television-friendly film of a] festival they could have lived with, but no one said I had to do that. The minute I sat down to edit it, I was editing a feature film."

Pennebaker's film, which became yet another blueprint for all festival concert films to come, was the first rock-concert film, and it looks the way it does in part, he says now, "because before then, it technically wasn't possible to record the music correctly."

He overcame that problem by borrowing two eight-track tape players belonging to Beach Boy member Brian Wilson. Pennebaker remembers his shock, upon flying to Monterey, to find out that the venue was essentially a livestock pen. "I'd never seen a concert with a lot of people at it even," he adds, "but when I walked around on what was going to be the stage area, and tried to visualize the number of people who would be there and the staging and how to shoot it—well, it all came together in my head."

Monterey Pop is a classic of the genre, mainly because the perfor-

mances captured in it were so spectacular. And the film itself was successful, grossing $2 million and spurring interest in the making of a
film of the Woodstock festival. (Pennebaker was offered the director-
ship of that one, as well, but he turned it down.) Most importantly,
however, the film played throughout 1969 at movie theaters across
the United States; it is clearly one of the reasons why so many young
people wanted to attend the many rock festivals that were organized
in its wake.

Thanks in part to the circulation of *Monterey Pop* during the summer of 1969, the appetite for attending rock festivals was peaking. Indeed, prior to Woodstock, there were rock festivals all over America
in 1969, and yet, surprisingly, most of them were unsuccessful: it was
actually dubbed the "Summer of Bummers" by *Rolling Stone* magazine (Hopkins, "Crashers, Cops, Producers"). Serious riots had broken out at festivals in Newport Beach, California, and in Denver. The
violence has generally been attributed to the cultural tension between
the cops (or "pigs") and the hippies, if not to the zeitgeist (as at Altamont). But, in fact, the root cause of most of the violence was often
the audience's collective refusal to pay an admission price. At every
festival that summer, it was the gate-crashers who would bring down
the wrath of the police, winding up in some cases, as in Denver, in
tear-gassing and worse.

The Denver Mile High Music Festival and the Newport Pop Festival (not to be confused with the Newport Folk Festival, in Rhode
Island) were the most violent festivals that summer, but such incidents marred almost all of the forty others listed in *Rolling Stone*.
Indeed, almost the only large festival that summer that lacked violence was held in Atlantic City at the Atlantic City racetrack, where
promoters had made a conscious decision to downplay security mea-
sures, allowing countless kids to crash the field (Lombardi, "Atlantic
City").

In the contemporary report of the Atlantic City festival, *Rolling
Stone* reporter John Lombardi astutely commented that one reason
why that festival was more successful than others may have had to
do with the cultural differences between East and West Coast audiences: "Unlike California, where everyone takes the sea for granted
and rides, walks or thumbs to the beach, the fifty- to sixty-mile trip

to the ocean for Philadelphia-area kids is still an excursion—the cultural revolution in the East is that far behind. [The kids] knew from experience the beach signs saying 'no people allowed on the beach from 10 PM to 6 AM'" (Lombardi).

Cultural conservatism may have played a role in the festival's success, but a more practical reason may have been that the local officials, who saw the festival as an opportunity for local businesses to profit, weren't worried about gate-crashers. In direct contrast to contentious battles in San Jose, Miami, and elsewhere, Atlantic City's city council almost uniquely came out in favor of granting the promoter an annual permit, on the grounds that "it was a well-behaved group and [we] do not feel it would hurt business" (Lombardi). The words "well-behaved" stand out here: clearly, the crowd was able to be "well behaved" because they were allowed to crash the festival. In all other accounts, when crashing is disallowed, the police are blamed for "overreaction" while gate-crashers are absolved.

Elsewhere, violence at festivals was a given, due in part to the deep-seated belief held by concertgoers that music should be available to them for free (a belief that would later surface in high relief at Woodstock). One gate-crasher at the Newport Pop Festival, which sparked riots, vandalism, and more than 300 injuries, told the reporter Jerry Hopkins, "I never pay to go to these things, man . . . why should I? I don't support these guys. I only support the people who need the money. I've been to every festival there is and I've never paid to get into one of them" (Hopkins, "Crashers, Cops, Producers"). This remark prompts the clichéd realization that the more things change, the more they stay the same: today, these music fans—and surely this particular music fan—would be downloading music illegally with similar self-justification.

Woodstock, held at the end of the summer of 1969, changed people's perceptions of rock festivals, but it was a unique event in that way. A more typical event—indeed, an event that showcased many of the same discourses that were circulating at rock festivals that year—was the Aquarian Family Festival, a two-day "free" event held on May 24 and May 25, 1969, on the football practice field of San Jose State University. The festival was held simultaneously alongside an event called

PRESENTED BY DIRT CHEAP PRODUCTIONS IN CO-
OPERATION WITH THE INSTITUTE FOR RESEARCH AND
UNDERSTANDING, THE THIRTEENTH TRIBE, THE DRUID
CORPORATION, THE SAN JOSE STATE EXPERIMENTAL
COLLEGE, AND THE SAN JOSE FREE UNIVERSITY.
LIGHTS BY MU, MASTER OF CEREMONIES:
ERIC "BIG DADDY" NORD AND NORMAN,
THAT FAMOUS WHIZ KID OF
FREE RADIO.

SONS OF CHAMPLIN - ACE OF CUPS - WOMB - LINN COUNTY
ALL MEN JOY - THROCKMORTON - TREE OF LIFE
WIERD HERALD - LAST MILE - CRABS - GENTLE DANCE
NYMBUS - CROW - DIVINE MADNESS - RUBBER MAZE
BIRTH - RED GRASS, GREEN SMOKE - LIBRAS - SABLE
GREATER CARMICHAEL TRAVELING STREET BAND
CLEANLINESS AND GODLINESS SKIFFLE BAND
GLASS MOUNTAIN - DENVER - BEGGARS OPERA
ELGIN MARBLE - JOY OF COOKING - LAMB
FRUMIOUS BANDERSNATCH - MOTHER BALL

**THE AQUARIAN
FAMILY FESTIVAL**

**MAY 23 & 24
FREE WITH LOVE**

LOCATED AT THE CORNER OF ALMA AVENUE
AND SENTER ROAD IN DELIGHTFUL SAN JOSE,
AT THE SAN JOSE STATE PRACTICE FIELD.
STARTS AT NOON ON FRIDAY THE 23RD
OF MAY AND GOES ON UNTIL - (?).

FREE MUSIC, FREE FOOD, FREE SUNSHINE.
COME AND BE WITH US.

SOUNDS UNLIMITED BLUES BAND - ZEPHYR GROVE
MORNING GLORY - RISING TIDE - OLD DAVIS -
MAD RIVER - HIGH COUNTRY - SANDY BULL
WARREN PURCELL - FLAMING GROOVIES
LIVING COLOR - STONED FOX - REJOICE
SOUTH BAY EXPERIMENTAL FLASH
MT. RUSHMORE AND
MANY OTHERS

SPECIAL THANKS TO THE DALY CITY HELLS ANGELS
AND ROGER CALLION MUSIC

Aquarian Family Festival, San Jose, 1969.

the Northern California Folk-Rock Festival, which was being held at
the family park adjacent to the Santa Clara County Fairgrounds, and
which featured Jimi Hendrix, Chuck Berry, and the Jefferson Airplane
as headliners. The Aquarian Festival is notable because it was almost
entirely absent from even contemporary media reports. With the exception of a few short newspaper articles and police reports, it's all
word of mouth from here on in.

Now, there's a lot of *Rashomon*-like conflicting detail in reports
regarding who played and what happened at this forgotten festival,
particularly because those I spoke with who were there are now in
their sixties and admit to ingesting large amounts of drugs at the
time. Although eighty thousand people were said to have attended
one or the other or both of these events that weekend, the *San Francisco Chronicle* makes no mention of them, since the newspaper was
taken up with more serious events, including protests in Sacramento
and in People's Park, that were going on simultaneously. The San Jose

Mercury did cover the Aquarian Festival, but called it the "AquariuM" festival—this is either a typographical or a reportorial error. The *Mercury* covers the festival in its issues of May 24, 25, and 26, with plenty of pictures with jolly captions making fun of hippie-speak, a small amount of attention paid to the violence and chaos that occurred in the neighborhood around the festival, and no mention of the dispute that sparked the festival in the first place.

These events seem to have carried no cultural weight at the time. But in fact, the Aquarian Festival was an almost spontaneous response to or protest against a promoter putting on the Northern California Folk-Rock Festival 2 at the San Jose Fairgrounds the same weekend. (Note the egregious use of the word "folk"—clearly a high art signifier that was meant to befuddle local opposition and borrowed from the Newport Folk Festival.) The year before, the first Northern California Folk-Rock Festival had been marred by a huge influx of PCP that sent one thousand people to the emergency room. It also had advertised numerous famous acts who failed to show up—since they hadn't been booked. In response to those abuses, a man named Dennis Jay contacted the promoter and asked if his organization, called IRU, could provide free medical help at the next year's festival. The promoter said, "If you pay me."[2] At the same time, radio station KSJO was warning listeners that the acts advertised on the poster—particularly Led Zeppelin and Jimi Hendrix—were not going to appear, since they were booked elsewhere for the same time. The latter situation resulted in a lawsuit against the promoter, who retaliated by paying Hendrix $30,000, an unheard-of amount at the time, to fly in by Lear-jet and play for half an hour.

Meanwhile, Jay and members of San Jose's Free University and the Druid Corporation, a nearby commune, and a few other groups (the Institute for Research and Understanding, the San Jose Red Eye, and Dirt Cheap Production) organized the Aquarian Family Festival to be held about a half-mile from the site of the Northern California Festival 2. The concert came about fortuitously. In addition to pissing off the promoter, the original point of this gathering had been merely to provide a place for hippies and travelers to camp and sleep between sets. Many of the attendees were expected to arrive from Berkeley, where they'd been protesting at People's Park, and this began a precedent: providing campsites near these events has now become the norm at festivals like Bonnaroo, Glastonbury, Roskilde, Coachella, and at least one playing of the World Quidditch Championships.[3]

Phil Sharkey was a member of the Druid Corporation at the time. In order to help people planning on coming down to camp, he used the then newly introduced Student Bill of Rights to requisition the San Jose State football practice field. But, he says, "the college, looking for an excuse to deny my request, but sensitive to the new Bill of Rights, laid down a rule that we could only use the field while there was music. I guess they thought that would solve their problem. [So] some of the Druid Corp and Dirt Cheap folks came up with the idea that we could use our weekly 'Be In' contacts to keep the music going. During this process, we found out that many of the bands who were on the bill for the Folk Rock Festival were not, in fact, planning on showing up. So the objective shifted to an alternative and free show."[4]

Because the conditions of the license were that music at this festival had to be continuous, the collective called up every band they knew. Ron Cook, a local luthier who performed at the festival and helped build its stage, recalls a list of bands' names taped to the sound board determining the order of play—similar to the way people now sign up for tennis courts. Moreover, more famous bands like the Jefferson Airplane rushed over from finishing their (paid) set at the Northern California Festival in order to show solidarity with the hippies. By all reports, the free festival drew approximately twenty thousand people (though Sharkey says it was eighty thousand). Although this number was dwarfed by the crowds that would go to Woodstock three months later, the concert is instructive because it exhibited many of the same narratives—yet none of the goodwill—of the later event. This may be because the goodwill stemmed from the film version of Woodstock, rather than from the reality.

The main theme that the Aquarian Festival illustrates is the tension between the "free" and the "paid" festival, which would play out to a greater degree at Woodstock, where concertgoers broke down the fences to attend. The genesis of this notion—that festivals should be free—seems to have arisen because some early psychedelic bands played for free in parks; later, when the bands became popular, the larger crowds required them to incur incidental expenses like sound systems and security. The early free festivals seem to have given your normative hippie a hazy (and self-interested) sense that they were "being ripped off" by "the man" if they were charged admission at outdoor festivals. It also seems to have something to do with nature: for some reason, audiences understand that they have to pay when the venue is indoors, even though an outdoor venue incurs all the same (if not more) expenses.

The Grateful Dead, obviously, fanned the flames of this when they "liberated" the equipment at the Monterey Pop Festival and played on it for free in Golden Gate Park: such acts gave rise to bizarre expectations of freeness on the part of their fans for the next thirty years. The film *Festival Express* documents a set of Canadian festivals in 1970 featuring Janis Joplin, the Grateful Dead, and others. Each festival is met with violence and protests from attendees who want it to be free. In one case, the bands play for free outside the grounds, thus angering those who'd already paid; in another, the promoter lets people in for free and winds up losing his shirt. The film has scenes of the musicians debating whether the fans should be paying to see them; their consensus is that they should. Needless to say, the fans don't agree — the trope of "free music in parks" had become too strong by then.

However impractical, the ideology of freeness was certainly well in play by 1969: a week before the Aquarian Festival, one hundred thousand people attended a free festival held in Grant Park in Chicago; it was considered a big success. An attempt to organize a festival called the Wild West Fest in Golden Gate Park in August that was to cost three dollars, however, met with such rancor and infighting from community members and promoters that it had to be canceled (Selvin, *Summer of Love*). During this period, the tension between paid festivals and free festivals was at the root of a number of very violent incidents; indeed, the violence that characterized the Aquarian Festival and later Altamont was not even remotely unique to those festivals.

The Aquarian Festival is also a useful lens through which to peer back at other non-"idyllic" discourses that were circulating at the time. Clearly race is one of those discourses. According to police reports, there were four stabbings at the festival — and two involved what were then called "negro" victims. (Moreover, Sharkey remembers witnessing three beatings, which he describes as retaliatory, if violent, in nature.) We know from this that African Americans did attend the festival, although probably not in great numbers. We also know there was some resistance to their presence—except, of course, on stage. Like Woodstock, this festival gave black performers a large performative role. In San Jose, at the main event (Northern California Festival 2) these roles were filled by Chuck Berry and Jimi Hendrix. At Woodstock, their roles would be filled by Richie Havens and Sly Stone, with Jimi making a reprise appearance.

As for women concertgoers, the newspapers in this era couldn't seem to get over the presence of topless women, and they foregrounded their presence in every article. In fact, it's hard to read archival reports of the Aquarian Festival without thinking that race and gender are—by their very absence in the record—central to the narrative. Today, *Rolling Stone*'s lack of outrage in its coverage of the festival is still startling: seven assaults, four stabbings, and fifteen attempted rapes merit the following lackadaisical report: "Stolen cars, property damage, stabbings, and one gang-bang with an involuntary chick headed the list of non-musical noise" (Hopkins, "Festival Shucks," 11).

The Aquarian Festival was a unique event, a weekly Be-In that successfully expanded into a giant festival, entirely run by volunteers, including the Hells Angels. (Sharkey says, "We did not 'hire' the Hells Angels. The San Jose Police were not permitted on the practice field, just SJSC security [and that was one guy]. The bikers [not just Angels, but Gypsy Jokers also] set themselves up in that role because it gave them access and a way to park their bikes on stage left. It was not possible to deny them under their understated but clear threat of violence.") And despite the body count, the Aquarian Festival was still largely characterized as "peaceful" by the press—since stabbings of negros and petty criminals—not to mention fifteen rapes—didn't seem to register much in the annals of the press at the time. Of course, in the same vein, it is necessary to bear in mind that "peaceful" may have been meant relative to the times. Just one week prior to this festival, the National Guard had teargassed five hundred UC Berkeley students, killing one of them; over the same weekend, seven thousand people, led by the Nobel laureate Linus Pauling, marched on Sacramento to protest police brutality to then-governor Ronald Reagan.

Three days after the festival ended, at a city council meeting, the Northern California Music Festival was chastised for the decibel level of the amps, in a hearing that has been reprised countless times since then at nearby arenas in the Bay Area and across the United States. Noise abatement has long been a tactic used to limit rock festivities: it would come, in later years, to be one of the main legal weapons in challenges to urban festivals, and noise is one of the main reasons why most festivals are held in rural areas: just recently, in 2017, Coldplay challenged a 10:00 p.m. curfew that could be said to have been first instituted by the Northern California Music Festival.

Despite all this, the very existence of the Aquarian Family Festival has almost been lost in the mists of antiquity; it is barely even a blip on the internet. Peering back in time, it is difficult to even imagine what it looked like, what it sounded like, and what it felt like to be there, because so much is different today. The entire region around San Jose State University has been swallowed up in the technology boom, and the idea of running a concert for twenty thousand people on *volunteer labor alone* simply does not compute. Instead, what we think of when we recall the summer of 1969 is a very similar (though infinitely larger) event that was held three months later in Bethel, New York. Like the Aquarian Festival, it was intended as a response to a canceled concert; it too "became" free by accident, and it required all kinds of negotiations with the community surrounding it. But the narratives emphasized by the mainstream press about what was officially called the Woodstock Music & Art Fair were entirely different than the ones at the Aquarian Festival. Instead of being critical of the event for its chaos, violence, traffic, and noise, the press championed the concertgoers for their peacefulness: the week after Woodstock, national magazines declared the "birth of a culture" (*Commonweal*), "a new culture of opposition" (*Current*), a "Whole New Minority Group" (*Newsweek*), and an "Underground Industrial Complex" (*Christian Century*). Why the change in tone?

One reason may have been the Woodstock festival's sheer size, which conferred on it the status of a "live media event." This in turn in some ways coerced the media into giving it their approval; and once they did that, Woodstock wound up as an anti–Cold War apparatus, reconciling young people who might otherwise have been put off by America's foreign policy problems to the joys of democracy, capitalism, and the "pursuit of happiness" proclaimed in the Declaration of Independence and guaranteed by the Constitution. Very soon after its occurrence, Woodstock came to stand in for America on the world stage, allowing the country to seem "free" at a time when it was in fact very much oppressed.

This shift may explain why Woodstock would soon become a catalyst or touchstone for forty years' worth of events that have capitalized on its success—not its monetary success (it didn't break even), but its ideological success. Visually, musically, and symbolically, Woodstock is now considered a culminating site of protest and social change, a utopian idyll where an entire generation was able to express its solidarity against the power elite.

Of course, the main reason why Woodstock, rather than the Aquarian Festival, is so well known is because of the motion picture made of the festival. Released a full year later, in 1970, the movie *Woodstock* (later called *Woodstock: 3 Days of Peace and Music*) would ignite a fifty-year-long glow in the hearts and minds of young people who saw it the world over. *Woodstock* has long served as a redemptive vision for a counterculture that might otherwise have to think badly of itself. It helped to popularize a number of long-lived bands. And it has inspired rock festivals ever since. In addition to its symbolic effects, the film has had a literal effect as well, by allowing the festival's promoter, Michael Lang, to recoup his losses (and then some). Prior to its release, Lang had lost an estimated million plus on the festival. The film earned $13.3 million in wide release and eventually grossed $50 million in the United States. *Woodstock*'s recorded soundtrack, in the form of a triple album, also sold well. These spectacular sales figures can only have been an incentive for future festival promoters.

The *Woodstock* film's most important function, however, has been discursive. The film was the most popular documentary of its era. *Woodstock* cast a far greater spell on those who saw it than did *Monterey Pop* (which came out a year earlier and was a considerably shorter film, clocking in at only eighty minutes long, as opposed to *Wood-*

stock's three hours). But the spell was not cast by the promoter's original vision of a hippie idyll, by the musicians' undoubted artistry, or by the audience's love-inspired behavior. The spell was cast by the filmmaker, Michael Wadleigh, who wisely used familiar nonfiction and fiction film conventions to shape an appealingly positive narrative out of a long and possibly not that pleasant three-day rock concert. Much of the film's success is due to its canny use of Hollywood tropes, to its anointing itself with the weighty title of a historic document, and to the way it flatters its audience, who are told over and over again that *they* are the stars of the event.

Truly, *Woodstock* is framed as a bildungsroman (novel of growth), with the festival itself standing in as Young Werther. It has a novelistic narrative arc, beginning with the construction of the stage on the site, and ending with its being dismantled. But this is not the only way in which the film frames itself as a novel of growth and discovery. Many of its images are directly linked to fictional devices, particularly the appreciation and worship of nature and the way that nature is linked in every frame to a teleological view of American history. The first twenty-five minutes of the film are devoted to shots of the pristine and empty green fields of Max Yasgur's farm in upstate New York. These shots are full of shimmering distant lakes and amber waves of grain— they are a course in American Idyll 101.

Gradually, these fields are invaded by handsome, shirtless young men on horses and tractors: it's like watching western expansion occurring right before our eyes . . . and guess what? It Is Good. A brief scene of these young men communally erecting the stage, lifting its framework high over their heads, is highly suggestive of old-fashioned barn-building or roof-raising; it implies that what is being built is not a stage, but a church. Not surprisingly, the men in these scenes are movie star handsome, strong and rugged, while the women in these shots (and in the film as a whole) are invariably shown as domestically contained, clad either in granny dresses or nothing at all. One beautiful young girl rides behind a craggy, bearded frontiersman on a horse; another, heavily pregnant, tends children.

Presently, the scene shifts to the arrival of the three hundred thousand young people who will fill the fields over the course of the weekend. An enormous amount of this footage is presented in split screen, a technique that will be much copied in rock films, which "quote" *Woodstock*; but here, it is a strategy that calls attention to Woodstock's dual purposes. On the one hand, the concert is spoken of as an organic, beautiful celebration of nature—of "going back to the garden," as the film's theme song puts it. (The song, "Woodstock," by Joni Mitchell, was written many months after the concert. It is sung here by Crosby, Stills, and Nash and then overlaid on the scenes of arrival, the first and most egregious instance of how music is altered in this film.) On the other hand, the festival is clearly a highly technical and technically mediated event. The film shows the mediation via complicated aerial shots that capture the traffic jams, through shots of the stage and of the amplifier towers, and many film-within-film scenes of the media interviewing people on the site. These reflexive moments allow the audience to see the concert as newsworthy and historic. But at the same time, the film's clever split-screen gimmickry and its use of hippie music and art shots serve to distance the filmmakers from mainstream media—a crucial move needed to woo its countercultural audience.

Another duality often brought to the fore in the film is the one between "the squares" and the "freaks"—that is, the townspeople and the hippies. Again and again, the film calls attention to the two "nations" that are merging here at Woodstock, as when townspeople praise the hippies and the hippies behave nicely in return. It is yet another fictional cliché from the genre of the western movie: the stranger comes to town; at first, he is looked at askance, but finally he is accepted and his difference is assimilated into the culture (as in *Shane, Stagecoach*, or *True Grit*). Over and over again, duality is on display, as when a shot of the moon is paired with a shot of the klieg lights, or when a shot of the vast crowd as seen from a helicopter is paired with the blissed-out face of an individual.

The film continues to purvey themes of duality, difference, and tolerance. The split screen continues to emphasize the size of the crowd and the duality of that size and individual moments: for a movie of a concert, there are fewer live shots than one might think (and quite a bit of the music was rerecorded). The weather comes in for a lot of airtime, as does female nudity. There are some famous performances, namely ones by the Who, Sly Stone, and Crosby, Stills, and Nash, but not all of the music we hear is presented live: much of it is used as background music for shots of concertgoers swimming, smoking, sleeping, talking, dancing, or doing yoga. The first performer, Richie Havens, is given an enormous amount of screen time, but he is almost de-raced by the film's obsession with depicting his feet and his hands. At the end of his set, Havens says, "This concert is about you . . . tomorrow people will be reading about you all over the world." This is the first sense that the audience gets that it, itself, is the star of the show. They have been invited into this space to perform as a rock crowd. It is an invitation they will continue to accept for the next forty years.

Another important visual argument that *Woodstock* (and to some extent *Gimme Shelter*) makes to viewers can be detected in its depiction of geographical space. In addition to addressing the more normative "back to the land" narrative that the counterculture was highly invested in at the time (see Fred Turner's *From Counterculture to Cyberculture*), *Woodstock*'s images of crowds in nature may well have addressed and even assuaged the public's growing fear of overpopulation. (The idea of a population explosion was very much in the zeitgeist at the time, thanks in part to Paul Ehrlich's enormously influential 1968 book *The Population Bomb*.) *Woodstock* calms these fears by showing a crowded world where everyone is still having a good time; a world where resources are shared and nature (in the form of the rainstorm that drenches the crowd on Saturday night) is benign. The aerial shots of upstate New York (and, in *Gimme Shelter*, rural Livermore) also assure viewers that the land is not under siege: over and over again we are reassured that it is endless, pristine, and there for the taking, once again evoking the epic American ideal (or idyll) of the West. This is Mohican territory, and one wouldn't be surprised to see Natty Bumppo (as played by Daniel Day-Lewis) charging into the scene.

Perhaps the most important assurance that Woodstock gives, however, is of America as a united nation. This is most evident in the final and most canonical scene in the film (a scene recreated in the 2009 film *Taking Woodstock*). In it, a farmer is interviewed about the concert. "I have two sons, one here and one in Vietnam," he says. "I wish they both were here." It is a comment explicitly meant to unite the two sides of debate—the counterculture and its opposition. That it worked is attested to by the wild success of the film, its longevity as a cultural referent, and the hundreds of recreations that take place every summer.

In sum, Woodstock's importance as a nonfiction film, as a vision, and as a marketing tool for rock cannot be overstated: it is the mainstay of the rock business's sense of cultural relevance and of its supreme self-confidence in its market. Joe Boyd, then manager of a band called the Incredible String Band, categorically believes that if that band had played in front of the cameras in the rain on Friday night, they'd have become the stars that Melanie—who took the Incredible String Band's time slot and is a central figure in the movie—became: they opted to take a later slot, weren't filmed, and flopped.

"We knew we had blown it," writes Boyd. "The extent of the error became clear in the months to come as the Woodstock film reached every small town in America and the double album soared to the top of the charts" (White Bicycles 223).

The film of Woodstock opened one year after the festival, in 1970, and it was immediately embraced by the public. The same cannot be said of Gimme Shelter, a film by the Maysles brothers about Altamont, a free Rolling Stones festival at which a young man, Meredith Hunter, was stabbed to death in the front row. Gimme Shelter, which chronicles another free 1969 concert, is Woodstock's Manichean rival, both in popularity and in spirit. Woodstock relied on filmmaking gimmickry and an underlying narrative point of view, while Gimme Shelter is a triumph of cinema verité filmmaking. Woodstock used typical news documentary techniques, while Gimme Shelter attempted to make viewers "live" the film: at the concert's height, the filmmakers deployed thirty-five camera people in the field (one of whom was a very young George Lucas) to capture crowd moments.

Because of these differences, on the surface, Gimme Shelter is the yang to Woodstock's yin, an unblinking depiction of the dark side of crowd gatherings, the concert that ended the Age of Aquarius and ushered in the tainted 1970s. In fact, a close reading of Gimme Shelter shows that it uses similar rhetorical strategies to make a similar point to that of Woodstock. Both films really valorize the idea of being part of a rock crowd.

Gimme Shelter began its life as a typical rock documentary about the Stones' 1969 tour. But halfway through, it morphed into something darker. This trajectory can be seen in its narrative, which begins with typical live-performance footage of the Rolling Stones. Then the mood darkens, as scenes are intercut with scenes of people attempting to set up the free concert that will later be dubbed Altamont. The arrangements for this concert—which first had to be moved thirty-four miles north from Golden Gate Park in San Francisco to Sears Point Raceway in Sonoma and finally fifty-six miles east to the Altamont Speedway—are portrayed as embattled, chaotic, and possibly not even in the band's best interest: lawyers and the media surround them, and there is a lot of shouting. And the mood darkens further as we "attend" the concert as it unfolds. We see people setting up stages, arriving at dawn, and partying. Gradually the images of peaceful attendees degenerate. There are a lot of freak-outs, naked people, and ugly images in the crowd: most of the individuals followed by camera people are visibly stoned and somewhat unhappy. We see shots of violence in front of the stage: concertgoers beaten by pool cues, Jefferson Airplane singer Marty Balin attacked when he attempts to interfere, other bands trying to calm things down, and more performance footage. Finally, we see the stabbing of Hunter, punctuated with scenes of the filmmakers, David and Albert Maysles, as they show the footage to the Stones themselves.

Because of that footage, *Gimme Shelter* has gone down in history as a dark film about a murder. But in the end, what is really upheld by the entire film is the Rolling Stones'—and live rock music's—mystique. The Stones, the film argues, are a wonderful live act whose decadent lifestyle and mesmerizing performances are a harbinger of moral chaos. The movie neither condemns nor praises the Stones or the violence at Altamont it depicts. Instead, it presents the Rolling Stones as atavistic romantic heroes from another age, and then, essentially, it exculpates them.

In short, *Gimme Shelter* takes familiar narratives from Hollywood and from fiction—in this case, the myth in which the powerful piper pipes the children down the canyon to their deaths—subjectively depicts it, and then dubs it a historic documentary. Also like *Woodstock*, *Gimme Shelter* presents the crowd as a distinct player in the proceedings. (The crowd: played by itself!) Somehow, then, *Gimme Shelter* argues that despite the violence at its core, attending festivals like Altamont is a crucial way of participating in American history. To have been there is to have been an actual actor in the scene: it is to have taken part in the shaping of a cultural moment. This is probably why, despite the film's stark portrayal of Altamont as the scene of a violent disaster, *Gimme Shelter* has not prevented generations of rock fans from eagerly plunging themselves into equally dangerous and potentially chaotic scenes. One leaves the theater thinking not "Gee, I'm glad I skipped Altamont," but "If only I had been there!" This is the thought that has fueled the engine of a thousand rock festivals across the United States and Europe and beyond: not just Coachella, Bonnaroo, Lollapalooza, and Austin City Limits, but Glastonbury, Sziget, Roskilde, and Rock in Rio. The early festivals at Monterey, Woodstock, and Altamont were just like puny little birthday candles, ranged across a decade of disaster. It's only thanks to the films made of them that they've turned out to be the relightable kind.

CHAPTER 4

Networks R Us: The US Festival, 1982–1983

OW DID WE EVEN GET THERE? That's what I can't remember. Someone's mother must have driven us, I suppose, all the way from our leafy green suburb, but I still find it baffling. There we were, four teenage girls in halter tops and cutoff shorts, carrying backpacks with simple Jell-O snacks and smelly suntan lotion (because SPF had not been invented yet). We weren't old enough to drive, so we must have been cursorily dropped off by someone at the crack of dawn on a freeway off-ramp in the extra-bad part of Oakland off International Boulevard. I wouldn't do it for my own daughter now, but I guess people did things like that in those days, because what I do remember is trudging across the parking lot of the Oakland Coliseum Arena with my friends and getting in line with a lot of other people to wait for the gates to open.

It was July 1978. The Oakland Coliseum was then, as it is now, the stadium home of the Oakland A's baseball team, but we weren't there to see them. We were there to see the Rolling Stones, along with Santana, Eddie Money, Peter Tosh, and Toots and the Maytals, at a Day on the Green, which passed for a rock festival almost a decade after

Woodstock. While we waited, a plane buzzed the parking lot, dropping party favors on the crowd. I got a fortune cookie, with the fortune, "Happy Birthday Mick Jagger." The gates opened at noon, and we all ran as fast as we could across the grass ("the Green") to get good places. The stage was somewhere in left field, and it loomed above us, miles high: even with a gap between it and the crowd, we realized that if we were too close, we wouldn't be able to see much without craning our necks, so we planted ourselves a bit farther back.

For the next four hours, we laid out towels and sunbathed and chatted with our neighbors. But after each act, the crowd would creep further and further up on us, until finally, after Eddie Money, we had to roll up our towels and stand. It was still a long three hours until Santana played, with the sun going down in the sky now, and our shoulders were all red and we were dying to go to the bathroom. Near the concert finale, I remember looking up at one point and seeing people on the third tier of the stadium, letting off streamers across the violet sky. They were actually unfurling rolls of toilet paper, which would float out in pretty patterns, crisscrossing one another, and I wished with all my heart that we had gotten to the stadium later, and were sitting up there—near a bathroom—instead of being where we were. The music would have sounded the same, and as it was I could barely see anything, so squished was I up against my neighbors, many of whom had big heads, in front.

Later on at school we bragged mercilessly about going to the Day on the Green. But I didn't rush back to one until years later, when I was able to get in for free. And by then I had a backstage pass.

Although I have fond memories of those ridiculous concerts, they illustrate how, in the 1970s, commodification overtook the rock market. By then, many large rock concerts that described themselves as festivals were reformatted as tours. They were held around the country in sports stadiums and speedways, becoming moneymakers for local (and national) promoters like San Francisco's Bill Graham and Boston's Don Law. Instead of representing some kind of countercultural community, large rock concerts became mere bacchanalias, where blue-collar youth could gather to drink beer and rock out. Throughout the 1970s and early 1980s, the rock festival moved further and further away from Woodstockian ideals and closer to what the filmmaker Jeff Krulik showed in his epic documentary about a rock crowd waiting to get into a Judas Priest concert, *Heavy Metal Parking Lot* (1986).

In 1985, this debased space was tweaked into a field rife for social change when Bob Geldof, the singer for a quite minor Irish rock band, created the world's largest audience for a concert he called Live Aid. The sheer size of this concert, held on July 13, 1985, dwarfed anything previously envisioned, but its importance as a rock festival is less as a live gathering and more as a mediated one: that is, as a live televised event. Before Live Aid, a person prized being present at a rock festival, as I had, so that one could say one had been there. After its occurrence, the rock festival was seen as an event that could live outside festival walls and inside homes, and it was also seen as a place where the naughty and rebellious elements of rock music could be chained to noble impulses and good causes. Such gatherings were events that could intervene in politically sensitive areas and mete out social justice, events through which power could be wielded in real-life areas. In other words, rather than, as previously envisioned, create utopias, some festivals were organized as a way to redress *non*-utopian spaces.

In subsequent years, Live Aid has been roundly criticized for how the money it made was used. But nevertheless, its achievement shouldn't be underestimated. What its organizer Bob Geldof did was to reenvision the festival space as one that could be used for education, consciousness-raising, and fund-raising. Moreover, Geldof saw that satellite television could be used to broadcast such a concert around the globe, live, to the inside of people's homes. These two ideas, conjoined, resulted in a sixteen-hour-long concert performed in two football stadiums on two continents that, through satellite feeds, reached an estimated audience of 1.9 million. Thirty years later, Live Aid is still a well-known event. But it didn't really come out of nowhere. In fact, like so many of the events that have informed the idea of musical pleasure in the twenty-first century, it was actually the natural outgrowth of an idea that Steve Wozniak, the cofounder of Apple Computers, had pioneered two years earlier: the US Festival.

The US Festival was the idea of a single person. It was enacted, however, through many links between a number of other institutions, including the U.S. Army, NASA, the Esalen Institute, and rock promoter Bill Graham. The festival that these weirdly assorted groups created led to some unforeseen outcomes. One outcome was Macworld, an annual computer exposition, and the profusion of technology-consumer expositions like it. Another direct outcome of the US Festival was CTC, the first FM radio and cable television station broadcasting in Russia and a precursor to detente. A less concrete but equally clear outcome that one can attribute to the US Festival is the symbolic linkage of money, music, and computer technology as a discourse that the culture at large now accepts as a natural, rather than artificial, triumvirate. Essentially, the US Festival was a space where these three entities were bound together in the mind of the populace in ways that differed substantially from how each had previously been imagined individually.

Lastly, the US Festival conjoined free-form radio and Apple computers in the public mind. Put simply, it anticipated a company called iTunes, and all that that implies.

Rock festivals always privilege a certain kind of imagined authenticity in commercial music, implying not only the idea that such festivals are a space of freedom and naturalness, but also that, by merely attending them, spectators are somehow taking part in a historic moment. The fact that the US Festival, with its corporate logo flag flying high above every crevice, was clearly a corporate event with a visibly corporate presence, made no difference to the attendees: if anything, it has simply made subsequent corporate events—like Macworld—seem more like rock festivals, rather than the other way around.

Although the US Festival demonstrates much that is pertinent to rock crowds and power, there is another important corollary inherent in this chapter about Apple's role in the music industry. With the invention of the MP3 and peer-to-peer file sharing and the subsequent change in how music is disseminated (circa 2000), some of the cultural significance and the emancipatory discourses that surrounded both radio and rock music have become obsolete: consuming music is no longer dependent on amassing large collections of records. Because of this, and because music can be distributed for free, young people no longer define themselves as much by the fashion, styles, and genres of said collections. Since the most successful commercial purveyor of digital music, signaling the death knell of the normative radio and record industry, has been Apple's iTunes, the US Festival's fusion of rock with the ideology of technological determinism is of particular significance to how music has evolved in the twenty-first century.

—

If you're under the age of fifty and you're not from California, you might not have heard of the US Festival. But this festival plays a significant role in the memories of many older southern Californians, especially among people (like me) who believe that the film *Fast Times at Ridgemont High* was an Oscar-worthy documentary—and that is not an insignificant number. The US Festival was held on Labor Day of 1982 and again for three days in May 1983, at Glen Helen Regional Park in Chino, near San Bernardino, sixty miles east of Los Angeles. The festival was spearheaded by Apple cofounder Steve Wozniak, who specifically conceived of it as a "Woodstock West." Each festival drew audiences of up to 170,000 people for a sum total of eight days (September 3–5, 1982, May 28–30, and June 4, 1983) and featured an eclectic array of popular white rock acts, including the Grateful Dead, the Police, U2, the Clash, Mötley Crüe, and Quiet Riot. The first festival was considered a rock festival, straight up; the second festival had a country-rock day added a week later. Although conceived by Steve Wozniak, the festival was run by a corporation called UNUSON.[1] According to his autobiography, Wozniak wanted to counter what he saw as the me-ishness of the 1970s by returning to the more collective vision he saw in Woodstock. Yet, in addition to whatever altruistic intention Wozniak may have had in attempting to create a collective atmosphere of peace and love, he clearly also wanted to create a forum to show off the possibilities of computers, specifically computers and music. Thus, the festival's main innovation over earlier festivals—an innovation that would be copied at later festivals and probably even more saliently at the annual Macworld conventions beginning two years later—was the inclusion of a series of tents and booths showing off computer technology and its possibilities in the realm of music.

Although the US Festival explicitly reneged on many of the utopian narratives of Woodstock and was considered a commercial failure in many ways (particularly fiscally), it did succeed in chaining the idea

of computer culture, and specifically Apple computers, to the popular vision of rock as rebellious, populist, and emancipatory. One year
later, in 1984, Apple's famous Orwell commercial first aired on commercial television during the Super Bowl; though to some the advertisement represented a groundbreaking narrative, it was actually just
an extension of the US Festival's computers-will-set-you-free rhetoric.
Both the ad and the festival used similar science fiction and futurist
motifs, emphasizing the idea that computers would change the world,
a narrative quite different from the utilitarian functional applications
touted by IBM and later by Microsoft and a key to the underlying success of the US Festival's rhetoric.

Moreover, the US Festival's protean linkage of music and computers can also be mapped forward into some of the applications
of the iPod. The festival's role as a "network forum"—the term used
by Fred Turner to describe objects or sites where such linkages are
made—is visibly enacted in iTunes, a literal network (that is, as a dis-
tributor of content) that is currently in the process of replacing how
popular music is disseminated.

The initial concept of the US Festival began, in its founder Steve
Wozniak's own words, as "a Woodstock West," though later on he
would disclaim that title and refer to it instead as "the Superbowl of
rock festivals" and "the world's biggest party." The festival—produced
twice in a nine-month period—drew a total of almost a million people,
cost over $40 million, and is mostly remembered today for the large
amount of money it lost. However, it was successful in other ways.

First, Wozniak's deep pockets showed subsequent promoters how
to create large rock festivals on "outside lands" and established them
as safe, hygienic, fun "parties." By showcasing popular, apolitical acts,
it expanded the type of audience attracted to these festivals to include
blue-collar and conservative young people, while adding to the sense
that such festivals were destinations well worth attending. Second,
by using the established countercultural tropes of communal utopia,
American idyllicism, and music as a "free" commodity, the US Festival succeeded in establishing a link between Apple computers (which
Wozniak cofounded), computer culture, and rock music, linking all
the attendant "hip" discourses of rock music to the essentially cere-
bral and scientific discourses of computers. The success of this linkage
cannot be overstated.

Finally, in a move spearheaded by the Esalen Institute, the second US Festival, partly sponsored by the U.S. Army and by NASA, created a satellite link with a Russian radio station to broadcast on the main stage to the crowd in San Bernardino a concert by a Russian band called Arsenal (as well as broadcasting back to Russia a performance by Men at Work). This groundbreaking event, though it certainly foreshadowed glasnost, also serves as a much-needed reminder that the US Festival (like Woodstock and Altamont) occurred during the Cold War. Broadcasting a rock performance to Russians—and forcing three hundred thousand Americans to watch Arsenal—is a marked example of the fact that the spectacles which draw rock crowds together are in fact instantiating American ideals of capitalism, freedom, and individuality, while at the same time injecting them with a capitalistic underpinning that allows for easy consumption. The rock festival is and always has been a visible metaphor for these ideas, but the US Festival makes the connections more visible than most.

The US Festival actually owes less to Woodstock than one might think. Instead, its genesis seems rooted more in the history and development of 1970s free-form radio formats. Like rock festivals, radio has always had the potential to create discursive communities, though it has seldom been used in exactly that way. Indeed, in his "The Radio as Communications Apparatus" (1932), Bertolt Brecht suggested that the radio of his day and age needed to be "transformed from a distribution apparatus into a communications apparatus. The radio," he added, "could be the finest possible communications apparatus in public life, a vast system of channels. That is, it could be so if it understood how to transmit, how to let the listener speak as well as hear, how to bring him into a network instead of isolating him" (43).

Brecht's call for radio to become a "two-way" system—for the audience to be able to "talk back" to it—is interesting for two reasons. First, this is essentially what the internet, particularly in its 2.0 version with tags, wikis, and blogs, has allowed for. However, it could also be argued that festivals preceded this development by some years, becoming an interim place between radio and the internet. There is an undoubted parallel between broadcast technology—that is, the distribution of sound to a wide geographical area—and the narrower "cast" of music broadcast live in the bounded space of the festival grounds. Both rely on amplified sound to project their ideas;

both are systems that distribute content. Another word for a system that distributes content is a *network*. Hence, the connection between radio broadcasting systems and festivals. Both are networks, with one (the festival) becoming the embodied form of the other (the radio).

Brecht's logic also precedes some of the new ways in which festivals configured audiences. In some of Brecht's earlier plays he asked for the audience to assume the roles of performers—by playing the airplane crew as well as cheering multitudes in *Lindberghflug*, for example. When festivals like Woodstock anointed the audience itself as a character in each performance, they made a similar Brechtian gesture, albeit with a more lasting effect.

Brecht's ideas for radio, however, were radical. The more conventional use of radio has often been characterized as a strong form of propaganda: from its early days carrying Hitler's message in Nazi Germany to present-day debates over talk radio shows hosted by Rush Limbaugh and Howard Stern, there has been little question that the form lends itself to ideological rhetoric.

Today, the days of radio as "a substitute for theatre, opera, concerts, lectures, coffeehouse music, the local pages of the newspaper . . . practically every existing institution that had anything at all to do with the distribution of speech or song," as Brecht put it, are almost over (41). And yet, there is no doubt that the US Festival was inspired in part by FM radio—that is, by one specific FM radio station, which exemplified the concept of the free format. The station in question was KFAT, and it was Steve Wozniak's favorite.

Wozniak has consistently cited KFAT as the direct inspiration for the US Festival. In his autobiography *iWoz*, he says:

> I was driving around in my car listening to a radio station—KFAT out of Gilroy, California—a station that had heavily influenced me during the Apple days. You see, I'd changed my music tastes from normal rock and roll to a type of really progressive country by then.
>
> This was a new and strange type of music I'd never been exposed to before—a lot of folk, a lot of country, and a lot of comedy. It wasn't some dumb old countryish beat and song and themes; these songs were a lot about life. They very much

reminded me of the sort of thinking Bob Dylan did, being as familiar with his lyrics as I was. And these songs went as deep—they pointed out what was right and wrong in life. The way they were written and the way I experienced them brought out a lot of emotion in me. I mean, there was a real meaning attached to these songs and I was heavily influenced by this station.

At around this time, I recall seeing the movie *Woodstock*. There was a meaning attached to that movie, too. A meaning that had to do with young people growing up and trying to find alternative ways of living. And so much of that was brought up in the words of these new progressive country songs I was listening to, like a music revolution was starting all over again.

And it hit me. I thought: Why not? Why not try to do a kind of Woodstock for my generation? I realized at this point that I had so much more money than I could ever dream of spending. I was thirty at the time and probably worth a hundred million dollars or more. I thought: My god, why not put on a big progressive country concert with these groups I loved? A lot of people might come. (245)

Wozniak's encomium of KFAT exemplifies how FM radio was viewed by many rock music fans in the 1970s. During that decade, hippie culture was in abeyance, and rock culture was at its most bland, white, and corporate. Yet this one station, KFAT, managed to bring together seemingly disparate musical ideals into a "free-form" ideology that contributed to its legendary status in radio. The station had a unique personality and a clear playlist of artists that spoke to a certain type of listener: often conservative, blue collar, or military, and what might be described as "redneck" by California standards. The station was beloved in its signal area (the southern Santa Cruz Mountains) and is still deeply missed there.

One of the most interesting takeaways from Wozniak's quote above is that he only saw the film *Woodstock* in 1978; unsurprisingly, one also finds out, he was a Republican as a teenager. Although in 1969, at the age of nineteen, he was living less than an hour's drive away from Golden Gate Park, he somehow missed out on the Summer of Love and was, in his own words, looked at askance by hippies, who, he says, "wanted him to do drugs." His heartbreaking description of himself at the time speaks to the difficulty he and others like him had with the counterculture:

> I would wear a little Indian headband, and I wore my hair really long and grew a beard. From the neck up, I looked like Jesus Christ. But from the neck down, I still wore the clothes of a regular kid, a kid engineer. Pants. Collared shirt. I never did have the weird hippie clothes. I was still middle ground; I was still the way I'd grown up. No matter how hard I tried, it was like I couldn't get outside of normal. (81)

This description pretty much fits the profile of many KFAT listeners. It also fits the description of most US festivalgoers (as depicted in the video footage). Furthermore, it entirely fits the description of Macworld attendees, the future computer geeks who will soon be born from the ashes of the US Festival. In fine, the US Festival was a boundary-buster—a gaudy, vulgar spectacle for the masses, a lowbrow version of Stewart Brand's more highbrow endeavors like the *Whole Earth Catalog*, the *Whole Earth Software Catalog*, the WELL, and the hackers convention. In his book on the history of those artifacts, Fred Turner notes Brand's connection to "culturally central institutions" like MIT, Stanford, and Hewlett Packard (*From Counterculture to Cyberculture* 4). But neither Wozniak nor his partner Steve Jobs was affiliated with these kinds of elite institutions: Jobs briefly attended Reed College before dropping out, and Wozniak attended De Anza Community College in Cupertino. In a very real sense, the US Festival's appeals were being made to the graduates of De Anza, not to graduates of Stanford; to listeners of KFAT—especially to those in the military—not to listeners of KZSU (Stanford's alternative radio station, one of the few places you could hear bands like the Clash and Gang of Four at that time). Thus, the US Festival was the moment when Woz's version of Brand's vision reached those educated at the De Anzas of the world, rather than the MITs. The US Festival's triumph may well have been that it took the edge out of rock festivals, allowing even those who, like Woz, "couldn't get outside of normal," to access them.

Radio itself as a broadcasting medium had long been one of Wozniak's underlying interests. Making a shortwave radio was one of his first engineering projects, which later inspired the digital circuitry ideals in the phone phreaking he did during his teenage years. KFAT's free-form ideology and progressive country music were also attributes Wozniak attempted to instill in Apple Inc., the company he began with his friend Steve Jobs in 1976, making him wealthy beyond his wildest dreams by 1980. That these ideals were central to his self-conception can be inferred from the importance he seems to have placed on the idea of a music festival that he funded himself (to the tune of $40 million). Even today, that is a vast amount of money to spend on a festival. Peter Ellis, whom Wozniak hired to produce the festival, recalls the absolute shock he felt when, after an initial meeting with Woz to discuss their plans, he left his home with a personal check for $2 million in his pocket to get the organization started. Ellis recalls that he and his friend, Jimmy Valentine, a local promoter, "drove over Highway 17 with that check in our pocket just not really believing it had happened." In his memoir, Wozniak reiterates that he "just wanted to throw a party." Truthfully, there is almost no rational explanation for the existence of the US Festival except that Wozniak was thoroughly convinced that rock music was of cultural importance as a meeting ground and communal space for all his own interests.

The US Festival was in fact not run by Apple per se, but by UNUSON, a separate corporation begun by Wozniak, who was already a multimillionaire when he quit Apple in 1981. According to his own documents, Woz developed his idea of a "Woodstock West" after meeting Jim Valentine, the manager of the local 1960s cover band that played at his (Woz's) wedding. Valentine introduced him to Peter Ellis, an EST enthusiast and former activist at San Jose State University who had organized a "survival fair" there in 1970. Although he had no previous concert organization experience, Ellis, who had a PhD in community organizing, had just finished creating—and selling off—the University of Phoenix. Because that idea had begun with a program pairing law enforcement courses with community education, Ellis had many, many contacts in local law enforcement and knew how to "work with city councils."

According to Woz:

Peter came up with the suggestion we call it the US Festival. At first I wasn't too excited—the name didn't have the futuristic grab of a science fiction title or the magic of a name like "Apple." He spoke of the progression from "me" thinking to "us" thinking in the 80s. I didn't think much of it, but found myself thinking how right he was continually for the next week or two. In order to promote the social significance of what we stood for, I required time spent discussing the US philosophy for a few meetings. Peter also came up with the idea of including a tech fair in the event of the 80s and attempting an unheard of satellite linkup with rock musicians in Moscow. (*US Festival*)

Ellis now says that he came up with the ideas of the US theme and the tech festival because he couldn't see any other way to sell the festival to the local (Glen Ellen) city governments from which they'd need to get permits. Once he'd cashed his large check, he had moved down to Glen Ellen for a few months to cultivate the locals (Ellis). The US Festival owes much of its success to the way he and his employees were able to sell those living in the area on having a giant rock concert in their county; the tech festival was, he says, key to getting them to agree to have it, in part because it seemed so respectable.

In addition to technology, another clear narrative of the festival was democracy. In 1983 the Cold War was still raging, so the satellite broadcast from the Soviet Union, the centerpiece of the second US Festival in 1983, was much more radical than it seems today.[2] The Russian-American exchange—first mentioned by Ellis—came about via the involvement of Jim Hickman and the Esalen Institute's Soviet-American exchange program. Peter Gerwe, a twenty-three-year-old communications major at the University of Santa Clara and a friend of Ellis, helped set up the satellite broadcast between the US Festival and the Soviets' Gosteleradio, or State Committee for Radio and Television. The transmission was aired twice, once live in the morning and once taped in the evening. What US Festival viewers saw on the giant video screens—some of the first used in large settings—was some Russians gathered in a Moscow television studio watching the US Festival live. (It is morning in California and evening in Russia.) The Russians were treated to the set by the Australian act Men at Work. Afterward, on the US Festival site a group of five hundred carefully screened students took part in a staged "conversation" with the Russians, which was also broadcast live on both the US Festival and the Russian screens. Incredibly, included in the front row were a Native American dressed in full war paint and feathers (in a twisted way, does this foreshadow Coachella's obsession with headdresses?) and several African American concertgoers pulled from the crowd and placed specially in the front rows of the broadcasting tent.

The talk-show style presentation featured astronaut Rusty Schweickart, cosmonaut Vitaly Sevastyanov, the U.S. congressman George E. Brown (D., Riverside), the Soviet scientist Evgeny Velikov, Wozniak, Maurice Mitchell of the University of Southern California, and the Soviet academician Zoya Malkove. It was moderated by Sam Keen, of *Psychology Today* (Krier, "U.S.-Moscow Hot Line"). Most of the official questions concerned the idea of peace, the use of nuclear weapons, and technology. But other questions—from the audience— were about the status of women, pop stars, college entrance exams, sports, *ET* (the film), and Atari. At one point, an American audience member asked the Soviets if there was much rock 'n' roll in the Soviet Union. "We like jazz and rock," was the response, "but what everybody likes best in the Soviet Union is rock 'n' roll" ("To Russia with 'US,'" quoted in US Festival program; private footage).

In the private footage that I watched of this event, one can see the American audience rising to its feet to cheer this remark, which was the only one that seemed to resonate with those not in the technology tent: indeed, there was a strong overall suggestion that the audience in the arena wasn't clear about what was happening on screen. Nevertheless, the question itself—and the scene—make two important points. First, it was an early grasping at the idea of the two-way communication that Brecht (and others) suggested would turn communications into a more socialist apparatus, preceding the internet's two-way affordances. Second, the broadcast underscored what exactly the US Festival was helping to make visible to the public. It emphasizes the longing of the audience to see its presence at this concert as meaningful—even though all they are doing is drinking, camping, and rocking out to silly music. Woodstock managed to elevate the audience's view of itself by inserting narratives of social change and communal utopia. Minus the countercultural subtexts, these activities at the US Festival can become meaningful only if they are displayed (via satellite) to people who—at least in the audience's mind—are *not* free to enjoy the same kind of freedoms at home.

Another important theme at the US Festival—spurred perhaps by the overall doctrine of utopia that festivals always invoke—was the Future. To that end, science fiction imagery and rhetoric were incorporated into the fairgrounds, starting with a fake UFO that hovered over the arena at night (it was attached to a helicopter that dangled it over the crowd.) A half-page ad taken out by the Church of Scientology ran in the *Los Angeles Times* on Sunday during the festival, advertising the appearance of Chick Corea (who, according to one observer, showed off his use of a Fairlight synthesizer in their tent while flanked by a giant statue of an alien and attended by scientologists dressed in kilts). The *Los Angeles Times* ad depicts the cover of L. Ron Hubbard's book *Battlefield Earth*, floating over a roughly drawn graphic of the US Festival grounds.

Although the scientologists' agenda was quite different from that of the US Festival, the ad captured the disparate jumble of US Festival ideology—from the "future is now" to the promises of outer space that hung over the festival. It even includes the word "free"—free cassette. Perhaps most important is its final plea: "multimillion dollar music computer extravaganza," which crowds the festival's three main appeals—millions, music, and computers—into its copy and by so doing begins the process of naturalizing these disparate themes. Nowadays these three things seem perfectly compatible, but in 1983, the extreme tension between them can best be felt in the arguments over commercialization that raged around the appearance of the band the Clash at the second US Festival in 1983. Criticism of the band for appearing on this bill reached such heights that the band eventually had to call a press conference in Los Angeles to explain why they were doing it. Joe Strummer, an electric guitarist who had rarely, if ever, performed unplugged, appeared at this press conference with an acoustic guitar slung over his shoulder, a gesture one can only presume was antitechnology. (It also brings to mind, doubtless deliberately, Woody Guthrie's acoustic guitar and his "this machine kills fascists" rhetoric.) According to Strummer, the band accepted a half-million dollars in order to "inject social realism into the scene." He also told the *Los Angeles Times*, "I refuse to be processed cheese. We want to stand up and be counted" (London, "Fear and Loathing"). He also claimed that the band's profits would be used to help struggling English bands.

The times are different now; plenty of theoretically "pure" bands are able to justify selling their songs to companies like Apple and Volkswagen as jingles. But back then, punk bands were supposed to eschew large paychecks, and it's hard to ignore the discomfort of the Clash with their role—not to mention their complete inability to justify their presence. In another (privately taped) film clip Strummer's manager, Kosmo Vinyl, can be seen decrying the US Festival and Wozniak in particular. He calls the festival "the biggest media joke ever," accuses the festival of selling (metaphoric) "Woz burgers," and says, "If he's so public spirited, aren't there better things to spend [this kind of money] on?" (*US Festival* footage).

According to the *Los Angeles Times*'s reporting of the event, "Strummer's most emphatic remarks addressed a key theme of the festival, the relationship between technology and progress. 'So we can mass program any information and send it in the wink of an eye,' he [Strummer] said. 'What's it going to say when it gets there? . . . I can buy a hi fi that plays music from every door of my car, but what's the music going to *say*?'" (London, "Clashing Opinions").

Ironically, Strummer, who passed away in 2002, is prominently featured in Julien Temple's film *Glastonbury*, raging onstage in the mid-1990s against the ejection of travelers, hordes of New Age hippies who attend Glastonbury each year for free. However, it is difficult to surmise what his opinion would have been regarding the digital downloading of music for free. If he was as against technology as his US Festival rant implies, he may well have been against digital downloading as well. However, if he wanted music to be available for free, as he claimed at Glastonbury . . . well, who knows?

Strummer's anticomputer remarks, however, are untypical, and controversy surrounding the tech festival was minimal. According to an article about the first US Festival published in the October 1982 issue of *Softalk* magazine, a decision had been made—almost certainly by promoter Bill Graham—a month before the festival to advertise it primarily as a rock show, rather than as a tech festival. *Softalk*'s report on the festival is one of the few that concentrates on the technology more than the rock. Like everyone else who wrote about or

attended the festival, the author, David Hunter, admits that the computer fair—housed in five huge circus tents—was mostly attended
by people attracted to the air-conditioning, rather than by the technology exhibits, but he waxes eloquent on the contents of the tents:

> A wildly diverse group of exhibitors spread their wares for the
> steady stream of sweaty bodies. Fox Video Games unleashed their
> "Games of the Century," including Worm War I, Deadly Duck,
> Beany Bopper, and Fast Eddie. Produced by Sirius Software, the
> games are compatible with the Atari Video Computer System and
> the Sears Tele-Games machine.
>
> Fox Video, a wholly owned subsidiary of Twentieth Century-
> Fox Film Corporation, must have been pleased at the attention
> awarded their new games at the Us Festival. Jerry Jewell of Sirius
> was in attendance and actually smiled once or twice.
>
> Computers, computer games, video arcade games, science,
> music, and science fiction were the main themes of the tech-
> nology fair. Apple, Atari, and Quantel Computers all had respect-
> able displays. Exhibiting products for the Apple were Link Sys-
> tems, Softape, Novation, R. H. Electronics, FMJ, Passport Designs,
> and Syntauri, to name a few. Three of the tents had several dozen
> standup arcade games each. Old and young alike tested their skills
> against Defender, Tempest, Zaxxon, Red Clash, Centipede, Crazy
> Kong, and others.
>
> Kittlevision had a small booth where they imparted information
> on various components for home satellite receiving stations. There
> were brochures for Television Receive Only, TVRO, billed as the
> "finest home entertainment system available today." From United
> Satellite Systems, TVRO features more than fifty television chan-
> nels and they're predicting one hundred and fifty by 1985. (Hunter,
> "Steven Wozniak Throws a Party")

From this description, it's easy to surmise that the technology on
display at the fair was both primitive and prescient. One of the technology tents was a big fake silver UFO with a slit window. Inside,
there were a number of robots that looked a lot like the robot in *Lost
in Space* or R2D2 and a futuristic-looking car. There was an exercise

machine that linked to a computer screen to track how much weight you've lifted—clearly predating the stuff you can see at any YMCA gym today. There was a mockup of the then-new *Challenger* space shuttle and a *very* primitive version of the video game *Street Fighter* and other Atari products. Judging from the archive, the graphics and colors on the computer screens appear to be totally primitive, and yet one has to acknowledge that most of these ideas—from the video games to the exercise machines to the cars injected with smart technology to the Roomba and the Prius—have become commonplace thirty years later.

On the other hand, Michael Moritz, whose book *The Little Kingdom* chronicles the rise of Apple, describes the technology fair as a sad disaster. The fair, he says,

> fell victim to the heat and the dust. It was no traveling Homebrew Club or West Coast Computer Faire. Some exhibitors failed to show; others found that their machines weren't designed to cope with the full might of Southland weather. Many of the visitors seemed to be as interested in the heaving air conditioners that struggled to cool the marquees as in the exhibition. There were some cheap examples of the power of technology, like the banks of telephones and the Walkmans and the women plugging their curling tongs into the electric cables that ran inside some of the theater sized marquees.
>
> But the triumph of technology was displayed late one night when three men were setting up a demonstration of a television satellite dish. They used a microcomputer to calculate the pitch and tilt needed to find a satellite floating twenty-five thousand miles high and monitored the results of their efforts on a color television. They adjusted the dish, skipping from one invisible satellite to another, until they found what they wanted: a Los Angeles porn television channel bouncing a signal more than fifty thousand miles so that three men in the California desert could watch a naked black woman perform cunnilingus on her equally bare, white, female partner. It was, at least, a marriage of community and technology and the festival organizers would not have been surprised to learn that the women worked well together. (315)

And yet despite his conclusion, Moritz's recounting of this incident, if accurate, shows that the technology on display was quite sophisticated and ahead of its time: Dish TV was twenty years in the future. It also surely foreshadows the intense interest and possibilities that porn would open up for the internet. Finally, and most importantly, it shows the coming conflation of information with entertainment. The porn incident in particular prefigures the adoption of computers as instruments of pleasure, as opposed to how they were certainly being sold at the time, as instruments to enhance work and crunch data.

That computers *could* be instruments of pleasure was clearly how they were viewed by many of their early adapters—Wozniak with his early dial-a-joke and phone-phreaking applications and Nolan Bushnell with Pong certainly saw this capacity very early on—but it was not how computers were viewed in the culture at large. Indeed, in the world of rock music, for instance, the use of synthesizers was particularly fraught. For many musicians, listeners, and critics, using a synthesizer in rock music defied the notion of "authenticity" defined by acts like Dylan, the Grateful Dead, Bruce Springsteen, and the Clash. Early critiques of synthesizer music tended to equate it with disco (which had its own built-in prejudicial narratives, some of them racialized). Indeed, almost every one of the synthesizer's best-known uses—click tracking, overdubbing, lip synching, and mimicking other instruments—were read as dehumanizing by music aficionados—at least in America. (In British popular music, synthesizers weren't nearly as frightening.) Yet synthesizers in rock became popularized in spite of this antitechnology mindset, and the US Festival alerted the market to them.

The US Festival may have done this accidentally. But it is interesting, given Wozniak's original statement that he wanted to "create a festival that was like KFAT's playlist," that the festival did indeed manage to confound musical conservatism and futuristic technology. By creating a nonbohemian festival—a festival for the ordinary, a festival with pretensions to capitalism rather than to art, a festival populated with a large percentage of young military men from nearby bases who'd been given discounts on tickets—the US Festival was able to widen the audience of potential computer users and video gamers considerably. Thus, just as KFAT's playlist invited unprogressive rock fans to consume its "outsider" image via silly scatological jokes, the US Festival was able to make ordinary people comfortable in ways that Woodstock never would have done.

Moreover, having done so, the festival was then able to display a new facet of capitalism—computer culture—in a way that made it perfectly clear that this was the road to wealth.

———

As previously mentioned, the US Festival is not well remembered by the culture at large, and one reason might be because of the very odd mix of acts that performed there in both years. To a young person used to hearing them all on Sirius XM's 80s station, they may just seem like a bunch of oldies acts, but at the time they were a hot mishmash of acts whose audiences didn't jibe. The first US Festival had what Robert Hilburn of the *Los Angeles Times* deemed "classy" acts like Gang of Four, the Police, and Fleetwood Mac—the very uncool (and, by the standards of the time, elderly) Grateful Dead were added at the last minute to help sell tickets. The second US Festival, which was booked by a different organization with an eye toward bigger ticket sales, included a Heavy Metal Day featuring Ozzy Osbourne, Mötley Crüe, and Quiet Riot (all of whom could be deemed AM radio staples). The second US Festival also included David Bowie, the Clash, and a country-music day featuring Jerry Jeff Walker, Willie Nelson, and Emmylou Harris.

Today, these lineups seem kooky and disparate, like an iPod on shuffle whose owner shares his library with his parents and his siblings. Rest assured, it seemed weird at the time, too: the aesthetics of the festival were confusing. What it wasn't confused about was the relationship it was trying to forge between music, money, and technology. In an interview with the *Los Angeles Times* after the first US Festival, Bill Graham said, "Over the years, people began thinking of Woodstock as this paradise, but it was far from pleasurable for most people. They sat 15 to 20 miles down the road. The real thing that Woodstock accomplished was that it told America that rock is big business. What we wanted to tell people here is that we've all matured—that people can be treated decently and that they'll respond decently" (Hilburn, "Graham's Really Big" 1). Graham's message in this quote—that music is business—was one that most people didn't want to hear, and still don't. It is a message that goes against the prevailing myths that underpin not just festivals, but rock 'n' roll—and FM radio. There's a pertinent parallel in *Revolution in the Valley* told about Steve Jobs: directly after the release of the Macintosh II, he and his colleagues rushed to New York City in order to present one in person to Mick Jagger, who was polite, but befuddled, incoherent, and unimpressed. That Jobs wanted Jagger to have a computer is pretty telling about the illusions that all these people—along with everyone who attends rock festivals—held about music and musicians. Wozniak himself expressed quite a bit of disappointment in the behavior of the rock bands at his festival. "It's funny," he told the *Los Angeles Times*, "but I go my whole life and think of musicians as musicians . . . performers, stars. The trouble is each one of these headliners is a corporation" (Hilburn, "US Success" 1).

This disappointment in rock bands may be behind the US Festival's eventual retreat into technology—and Apple's concentration on the dissemination of music, rather than on the music itself. At a press conference held after the second US Festival, UNUSON president Peter Ellis said that he hoped the corporation would move into "other video/computer educational and research areas." It didn't. (Ellis now runs a nonprofit educational business in Oakland, helping disadvantaged youth get scholarships.) On the other hand, in the same article, coproducer Peter Gerwe told the *Times* that he thought the festival's future lay in UNUSON's ability to use the weekend events as the basis of a worldwide pay-per-view cable program and a theatrical film.

"At this point, we're known as something that draws a huge amount of people and treats them well—but that's it," he said.

> We've got to move more aggressively into video so we don't have to depend solely on drawing huge crowds. It's too dangerous, emotionally and financially, to go after the biggest possible audience. . . . To make it work as a film and as a broadcast, we've got to make it more than a concert. It's got to be an event. That's why it's essential that we develop more things like this year's Russian-US broadcast, more video and computer effects, perhaps even cut away to a band that is playing in London. (Hilburn, "US Fest Ends" 1)

What Gerwe is describing was the exact model for the next big event to sweep rock festivals, Live Aid, which was held over the Fourth of July weekend in 1985. Gerwe himself moved to Russia soon thereafter and established the first Russian radio and cable networks, and he went on to join Crown Point Ventures, a venture capital firm. By the year 2006 he was worth millions; incidentally, Michael Moritz, the author of *Little Kingdom*, also became a billionaire venture capitalist whose best-known investment was in Google. In some ways, this is not surprising, since ultimately the aspect of capitalism that the US Festival made visible (both to the Soviet Union and to the festival's attendees) was not so much technology, but the acquisition of wealth through technology and the uses to which that wealth could be put thereafter.

In the end, Wozniak's dream of "the biggest party on earth"—of himself on stage introducing rock stars—was one he was willing to pay an enormous amount of money for (Wozniak, *iWoz*). To critics who saw that personal dream as socially unworthy, the US Festival was meaningless. But to those who aspire to this kind of wealth, Wozniak's highly publicized presence at the festival and his personal use of his fortune to produce it underscores one of the US Festival's unacknowledged narratives: technology as a route to wealth. Not only was this route made visible via the reconfiguration of Wozniak as a kind of temporary rock star, but the US Festival also kindly included a career fair to help those beguiled by that vision to become wealthy. By 1983, the technology fair included a heavy career component, described in the following manner by the second US Festival program:

> The thing that makes this Expo a little different is the Career aspect. Many companies will have their representatives at the Expo to talk with festival-goers about career opportunities. Where does one go to get the education for that particular industry?
>
> Further in league with this school of thought, several universities, academies and school districts will be in the tent, ready to answer any questions. Where could it all lead? Everywhere one turns in the Career/Tech Expo, there will be food for thought. Whether it is the new robotics on display, the computer banks, the satellite phone connections, or even the new computer-assisted Ford Thunderbird, the expanding world of high-tech life will be open for free examination. (*US '83*)

Although it's difficult to assess how many attendees may have taken advantage of these services, some definitely did, as attested on the "US Festival memories" website (www.usfestivals.com). And there is certainly no doubt that work in computers would be the path to wealth for many young people in the years to come: the US Festival made visible the trend of postindustrialization to American workers who might otherwise not have noticed its encroachment.

The technology-equals-wealth narrative that underlay the more obvious themes could be summed up by the music of another performer at the second US Festival: Joe Walsh, a part-time member of the Eagles who had a solid solo career of his own at that time. (The Eagles were Wozniak's first choice for a headliner, but they declined to perform.) Walsh's big hit, "Life's Been Good," is a celebration of wealth and heedlessness: "My Maserati goes 185/I lost my license, now I can't drive. I have a limo/ride in the back/I lock the doors in case I'm attacked."

Walsh's provocative epigrams about the ironies of being a rich white rock star would later be equally apropos during the dot.com era, when computer programming replaced rock stardom as a route to fame and fortune.

Meanwhile, the US Festivals may have been the first place where the value of music and money began to go askew. From the bands who demanded four to five times their normal paychecks to play it—Bowie commanded a million dollars, well above his price tag at the time; the Clash's $500,000 was ten times their normal paycheck—to the consumers cheering Woz in the audience for providing them with the "great party" . . . the very existence of the US Festival was visible proof to much of the audience that computer expertise had become the quickest route to great wealth—especially when the festival itself provided career counseling on how to become a computer expert.

As for Joe Walsh, he can be seen wandering around the backstage area of the festival in a long sequence of video footage, pestering the MTV cameramen. He is dressed head to toe in army fatigues, while everyone else present is dressed in white. Even Ozzie Osbourne. Even the Clash.

———

As a cultural touchstone or iconic musical marker, the US Festival is now almost lost to history. As Robert Hilburn pointed out in a column that ran a few days after it was over, its music wasn't adventurous enough to matter; moreover, its dissemination on film was confined to four showings on Showtime. (None of the artists involved allowed any licensing of their performances beyond that, being fearful at the time of the potential theft of their "intellectual property" via video recording in much the same way that artists today are afraid of digital dissemination.) There was no auteur like the Maysles Brothers or Michael Wadleigh (the directors of *Gimme Shelter* and *Woodstock*, respectively); thus, there was no lasting mental footprint. If anything, where the US Festival's ideas all came to rest was not in future festivals like Live Aid but at future tech conventions like Macworld. This computer expo, started by *Macworld* magazine two years later in 1985, combined central elements of the US Festival and the *Whole Earth Catalog*. Like the US Festival, it was tied to, but not explicitly funded by, Apple; like the US Festival, it also promoted Apple products, but in an entertainment-oriented way that emphasized their pleasurable features. Although in 2010, Apple decoupled itself from Macworld and no longer plays an active role in it, in previous years the convention has been the site of important technological announcements, such as the introduction of new products—the iPod, the iPad—by Apple. Much like rock tours, Macworld Expo has offshoots all over the world, and it has been held in Boston, New York, Sydney, and Tokyo. It generally draws upward of thirty thousand people each year, and also features performances by prominent rock bands. In 2010, for instance, Aerosmith performed for the Macworld elite in a special performance on Treasure Island in San Francisco Bay.

Another important conjunction heralded by US Festival was between computers and pleasure. At the same time that computer technology in the early 1980s was usually touted as a force that would revolutionize ordinary lives, MTV was making similar claims—about cable television, music television, and rock 'n' roll. But while it is hard to deny the revolutionary potential (and effects) of computers on labor, the case is somewhat harder to make for MTV. That said, the US Festival's almost inspired conjoining of these two narratives allows one to argue that the connection Wozniak clearly drew between computers and culture is in fact both artificial and extremely appealing. That he did so under cover of the Woodstockian ideals of community, sharing, and ritualized utopian ecstasy is a tribute to the power of the original vision of music festivals.

Today the measure of success in popular music is not just financial but psychological, and in both ways the US Festival was a failure. It lost money, and it also left no lasting memory in the public sphere: hence, the difficulty in finding T-shirts, posters, or other ephemera from it. This is partly because many of the bands on the bill were aesthetically trivial and partly because—despite Peter Ellis's conscious decision to brand the festival to the "US" philosophy—the festival as a whole didn't manage to create a single overwhelming sense of social cohesiveness with which audiences could identify. (Ellis says now, "It didn't turn out to be the US decade, more like the me-me-ME decade.")

Another reason that might be suggested for this erasure, however, is that, because rock music is at bottom an African American idiom, all formats that forget this are doomed to failure. At most festivals, black artists have always been more than welcome to play to predominantly white audiences, although black audiences were (and still are) essentially prevented from gathering at festivities similar to the ones described here. Monterey Pop had Otis Redding and Jimi Hendrix, and Woodstock had Richie Havens, Jimi, and Sly Stone, and their performances were essential to the reception of those festivals as cultural events that mattered. But the music at the US Festival was made entirely by white male artists. Of the fifty-two headlining acts that played over the seven total days at the two festivals, many featuring five or six band members for an approximate head count of three hundred musicians, there was exactly *one* nonwhite artist on stage: Rankin' Roger of the tutone ska act the English Beat.

The lack of diversity at the US Festivals—which, incidentally, would carry over to computer culture—is worth thinking about. It's a sad but observable fact that rock festivals like the US Festival draw predominantly white crowds. Less obvious, perhaps, is this observation: if they leave out black acts, as the US Festival did, they are ultimately doomed to failure, irrelevance, and consignment to the dustbin of history. To be properly understood, the racial narratives inherent in the history of popular music in America must always be front and center. And the same is true of rock festivals.

CHAPTER 5

The Chevy and the Levee

O NE WEEKEND IN THE MIDDLE of the last century, an outdoor concert for twenty-five thousand people was held in a small Catskills community within easy driving distance from Manhattan. The concert was sponsored by radical leftists and featured wildly popular artists, some of them African American, whose music drew on traditional American folk vernaculars. The concert caused some consternation among locals, who pledged to boycott its "commie-sympathizing" platform of artists and to drive off those who dared to attend.

No, it wasn't Woodstock, and it didn't end up as a giant love letter to the counterculture, although the foregoing description mirrors in almost every particular the rhetoric that preceded the events at Bethel in 1969. This concert—held in Peekskill, New York, in September 1949, twenty years before Woodstock—ended in a bloody riot with over 150 people injured and enormous amounts of property damage. State police, who'd been called in to quell the violence, were seen to beat concertgoers as they left, and local residents who had condoned the concert were driven afterward to sell up and leave the area

(Balaji, *Professor and the Pupil* 275). Local Jews were terrorized for weeks beforehand; according to one witness quoted in Howard Fast's memoir *Being Red*, "it was like living through a pogrom" (239). Leslie Matthews, an eyewitness and staff correspondent for the black newspaper *New York Age*, wrote:

> I hear the wails of women, the impassioned screams of children,
> the jeers and taunts of wild-eyed youths. I still smell the sickening
> odor of blood flowing from freshly opened wounds, gasoline fumes
> from autos and buses valiantly trying to carry their loads of human
> targets out of the range of bricks, bottles, stones, sticks. (Salkin,
> "Sixty Years")

Eventually, the events in it would be represented fictionally in E. L. Doctorow's *Book of Daniel*, while headliner Paul Robeson later called the concert a landmark event in the Cold War, and one, he added, that went "to the root of the whole struggle for freedom of speech and freedom of assembly, but [that] especially concern the struggle of we Negro people" (Balaji, *Professor and the Pupil*, 288).

Robeson would no doubt have been surprised by the different reception given to Jimi Hendrix, headlining a far larger concert in the same locale twenty years later. Though by then the civil strife that undercut society far outweighed the Cold War politics of the late 1940s, Hendrix, the highest paid performer at Woodstock, was given license to strip "The Star Spangled Banner" of its leaden pomp and circumstance, shredding the very fabric of the song in a performance hailed by many as the sonic equivalent of the political zeitgeist (Gilroy, "Sounds Authentic"). Few things better illustrate the cultural shift that had occurred since Robeson's performance at Peekskill. And yet, the shift may not have been so much in the cultural values of people in the Catskills, who in 1969, according to the local inn owner and memoirist Elliot Tiber, were as bigoted and right-wing as ever, but in the presentation and dissemination of these new, contentious values through a medium—the rock festival—that allowed audiences ways of processing contested ideas about society that were very different from earlier outdoor musical events (Tiber and Monte, *Taking Woodstock*).

The events at Peekskill emphasize this difference. In 1949, an overtly communist-sympathizing event sponsored by Artists International resulted in a serious riot. Twenty years later, in an era of similarly contested ideas and in an equally polarized location, audiences (and locals) at Woodstock were able to reconcile their deeply negative feelings about America and its Cold War mission with their own values and beliefs. Woodstock was (and is) deemed a success because it fostered this and because of its pervasive iconography: forty years on, the culture of Woodstock and its cultural values are invoked with reverence, and Woodstock-like festivals, in a more commodified form, have proliferated across the globe with varying degrees of success. Festival organizers are now able to use the model to promote sometimes contentious ideas—about ecology (Live Earth), social justice (Live Aid), and the legalization (and valorization) of drug use. The difference is that today they pin their ideological discourses not on the transgressive nature of artists (as we saw with Robeson or Hendrix), but on the representational dominance of festival ideology itself.

This is one of the most substantial, and understated, facts about the ideological work done at today's rock festivals. But there's another even more nuanced and less mentioned aspect of how these events work: the truth is that the Woodstock model for a discursively powerful rock festival is only successful under certain conditions, namely, when "culture" is aligned with white middle class norms. It becomes a more fragile model when it is interrogated alongside ideologies of difference, such as race, class, or gender. Rock festivals see themselves as spaces of freedom. But the fact is that their audiences are generally not nearly as diverse as their lineups.

As seen in the last chapter, rock festivals that draw predominantly white crowds are doomed to cultural irrelevancy if they leave out black artists and black popular music idioms. But what happens when, in addition to the artists on stage, the audience itself is largely black? Sadly, until recently, there have been very few examples of large-scale festivals with this kind of configuration, so few that it's a difficult question to even hypothesize about. First and foremost among historic all-black, all black-attended, rock festivals, however, was Wattstax, a one-day festival held in Los Angeles at the Memorial Coliseum in 1972. Occurring only a few years after Woodstock during a period when the rise in urban black poverty was very much in the news, Wattstax—as memorialized in the film *Wattstax*—makes a harsh comment on many of the contradictions inherent in rock festival rhetoric, particularly their ideas about community, freeness, and utopia.

Despite the fact that the 1960s were a time when black music was appreciated and courted at festivals like Woodstock, the majority of festivals have never seriously courted or embraced black audiences, and famously at Altamont, a lone black audience member, Meredith Hunter, was murdered in full view of the stage. Worse, his aggressor, a Hells Angel, was acquitted. This in itself could not have been an encouragement for young blacks to attend festivals, which had already by 1969 entrenched themselves in the collective American psyche as largely white enclaves. *Time* magazine, for example, famously called Woodstock attendees "pilgrims," an unconsciously racialized word that would not have been applied to attendees of Wattstax, even if they'd been wearing wimples. The absence may also have its roots in Woodstock's ties to the back-to-the-land, new communalist movement of the late 1960s (Turner, *From Counterculture to Cyberculture*). These festivals, particularly Woodstock, looked to nostalgic images of rural America to bolster their utopian and antimaterialist rhetoric.

For anyone who has attended them, it does not seem particularly insightful to state categorically that rock festivals are largely white male spaces. It's not even that hard to figure out why this is so. Audiences at rock festivals like to think of them as particularly free and open to everyone, but actually, three specific rhetorical appeals have shaped exactly what kind of American goes to a rock festival and who makes up the vast majority of the audience. Those appeals are cars, nature, and drugs.

The first of these, cars, could also be phrased as automobility, that is, having access and the ability to become a member of what Cotten Seiler calls "the republic of drivers" ("So That We as a Race" 1091) or as Philip Fisher has described it, "a democratic social space in which the right and even the ability to move from place to place is assured" (quoted in Seiler, "So That We as a Race" 1092). Woodstock's undoubted image as a space of whiteness is partially a reflection of its rural location. New York City–area blacks may not only have had difficulty accessing that location without public transportation, but they would have felt uncomfortable in the rural townships they'd have needed to traverse to get there as well. And although obscure site locations ought to create prohibitions to *all* low-income concertgoers, surely the rural settings of many rock festivals—Woodstock, Watkins Glen, Altamont, Bonnaroo—make festivals more attractive to middle-class white members of this imaginary republic, particularly those who partake of American idyll fantasies about nature, wildness, and a kinder, gentler, *rural* past.

This leads to the second appeal, nature. Certainly in the 1960s the fantasy of a rural idyll might not have played as well to potential middle-class African American concertgoers whose memories of rural America were less than idyllic. For them, the prospect of long automobile trips to rural places can hardly have been as inviting, even if the end destination wasn't a festival, but a national park.[1] Evelyn C. White has written movingly about her inability to join in the pleasures of outdoor life while teaching a writer's workshop in Oregon. White says the memory of Emmett Till's fate, and the photo of his body she saw in *Jet* magazine in the 1950s, haunts her and others of her generation: "I was certain that if I ventured outside to admire a meadow or feel the cool ripples in a stream, I'd be taunted, attacked, raped, maybe even murdered because of the color of my skin. I believe the fear I experience in the outdoors is shared by many African American women and that it limits the way we move through the world and colors the decisions we make about our lives," she writes (White, "Black Women and the Wilderness" 378). That fear would not lend itself to a fantasy about spending three days at a rock festival.

The final rhetorical appeal holding potential African American festivalgoers back has to do with the valorization of drugs. This discourse has its roots in Woodstock's outright celebration of drug use—particularly of marijuana—as an almost necessary mechanism of psychological and physical liberation; today's festivals are awash with that drug's presence. But it is no secret that minorities in America incur the legal penalties imposed for drug use far more frequently and are treated with far more severity by the law than are white people: a

2008 study showed that a black male born in the 1990s faced almost a one-in-three lifetime chance of ending up in jail.[2] To such a person, the constant valorization of drug use at festivals may not seem quite so banal. Rather, it is another area in which the discourse is normed to a white middle-class audience.

These three factors go far toward explaining why audiences at both Woodstock and Bonnaroo are less diverse than the music on offer. But the fact that there are few black bodies present at the New Orleans Jazz and Heritage Festival, the Brooklyn African Pop Festival, or All Points West when headlined by Kanye West, bespeaks a deeper problem. Because ticket agencies don't profile the races of their customers, scarcely any data exists that tallies the current racial makeup of festival audiences. Prevalent record industry statistics, however, say that 70 percent of American hip-hop sells to white people, backing up the claim made by Boots Riley of the radical Oakland hip-hop group the Coup, who says "my audience has gone from being over 95 percent black 10 years ago to over 95 percent white today" (Kitwana, "Cotton Club"). Of course, the audiences for black acts at small jazz and R & B clubs—particularly urban ones—are just as likely to be black as white. But surprisingly, the racial makeup of (live) music fans changes when it comes to acts that play youth-oriented music. Anecdotal evidence reveals that young black audiences—the all-important eighteen-to-thirty-four demographic—don't turn out in large numbers for live music by black hip-hop acts, whether they are playing small club dates or larger venues, and this is especially problematic for black artists in this age of digital downloading: it's why acts like the Eagles, the Grateful Dead, and U2 potentially can earn more than Kanye West and Jay-Z in any given year.

This is a problem for hip, alternative acts like Brand Nubian, ded prez (sic), and de la soul (sic) as much as it is for huge superstars like Black Eyed Peas and 50 Cent. At arena shows for the latter act, observers have speculated that up to 70 percent of the audience is white.[3] At smaller shows, the percentage of whites is, if anything, even larger (Dowdy, "Live Hip Hop"). Riley, says Kitwana, jokingly calls his audience "the Cotton Club," a reference to the affluent whites who went slumming in the clubs of Harlem in the 1920s.

Economics may explain some of this disparity. Large shows by artists like Jay-Z or 50 Cent can cost nearly $100 per ticket, and that's not including transportation, parking, and other expenses.[4] Some hip-hop aficionados, like Brother Ali of Rhymesayers Entertainment, claim that black people don't turn out for hip-hop shows because they "see through" the marketing strategies of the white record-label owners (Kitwana, "Cotton Club"). But when it comes to festivals, all these claims are magnified. Moreover, discourses of nature and drugs, along with other factors like economics, travel logistics, and security issues, work to prevent rock festivals from drawing large crowds of black youth. These youth are then in effect prevented or discouraged from taking part in the circulation of the cultural currency that such festivals hold out to their adherents.

This would be less disturbing if such festivals didn't actually use the idea of multiculturalism, diversity, and the supposedly risqué qualities of black music as one of their main selling points, especially since the popularization of hip-hop, a genre that sees its mission as chronicling the black experience in polemicized ways. With its un-doubted emphasis on poverty, gangs, gun violence, and misogyny, hip-hop has also served to increase already-extant anxieties in the white community about the nature of black culture, making its pre-sentation in a live setting more difficult to accomplish.[5] Certainly a festival like Wattstax could not exist in a post-hip-hop world.

———

This preamble is intended to explain what's still so important about Wattstax. Wattstax demonstrates some of the liminal aspects of the rock festival, and not only because it is one of the only concerts of its kind but because it shows the ways in which much of the rhetoric and many of the assumptions about rock festivals *can* work when decoupled from some white middle-class norms and reanimated with others. Whereas Woodstock worked to encourage skeptical youth audiences to extol the pleasures of a free-market society without assuming the guilt that more overt displays would have elicited, Wattstax exhibits to its audience a differently nuanced facet of capitalism: the idea that black culture was (and is) saleable and that black-owned businesses can succeed in America. Wattstax claims that the Woodstock model can also be applied to an African American audience, allowing them the pleasure of reconciliation to and resolution of an unhappy historic residue. In this case, the conflict to be resolved wasn't the Cold War, it was the success of the civil rights movement, narrowly interpreted through race relations in Watts; but the festival's rhetoric still allows its audience to process and accept the status quo idea of blacks as successful entrepreneurs disseminating their own culture, despite some evidence to the contrary. That Wattstax allowed for this resolution is probably why, despite contemporary evidence to the contrary, it is now considered one of the finest examples of a post-Woodstock festival and is called by both blacks and whites "the Black Woodstock."

Wattstax, a benefit concert and commemoration of the seventh anniversary of the Watts riots, featured performances by many of the most famous artists on the Memphis-based record label Stax. It was held at the Los Angeles Memorial Coliseum on August 9, 1972; tickets cost only one dollar, and the concert was sold out to a largely local, African American crowd. The writer and historian Nelson George calls Wattstax "a symbol of black self-sufficiency" (George, *Death of Rhythm and Blues* 25), although Brian Ward points out that it was largely underwritten by white corporations, including Columbia Pictures, which bought the film rights, and Schlitz beer, which rented the Coliseum in an attempt to diffuse a boycott of their product proposed by the black community at the time. (In prepublicity, the *Los Angeles Sentinel* was careful to call it "the Schlitz-sponsored festival" as a warning to potential patrons.) Still, Ward adds, "On a number of levels the politics, economics, iconography and almost sacramental ritualism of [Wattstax] vividly illustrated the relationship between rhythm and blues, black consciousness, corporate commerce and the freedom struggle in the heart of the black power era" (Ward, *Just My Soul Responding* 222). The festival raised about $100,000, which was divided between Jesse Jackson's Operation PUSH (People United to Save Humanity), the Watts Summer Festival fund, the MLK Jr. Hospital Fund, and the Sickle Cell Anemia Foundation (Berry, "How Wattstax Festival Renews" 14).

Wattstax differed from the whiter rock festivals in several crucial ways, most importantly because it was held in a stadium. Stadiums have their own acoustics, crowd dynamics, and even theorists: Canetti, for example, makes a distinction between what he calls open crowds and closed crowds. The open crowd, which one observes at festivals like Woodstock and Altamont, where fencing is either non-existent or far enough from the music to seem nonexistent, is one which at least gives the appearance of growing indefinitely. The open crowd, says Canetti, wants to consist of more people: to "seize everyone within reach; anything shaped like a human being can join it" (*Crowds and Power* 16). In contrast, the closed crowd—like the one at Wattstax—is bounded, in this case by the walls of the stadium, and the boundary not only prevents the crowd from increasing—and postpones its dissolution—but more importantly, creates a kind of bond between those on the inside versus those on the outside. Says Canetti:

> Outside, facing the city, the arena displays a lifeless wall; inside is a wall of people. The spectators turn their backs to the city. They have been lifted out of its structure of walls and streets and, for the duration of their time in the arena, they do not care about anything which happens there; they have left behind all their associations, rules and habits . . . there is no break in the crowd which sits like this, exhibiting itself to itself. It forms a closed ring which nothing can escape. The tiered ring of fascinated faces has something strangely homogenous about it. It embraces and contains everything which happens below; no one relaxes his grip on this; no one tries to get away. Any gap in the ring might remind him of disintegration and subsequent dispersal. But there is no gap; this crowd is double closed, to the world outside and in itself. (Canetti, *Crowds and Power* 28)

By closing out the world, the stadium creates an "us and them" dynamic, much like the "us and them" dynamic created by segregation. More importantly, however, unlike Yasgur's farm, the Altamont Speedway, the Glen Ellen Regional Park, or other sites of famous festivals, a stadium is an implicitly political location, an architectural reminder of the repressive nature of power. From images of Roman emperors watching their captured slaves battle to the death to stadiums crowded with political rallies in Nuremburg to refugees from Hurricane Katrina, stadiums echo not only with bygone cheers but with the silent memory of oppression. They are steel-and-cement reminders of suffering and surveillance, architectural structures of discipline. It is not surprising, perhaps, that the largest rock festival catering exclusively to a black audience took place in a stadium located in a poorer part of Los Angeles. Here, blacks gathered in safety and in comfort, entirely estranged from nature—not just the false nature that the US Festival or Woodstock provided people with, but any nature at all.

That the stadium is an essentially urban apparatus is a fact that the filmmakers of *Wattstax*—directed by Mel Stuart, a white director best known for directing *Willie Wonka and the Chocolate Factory* around the same time—never forget.[6] In direct contrast to *Woodstock*'s "back to the land" opening shots with their pastoral, sunshine-bathed sequence and the chorus of Crosby, Stills, and Nash singing "we've got to get back to the garden," *Wattstax* begins with a montage of urban scenarios: storefronts, sidewalks, parking lots, and cement "playgrounds" peopled with African American city-dwellers.[7] After a brief look at the Watts Towers, we see the streets, cars, housing developments, wire, fences, welfare lines, nurses, misshapen elderly people, ragged children, drunks . . . and riots. In the background, the song "Whatcha See is Whatcha Get" by the Dramatics plays: "Cos what you see/is what you get/because I'm as real/as real can get/and real . . . is the best thing yet." Here, the filmmakers declare, is the opposite of the utopian dream of "the garden": what Althusser would call "the real conditions of our existence." In the terms of this film, the real conditions of existence are "the best thing yet."

This visual comment on the disjunction between Woodstock and Wattstax continues with the next shot, which shows the stage being built at the Coliseum. In *Woodstock*, the erection of the stage was depicted as a barn-raising done by gorgeous, bare-chested blonde youths in a holy spirit of communion. At Wattstax, the stage is erected by burly white union guys. In this universe—the universe where "the real" is as "real can get"—work is depicted not as religious but as labor. Even when it's done by whites, work is work.

As this sequence indicates, *Wattstax* differs in every particular from *Woodstock*, from the national anthem, sung respectfully by Kim Weston—as opposed to Jimi Hendrix's famous shattered version—to its final dystopian vision of America: a helicopter shot of the Coliseum which pulls slowly away to show the urban wasteland that is south-

central Los Angeles. It also moves away from the idea of the concert
field as a separate community, instead combining concert sequences
and crowd shots intercut with scenes of a Richard Pryor monologue
and with interviews with local Watts residents. The effect is to emphasize the fact that music and community are intertwined. As the
writer Scott Saul says:

> By cutting dynamically between music onstage and interviews over
> the course of the film, *Wattstax* establishes a sociological vision of
> the music: a vision that appreciates its artifice—its power as music
> and as costume drama—while grounding our understanding in the
> attitudes of the community from which it springs. *Wattstax* frames
> the music not as a means of escaping the pressures of the world but
> as a means of handling them. ("What You See Is What you Get")

This was a radical notion and an even more radical film, one that,
as Saul says, "confronted a crucial turn in early '70s culture and politics: the hardening of white-ethnic identity and the rise of what historian Rick Perlstein has called 'Nixonland'" ("What You See Is What
You Get"). In 1972, Nixon had secured his reelection through a combination of patriotic pageantry and tough-on-crime rhetoric that
Wattstax, with its black working-class subjects at the fore, pointedly
rejected, and it makes sense that a white public polarized along lines
of racial resentment and gravitating to the suburbs would be reluctant to pay money to see blacks "do their thing" in the inner city. And
this proved to be the case; the film was unable to cross over to a white
audience. The ending of the film is particularly contested, since there
are two versions: the original, which featured a faked sequence with
Isaac Hayes playing "Coming Down the Mountain" on a soundstage,
and the anniversary release, which features the concert's real ending, with Hayes entering the stadium with a police escort in a gold-
painted station wagon and bursting onto the stage to sing "Shaft." The
second ending makes the film into a powerful statement, but it was
only added to the DVD release in 2003. *Woodstock*, of course, left us
with a shot of a pristine forest.

These filmic differences are striking and intentional, and they
underscore the many ways that the audience at Wattstax differed

from the one we witnessed, on film, at Woodstock. For example, the entirely black audience of ninety-two thousand dances respectfully, even decorously, in the stands and on the field, a very different vision from the naked hippie chicks and stoned young men who make up Woodstock's cast of characters. Unfortunately, the decorum exhibited by the audience at Wattstax underscores not Woodstock's anarchic pleasures and societal defiance, but the fact that such behavior is a privilege unavailable to the African American community. Woodstock's defining moment happened when hippies broke down the fences so they could attend for free. At Wattstax, when the crowd bursts onto the field to dance to Rufus Thomas's "Funky Chicken," we hear Thomas enjoin them all back to their seats: "More power to the folks going back to the stands. More power to the folks going back to the stands" (*Wattstax*, dir. Stuart). The crowd files amicably back to the stands, leaving one exuberant dancer with a broken umbrella on the field. "That's a Brother all right," says Thomas to a delighted crowd. "But I be damned if he *my* Brother" (*Wattstax*). This is not a sentiment you will hear at Woodstock, which spent an inordinate amount of time emphasizing brotherhood.

But if *Woodstock* implied a hippie utopia, *Wattstax* acknowledges a past that is truly dystopian. The final sequence of the remade version—that is, the film of what *really* happened at the end of the concert—shows Isaac Hayes, at the time one of Stax's biggest stars, arriving on stage in a black and red cape, his bald head and reflective sunglasses shining ominously in the lights, as the ninety-two-thousand-strong crowd leaps to its feet and the scoreboard flashes the words "THE BLACK MOSES." As the rhythm section roils up the opening riffs of "Shaft"—that unforgettable, irreplaceable sequence of bass notes that is now one of pop's most iconic riffs—Hayes steps up to the microphone, throws off his cape, and intones the opening line: "Who's the private dick who's a sex machine to all the chicks?" He is clad entirely in golden chains.

Today, this image of Hayes—powerful, gilded, iconic, enchained—seems to encapsulate some nostalgic notion that the concert is allowing its attendants to somehow engage with black history in a new, compelling way. This belief may be what gives *Wattstax* such power. Yet the written record of Wattstax, the concert, gives a far more con-

Shaft! Jackson and Hayes, Wattstax, 1972.

flicted version of events. The article in the *Los Angeles Times* describing the concert itself, for example, was downright negative, and the review of the movie, released six months later, was if anything even worse, taking Hayes himself to task for a performance it calls "overblown." The film itself was characterized by the critic Dennis Hunt (who was himself African American) as "fragmented and skittery" ("Pryor Highlight" 80). He calls it chaotic and tedious and says it is full of "long stretches of boredom that occur when an interviewee lapses into rhetoric or a singer lumbers through a number" (Dennis Hunt, "Pryor Highlight" 80). Hunt also calls most of the musical performances "inept." Yet in 2004, the movie was rereleased and broadcast on PBS, to an ecstatically positive press. Indeed, it is now generally spoken of with reverence.

One reason for this change in tone may be that the rerelease has a different ending: at the time of its original release, the licensing of the song "Shaft" prevented this sequence from being shown. It was replaced with Hayes performing the song "Coming Down the Mountain" on a soundstage. But although this certainly is a far less powerful finish, it cannot quite account for the vastly different tone surrounding the film today than originally. The review in the *Los Angeles Times*, for instance, complained that the concert suffered from poor staging, poor acoustics, and too many acts. The writer Lance Williams grudgingly admitted there was "a mood of camaraderie" in the crowd, but he also claimed that the crowd was "bored" much of the time and that it seldom got to its feet to dance. He also took Hayes to task, saying his act was a repeat of a recent performance at the Hollywood Bowl, giving it a sense of "colossal déjà vu." Hayes, he adds, did two takes of "Shaft" for the cameras (Lance Williams, "Wattstax").

That the *Los Angeles Times* was skeptical of this endeavor is not surprising. But the *Los Angeles Sentinel*, L.A.'s largest black newspaper, took a similar tone. Prior to the festival, the *Sentinel's* coverage of the event was confined to ads placed by the Wattstax organization. The *Sentinel* is a weekly, and in the two issues prior to the festival, August 12 and 17, the paper ran two large ads for the festival. On August 17, it also ran a very small one-column article on the front page announcing the Watts Summer Festival lineup of events. On August 24, the week after the festival, the *Sentinel* ran a few photos of festivalgoers on page 12 and a full-page "Thank You" ad from Stax Records.

The *Sentinel* did not run reviews of concerts in its pages (and if it had, it might have concentrated on the Jackson 5 concert that occurred the same week at the LA Forum). However, on August 31, the paper, which was now taken up entirely with coverage of Watts-area Olympic athletes and back-to-school issues, ran an editorial by Emily F. Gibson entitled "Annual Watts Summer Festival Has Come and Gone," in which the writer called Wattstax "a diversionary tactic" and claimed that the festival "helps to silence dissent in the ghetto by keeping the summer cool" (A7).

"What is there to celebrate?" she opines. "Are the conditions which gave rise to an unparalleled unleashing of tempers then any different than they are now . . . ? Have [the Watts Summer Festivals] been instrumental in bringing about black unity for the purpose of strategizing the liberation?" (A7).

"As far as this writer is concerned," continues Gibson, "the opportunists and demagogues who perpetuate the idea of the Watts Festival are as guilty of the crimes committed against black and poor as the most vicious racists, money hungry merchants, blood thirsty police, and panhandling politicians." She goes on to call Jesse Jackson "a pimp of the people" and claims that the money used to present Wattstax could have been better spent to alleviate suffering in the neighborhood (A7).

Between the *Los Angeles Times*'s tepid coverage and the *Sentinel*'s open hostility, one gains the impression that Wattstax was far from the success it seems in retrospect. In fact, it was better received from afar. The concert received a rave review from the syndicated columnist Bob Considine, for example—although he did not actually attend it. In an October 1972 issue of the Wisconsin *Phairos-Tribune*, he announced the occurrence of the then month-old concert. "There was little press coverage, and no TV coverage at all to record a truly historic event," he writes:

> In my opinion, the media ignored the event because there were no fights, no riots, no one was injured and no one killed.
>
> Al Bell, the dynamic head of Stax and everybody else who created that great day got little or no attention. But if one bottle had been thrown, if one policeman had clubbed one teenager, Wattstax '72 would have been all over the front pages and received sensational coverage from TV. ("There's Good News Today" 4)

By 1973, the impression that Wattstax had been a big event was already in play (thanks no doubt to the power of Columbia Studios). Marilyn Beck's syndicated column devotes quite a bit of space to the movie's January 1973 premiere, including concerns that it will receive an R rating (for language), thus preventing "an audience of young people from seeing it who would benefit from the portrait of the black experience" ("Hollywood Hotline"). A few weeks later, Sandra Haggerty of the *Tucson Citizen* chimes in, calling it a "moving documentary of the black experience in America" ("Black Tragedy" 19). Once opened, the film received many rave reviews, including ones in the *Wall Street Journal* ("*Wattstax* shows us blacks laughing at themselves and inviting other blacks to share that laughter with them": Boyum, "A Bit More Than Just Music" 12); *Newsweek* ("1,000,000 flamboyant foxes and dapper dudes enjoying themselves in a hip-stomping, hip shaking celebration": Cooper, "Watts Happening" 88); and the *Saturday Review* ("A film of incredibly vitality, pertinence and humor!": Knight, "Facing Reality" 71). Wattstax is also known for being the site of Jesse Jackson's resounding "I AM somebody" speech. Jackson was at the time head of Operation PUSH and was clearly using the concert as an overt political platform for his own ambitions.[8] He isn't shoved off the stage, like Abbie Hoffman at Woodstock. Instead, Jackson's speech—like Weston's performance of the black national anthem—is taken by the crowd at face value, as "a soulful expression of the black experience," to quote Richard Pryor (*Wattstax*, dir. Stuart).

Wattstax ought by rights to have been an apotheosis, rather than a unique event, for despite its contemporary critics, it was everything that subsequent rock festivals purport to be: it was authentic, transgressive, utopian, and even (almost) free. It highlights the way that, whereas white audiences have interpreted the ideal of freeness as a monetary value—"music should be free"—black audiences have interpreted it as a form of liberty—freedom as a quality of life. This is the essential difference between *Wattstax* and *Woodstock*. *Woodstock* (and the US Festival) displayed a free market. *Wattstax* tells an alternative history of America, one that is very different from the ideologically fantastic one on display at Woodstock. Where *Woodstock* heightened the idyllic aspects of the American spirit—its natural beauty, its independence, and its reliance on individuality—*Wattstax* reminds the audience of African American history: of slavery, segregation, and, ultimately, the fight for civil rights. The experiences of the Watts residents who are interviewed throughout the film speak of an American experience very far from the one alluded to in Woodstock, and as they do so, they help illustrate the way that culture is intimately bound up with community. By so doing, the film reveals the absence of this connection at the heart of Woodstock and other festivals. The community depicted in Woodstock was a fictitious construct, set to dissipate come Monday morning. The community at the heart of Wattstax—Compton, standing in for countless other urban black neighborhoods in the United States—is, as the movie promised, "as real as real can get."

Wattstax is now celebrated as one of the finest concerts and *Wattstax* as one of the finest concert films of the era. Forty years later, no other vast rock festival featuring all-black acts has called to an all-black audience in the same way. Black acts like Jay-Z, Kanye West, and Chance the Rapper can now headline stadiums, but these acts play to largely white audiences, and their earning capacity pales in comparison to white rock giants like U2, Bruce Springsteen, the Eagles, and the Grateful Dead. And while many individual acts like Snoop Dogg, West, and Black Eyed Peas have all been served up as headlining acts at festivals, none of these festivals has hosted largely (or even somewhat) black audiences. Rock the Bells, a yearly tour featuring cutting-edge black hip-hop acts, has a majority of whites in the audience, while Paid Dues, an independently promoted rap festival held for four years running in San Bernardino, California, drew only a couple of thousand attendees to a forty-thousand-seat venue before folding (Weiss, "Paid Dues"). Granted, Chance the Rapper's Magnificent Coloring Day festival at U.S. Cellular Field in Chicago, held in September 2016, an event that drew forty-seven thousand fans and featured performances by Tyler the Creator, Alicia Keys, John Legend, Common, and Kanye West, among others, can be said to have changed this paradigm. But Chance has since turned his genius toward promoting very small secret festivals held at secret locations. These may well be the wave of the future—but if so, it's the subject of a different book.

That Paid Dues was not successful can be attributed to all of the factors already discussed—its rural location, its emphasis on drugs, and the by-now established estrangement of young black audiences from the appeals of the rock festival—and all of these factors don't apply to Magnificent Coloring Day, which could be easily reached by traveling on Chicago's mass-transit system. But a more disturbing situation surrounds the dearth of black festivalgoers at a more mainstream, famous, and annual event: that is, the New Orleans Jazz and Heritage Festival, one of America's largest urban music festivals and one that not only purports to create bonds between music and community but that also has a foundational mission to celebrate black heritage. This festival's failure to engage black audiences in the midst of a predominantly black community highlights all the failures of festivals in general to fulfill their promise of "giving back" to the community.

The New Orleans Jazz and Heritage Festival is a permanent fixture with very different aims from most commercial or free rock festivals, but it also rests on black musical idioms and white appreciation of those idioms. In their article entitled "Producing the Folk at the New Orleans Jazz and Heritage Festival" in the *American Journal of Folklore*, Helen Regis and Shana Walton have argued that the festival's mission—"interpreting and presenting tradition to the general public" (401)—presents an ideological predicament about how culture is reproduced for public consumption, particularly since the festival exists in the competing realms of "heritage" and hipness, pop culture and entertainment. The Jazz Festival's ideology is to present new social and racial possibilities—that is, an imagined space where race disappears, through the preservation, interpretation, and celebration of American music. But while it is powered by nostalgia and underpinned by a sense of urgency, it still embodies real contradictions in the face of social reality. In the wake of Hurricane Katrina, when it was seen as reviving the elusive spirit of New Orleans, the Jazz Fest (as the authors term it) is now required to uphold imagined standards of authenticity while at the same time shouldering the burden of a disproportionate amount of New Orleans tourism income each year.

The Jazz Fest takes place every year in April on the same site, the Fair Grounds Race Course. It draws between 375,000 and 664,000 visitors over the course of seven days, reaching a high of 160,000 on a single day, and it brings upward of $300 million into the city's coffers each year. Like other ticketing agencies, Jazz Fest doesn't keep records of the race of purchasers (nor, since 2003, will it release any sales data). But Regis and Walton assert that in a rough head count over the course of three days in 2004, the percentage of African Americans in the audience ranged from 3 percent to 30 percent—and more than half the time, they say, it was less than 10 percent, a disturbing percentage given that the African American population of New Orleans is somewhere around 60 percent (Regis and Walton, "Producing the Folk" 435). In 2006 (post–Hurricane Katrina, when total attendance dropped significantly), black attendance dropped to less than 5 percent. Thus, Regis and Walton write, "in the Jazz Fest setting, middle class white people get the opportunity to partake of otherness in a space where difference is recognized because it is labeled, tamed, and domesticated" (422), and this trend has only continued, since the steep increase in ticket prices—and a reduction in the number of community ticket programs—have helped remove less affluent and marginalized communities from the fairgrounds, in the process erasing "any uncomfortable references to poverty, inequality or structured privilege" (429).

The main problem with the Jazz Fest is that although the festival features music and musicians of all stripes and races—country, rock, funk, soul, jazz, R & B, gospel, bebop, and superstar rock with headliners like Sting, Bruce Springsteen, and Dave Matthews—it is the musicians who appear to be both poor and black who serve to "ground the festival's commercial and popular music in incontestable authenticity" (Regis and Walton, "Producing the Folk" 402). Jazz Fest's task, Regis and Walton remind us, is to "produce the folk"—a task it does via a complicated acting out of the social structures and experiences of the social geography of New Orleans. There are many ways in which this occurs—for a fuller account, one should read the book—but suffice it to say that at Jazz Fest, racial oppression is meant to appear as something safely in the past, with the result that it disallows the meaningful engagement of black people with their own culture.

Although the New Orleans Jazz and Heritage Festival has its own specific history, location, and mission statement, the complex relationship between race and class that occurs there can be said to apply to all other rock festivals in far broader strokes. For example, Jennifer Stoever's work on the very different Lollapalooza Festival highlights these similarities. Today's Lollapalooza is a yearly rock festival held over a single weekend in Grant Park, Chicago, that draws some seventy-five thousand attendees per day, adding $13 million to the city's coffers. In the 1990s, however, the festival was a touring unit that played in some thirty-six cities each summer; total attendance was approximately eight hundred thousand in 1992. Stoever contends that the inaugural years of Lollapalooza ("Experience Music Project" 91–96) "served as a racializing engine . . . constructing 'multiculturalism' as a bounded, spectacular performance removed from the rigors of real life." Stoever points to the tour's defining moment as a duet performed at each stop by the Jane's Addiction vocalist (and tour organizer) Perry Farrell and Ice-T of Sly Stone's 1969 song "Don't Call Me Nigger (Whitey)." About this nightly moment, Stoever writes:

Far from merely a straight cover, Farrell and Ice-T's version completely rearranges Sly Stone's original, both sonically and ideologically. Typical of Lollapalooza itself, this duet is both provocative
and problematic. The central verse of the song remains intact, but
what sounds like tense quotation when filtered entirely by Stone's
voice becomes snarling social confrontation by T and Farrell. It is
ambiguous whether the performance mocks hypermasculinity or
enacts it; perhaps it does both. Although Farrell's dramatic delivery
tends to overwhelm Ice-T's more understated vocal style, positing
these lyrics as a verbal exchange rhetorically equates the two racial
epithets (not to mention Nazism with Black Power). Evading history *and* power dynamics, the duet re-frames racism as an isolated
schoolyard brawl rather than a system of structured inequity. Perhaps most importantly, there is the matter of the audience, whose
chants and cheers heartily anticipate the "n-word," suggesting a
mixture of shock, desensitization *and* titillation. (Stoever, "Experience Music Project" 5)

Stoever interprets this event and the frenzied media coverage of it
as a gloss on the idea of multiculturalism, although the headlining bill
(of eight bands) featured only guitar-based rock music, one female
singer, and the (black) artist Ice-T, who is fronting not a rap band,
but a hard rock band called Body Count. Yet the media accounts of
this festival framed it as a triumph of multiculturalism. As Stoever
points out, the press coverage describes the event "as an allegorical
and performative exhibition of multiculturalism, usually cast as a limited black/white unity." Pictures of the event depict Ice-T and Perry
Farrell with their arms raised in a Black Power-style salute.

Perhaps not surprisingly, this gesture is interpreted witheringly in
most press accounts as shtick on the part of Ice-T (*Los Angeles Times*,
Billboard).

In 1992, a few months after the Los Angeles riots that followed the
acquittal of four L.A. police officers in the Rodney King beating trial,
Lollapalooza became an even more lionized location of multiculturalism and sanctioned rebellion—despite a lineup of performers even
less diverse than the previous year's, and audiences were, if anything,
even whiter. Moreover, in 1992, Stoever tells us, the press constructed

the event as a "sanctioned and contained national riot of which local audiences can partake." *Spin* magazine, for example, titled its feature story "Power to the People: A Lollapalooza Diary" and focused its photo essay on scenes of the audience mayhem. The photos tell a tale of whiteness and masculinity, even as publications like *Melody Maker* claim that "all of the Lollapalooza tours crossed lines of class, race and gender in ways that most tours would have avoided like the plague."

Twenty years later, Lollapalooza eschews a white/black music binary that is, ahem, pretty much just about green (that is, money). But it's worth remembering that, over the last three decades, festivals like Jazz Fest and Lollapalooza have provided an entirely white-managed vision of cultural diversity. And black-managed events aren't simply whitewashed, they are also erased. If anything, they are doubly erased: once from the public record, when black-centric festivals like the Oakland Street Scene, Power to the Peaceful, and even Magnificent Coloring Day don't get mainstream coverage, and a second time, because gatherings with a black heritage mission—like the Jazz Festival—no longer count as rock festivals in the same way that Woodstock and Wattstax do. Moreover, this erasure has some social repercussions, since it means that large black audiences have lost that space for reconciliation that white audiences take for granted.

One of the points this chapter has tried to make is that the monolithic vision of American culture that festivals embrace is invariably normed to the middle-class white male. Any marked, alienated group that can't fully embrace the appeal of that rhetoric—not just African Americans, but also women, Asians, Hispanics, the elderly, and the poor—will not be drawn by this festival rhetoric in the same way. But this doesn't mean that the festival space cannot, under certain circumstances, work as the utopian, multicultural ideal that it claims itself to be. Indeed, it can, particularly if it removes the mechanisms that keep nonwhite crowds from easily attending them. This can best be seen at a music festival that took place in 2009, two days prior to the inauguration of President Barack Obama, at the Lincoln Memorial along the Washington Mall. Called We Are One, the concert featured performances by giants of popular music, including U2, Bruce

Springsteen, Stevie Wonder, Beyoncé, and many others. Their music was interspersed with speeches by actors and celebrities such as Jack Black, Kal Penn, Tiger Woods, and Marisa Tomei.

Few people would consider We Are One when thinking about rock festivals, not least because it was subsumed under the rubric of "Inaugural Festivities." Many presidents have held similar concerts, most notably Bill Clinton, whose first inauguration featured a similar event termed "A Call for Renewal," and which drew two hundred thousand to the Mall for a nighttime performance by Bob Dylan (Clinton, *My Life* 4). Still, there is a case to be made that Obama's inaugural concert not only falls into the category of rock festival but that it was the apex of the form. Whereas the Clinton events took place at night and stayed strictly within the parameters of a staid public ritual, the Obama events transcended that protocol, becoming more of a Woodstock event than . . . well, Woodstock itself.

Just think about it. Because the Obama concert took place in an urban center near a subway, neither nature nor automobility was a factor here. Nor were drugs valorized: the nature of the proceedings saw to that. Finally, despite the presence of many artists who normally trade in some degree of sexual display, a combination of the weather (freezing) and the dignity of the event removed all trace of sexual posturing. The result was a festival that provided Gilroy's space for "listening together," only rather than refer to a single community, We Are One referred to the *whole dang United States*.

The We Are One Concert was simultaneously broadcast on HBO, PBS, and NPR and was available for free viewing for a week on HBO. In addition, the concert left an enormous record in the form of homemade videos on YouTube. These are interesting, since they give an intimate picture of the crowd itself interacting with the concert's goals. Most of these videos are shot thousands of yards from the stage, so although the music can clearly be heard, they provide no visual record of what's happening onstage. Some include screen shots of the giant video screens; others concentrate on panning the crowd, recording, for posterity, the sight of a distinctly multiracial crowd jumping up and down, singing and emoting to the music wafting through the air around them. The overall impression of goodwill and exuberance is repeated in every video; moreover, the lengthy blog comments that both viewers and authors have left at these sites clearly mark them as historically significant in a particularly emotional, almost innocent, way.[9]

The concert itself has another unique visual aspect that sets it apart from all other rock festivals. Held on the steps of the Lincoln Memorial—a setting with a symbolic meaning that cannot be mistaken—the stage consisted of only a stark white marble proscenium. The monumental nature of this location served to heighten the sense of the monumental nature of the proceedings, as did the sober costumes of the performers; because of the weather—twenty degrees—the performers were mostly clad in dark overcoats and hats. The result was to erase the visual rhetoric of sexuality on which rock often depends. This effect is especially noticeable in the performance of the song "Higher Ground" by its author Stevie Wonder and the pop stars Usher and Shakira. The song begins with Usher—an often-shirtless rap idol known to perform risque bump and grinds—striding on stage, wearing a suit and tie and bundled up in a double-breasted, floor-length woolen overcoat. The camera pulls back to show us the statue of President Lincoln, hovering above him; then a bank of American flags pulls aside to reveal Stevie Wonder, also being hovered over by Lincoln. Usher begins to sing the song, joined by the Colombian singer Shakira, who is also (very unusually) wearing a modest long dark coat. Presently, the camera shoots them from beneath, so that the monument looms over them; eventually it cuts away and shows us the president-elect, Barack Obama, singing and dancing to the music. It is difficult to find nonhyperbolic terms to convey the weighty impact of this image, but suffice it to say that the sequence—the blind black man playing beneath the statue of President Lincoln flanked by two soberly dressed yet wildly charismatic young people of color, being applauded by the first African American president—makes perfectly visible not only the promises and ideals of civil rights, but also, as we've come to expect from festival rock concerts, the promise of success in America as well.

As this transcendent image indicates, the success of the We Are One concert cannot be overstated. It drew approximately half a million people to the Washington Mall, the same number claimed for Woodstock, albeit for a far shorter space of time. True, in the nearly fifty years since that historic event, concert organizers have made incredible progress on ingress and egress, acoustics and toilets, and it surely helped that the inaugural concert was in an urban location, near a subway, thus diversifying the audience's racial makeup. However, part of its success may have been due to the very different goals and rhetoric suffusing the scene. Rather than creating a utopian, antimaterialist narrative that mistakenly locates American values in nature, drugs, and sex, the We Are One concert merely sought to portray the election of Barack Obama as a symbol of the success of the civil rights movement. To that end, many artists sang songs that fit into that discourse: "Pride" by U2 (which invokes the death of Martin Luther King), "Higher Ground" by Stevie Wonder, "Lean on Me" performed by Mary J. Blige, and "The Rising" by Bruce Springsteen all address this notion explicitly. Other songs, like James Taylor's saccharine "Shower the People," John Mellencamp's bitter criticism of suburban American conformity in "Pink Houses," and Don McLean's "American Pie" (as sung by the country artist Garth Brooks) struggle to reconcile a different history—one of white cultural supremacy, disappointment, and timidity—with the concert's premise.

Clearly, like all the other festival narratives we've looked at, this narrative owes more to imagination and desire than to reality. Yet, I would argue that this festival succeeded better than most at making a reality (however temporary) out of that imaginary space. The song "American Pie," for example, is generally acknowledged to be an allegory for historical events in the 1960s. It situates 1950s America as a place of innocence destroyed by the counterculture. In its normative reading, "the good old boys" of the chorus are white fans of Buddy Holly mourning his death in a plane crash. But on this day and in this place, the crowd seemed to be celebrating something else. Was it the idea that a *dry* levee would have held during Hurricane Katrina? Was it the end of Bush's "American Pie" rhetoric and democratic ideals that had failed so signally? Was it the (metaphorical) death of the good old boys themselves? It's unclear. But certainly when good ol' boy Garth Brooks, raucously accompanied by the entire audience and, incidentally, by Barack Obama,[10] sang the chorus,

Bye, bye, Miss American Pie
Drove my Chevy to the levee but the levee was dry
Them good old boys were drinkin' whiskey and rye
Singing, "this'll be the day that I die."

it came as near to a raceless moment at a music festival as it is possible to imagine.

The We Are One concert shows that discourses of the music festival, when presented without rhetoric aimed solely at white males, *can* cut across all age groups and all social classes. But that concert was unique. Indeed, the absences that this concert highlights can help us to see the more usual desire, on the part of both audiences and festivals, to either dismiss or hide their essentially middle-class orientation. Rock festivals that have modeled themselves on Woodstock expose this longing and contain within them the fiction that rock, rock festivals, and rock fandom are a working-class preoccupation that somehow stamps its patrons with a kind of cultural or social authenticity. In fact, the working-class nature of rock seems to be most important in the genres where it is the least probable of origins: today's young artists need rafts of equipment, rehearsal space, and free time to develop their craft. Similarly, in order to attend a rock festival, a potential concertgoer needs leisure, cash, and a car. Rock festivals that evade these structures—like Wattstax and We Are One—tend to be less conflicted in their aims and hence more rhetorically powerful.

That these two concerts also happened to be genuinely multiracial affairs speaks once again to the connection between race, class, and cultural artifacts in America while also exposing how more normative rock festivals put the rhetoric of difference to work. If we turn our minds back to 1949 and the tragic violence that marred the Paul Robeson concert at Peekskill, it's easy to consider the modern-day music festival as both progressive and liberating. But as long as festivals are not for everyone, they have very serious limitations.

CHAPTER 6

Girls Gone Wild

ONCE MET AN ELDERLY MAN at a grunge party in Seattle who had in the long-distant past attended the Sky River Rock and Lighter Than Air Festival, a pre-Woodstock-like gathering held near Chehalis, Washington, over several rainy days in August 1968.

Today, organizers proudly recall that the Sky River Rock Festival is notable for being the first multiday rock festival on an undeveloped site and note that (unlike Woodstock) all profits were earmarked for donation to the Mexican American Federation of Washington, the Foundation for American Indian Rights, and the Central Area Peace and Improvement Cooperative.[1] However, this man's main memory of the festival was of spending the night in a teepee and waking up with a strange, naked woman leaning over him. Her breasts were therefore thrust into his face, and this, he said, was the *greatest thing that had ever happened to him before or since.*

Nothing sexual occurred during this encounter. She just got up and left the tent. But even so, the gesture was incredibly powerful. "You just can't imagine what it was like," he said. "We lived in such uptight times, and nakedness, open sexuality, women being available . . . it was this amazingly powerful thing, this completely transformational moment."

This story is a good reminder of the groundbreaking feeling of liberation that festival culture seems to have generated among its earliest attendees. Thanks to the invention and circulation of the Pill beginning in 1959, the 1960s were inevitably going to be a time when sexuality would be redefined: the utopian dream of a sexually free society was one that festivals were supposed to make flesh. The Sky River Rock Festival, like so many festivals of that era, exemplified utopianism, optimism, and hope, charging attendees with a long-lasting belief in the counterculture as an agent of societal change. But at the same time, it is both disturbing and inevitable that fifty years later, the single thing that this festival attendee remembers most clearly are a woman's breasts. It's especially weird since, although nudity is definitely one of the images most people associate with Woodstock, the cinematic record of the event doesn't contain much evidence to that effect. A few long-distance shots of people bathing in ponds during rainstorms earned *Woodstock* an R rating, but it's not titillating, and it's definitely misleading: according to an Associated Press article from 2009, most of the five hundred thousand attendees at Woodstock never saw a naked person. In the *Life* magazine special issue devoted to Woodstock, there is only one shot of full frontal female nudity; throughout the rest of that magazine and in other photo essays on the event, people are shown clothed.

And yet, the historical record of the counterculture in general and of Woodstock in particular generally includes the acceptance of public nudity as one of the festival's main features. Indeed, most people today agree that early rock festivals were able to concretize the concept of free love in a congenial public setting: as the Woodstock Preservation organization puts it, the Woodstock Festival's apparent abundance of what they call "unashamed social nudity" established a trend for those who attended subsequent festivals, and it did so well before the movie was released. And an issue of *Today's Health* from 1970 states that "since Woodstock, drug use and nudity have become barometers of a festival's success" (Keister, "Woodstock and Beyond" 20).

In fact, the concept of festival nudity wasn't so much a reality as it was a media construct, circulated through photographs from the events that featured naked women. Unlike the pornographic images one sees in the media, which invariably contain within them unspoken questions about power and its deployment in the sexual arena, the naked breasts of the hippie chicks at rock festivals were displayed in a way that echoes nature photos in *National Geographic*. They were depicted as anthropological, and thus educational, rather than erotic.

What may have been more important about these images was that they were clearly attached to women who were obviously willing to be on display for free. This may explain why they were far more powerful than those seen below the obsequious grins of girls in *Behind the Green Door* or *Playboy*'s playmate of the month: early rock festivals spanned an era that one might term the Pornographic Turn; that is, the years between 1953, when *Playboy* began, to 1972, when the popular film *Deep Throat* brought porn into the mainstream (McNair, *Porno? Chic!*).

According to some after-the-fact historians, the counterculture embraced nudity for a wide variety of reasons, including, but not limited to, a rejection of mainstream values, a symbol of truthfulness, a protest against harsh obscenity laws, and an outward display of the antiplastic/anticorporate/antitraditional mores of the time. Just as the 1990s' grunge movement was co-opted by fashion, in the late 1960s fashion magazines began to create a link between the popularity of early ecology books like Charles Reich's *The Greening of America*, Rachel Carson's *Silent Spring*, and the *Whole Earth Catalog* and the hippie movement's subsequent rejection of many of the outward trappings of fashion—like wearing regulation skirt lengths, hats, ties, and makeup. These rejections, when added up, would later be culled and commodified by advertisers and fashion magazines into "the natural look," that is, fashions that used natural fibers and muted colors (denim, burlap, linen; beige, brown, cream) and that didn't force the female figure into contorted forms.

But it's a long way from refusing to get your hair set or to wear a slip to the discarding of clothes entirely. A relatively small number of hippies actually did that, at Woodstock or elsewhere. Those that did—like the members of the Sexual Freedom League, a registered club at UC Berkeley, which in 1966 sponsored nude "wade-ins" at nearby beaches—did so as a political gesture (even when it was made with what appears, in hindsight, to have been a calculated desire to have sanctioned orgies).

Even so, the idea that nudity was a feature of early music festivals is an enduring one, repeated over and over in the literature historicizing them. The counterculture, we are told, and specifically the music festival, was a place where we can see the times' stultifying social conventions around sex being ground into dust. But they didn't, like Longfellow's mills of God, grind slowly or exceedingly small: instead, they may have unwittingly taken away as many freedoms as they gave.

———

Perhaps it's not surprising that rock festivals would become the place where such sights would signify so much about the sexual revolution. After all, as Linda Williams has argued (paraphrasing Sallie Tisdale), because Americans find it impossible to talk openly about sex, they exist in a state of "cultural puberty, simultaneously sex drenched and sex phobic" (*Porn Studies* 489), and "cultural puberty" is certainly a good description of much that goes on at rock festivals.

Moreover, sexuality has always, rightly or wrongly, been considered a cornerstone of what distinguishes rock music from other musics: for example, in her study of what she calls "collective joy," Barbara Ehrenreich has argued that the rock rebellion of the 1950s and 1960s wasn't just a move against mid-century sexual repression, but against the repression of physical motion in general, sexual or not. She points out that the era's bans on movement were particularly hard on women, citing rules in girls' sports restricting the number of dribbles in basketball, as well as common advice against female "movements" during sex (212). Building on the record of these kinds of restrictions, Ehrenreich characterizes early rock festivals (like Woodstock) as "beachheads of a new ecstatic culture meant to replace an old repressive one" (Ehrenreich, *Dancing in the Streets* 223). And the film of the festival certainly conforms to this view of the event, elevating it to a record of a sublime new community being formed on the wreckage of an old one.

But that perspective is embedded in the film's narrative, not in its visual rhetoric. Visually, *Woodstock* conforms to a very old model of film authorship; namely, the dictum that, as Laura Mulvey stated in 1971, the camera's gaze is always male. In her influential article "Visual Pleasure and Narrative Cinema," Mulvey showed that in the majority of films, women's bodies are used as a focal point around which male action occurs. Of course, not all films conform to her argument, and often (as, for example, in James Bond films) there are complex negotiations of voyeurism and pleasure that supersede typical gender categories; but overall, as Mulvey argues, film history has naturalized an order of events and a way that we view them. Thanks to Woodstock, the same can be said about how we view women at rock concerts. Today, the festival gaze is still overwhelmingly male — and for the same reason: because the lens through which the public viewed festivals was created by cameras, and their cameramen, at Woodstock.

Woodstock was released just prior to Mulvey's article, and it could easily have been one of her case studies, since it focused on muscular men energetically doing things (building stages, playing guitars, singing, drumming), while pretty women watch them. In a famous sequence, courtly, bearded men on horseback ride across the fields of Woodstock, with lovely long-haired ladies riding pillion behind them, and the passive nature of women at Woodstock is underlined by the dearth of women performers in the movie (and on stage). Again and again, in this as in other movies, the camera essentializes activity in men, passivity in women. The beautiful, contemplative shots of Joan Baez singing "Joe Hill," or the super-close-ups of Janis Joplin, don't exert the same kind of physical energy as Roger Daltrey, with his whirling arms, or Michael Shrieve, the wild-haired young drum soloist during Santana's set. Richie Havens's guitar-playing is a whirl of action, as shots of his fingers flying up the fretboard underline the physicality of music. But active women are few and far between in the film.

At Woodstock, the camera's gaze was male, but at least it wasn't prurient. The nudity at Woodstock wasn't limited to women, and it came about organically, due to features of the park (three large ponds) and the weather (rainstorms caused a great deal of mud, which had to be washed off somehow), but in subsequent years, that's become the norm at music festivals: sexuality is often on display in the audience, and it's not the sexuality of men. As early as the mid-1970s, women in tiny bikinis, sitting on men's shoulders, dominated photos of rock festivals. Indeed, topless women are a feature of festivals that practically replace the narrative itself, so insistent are they on being seen and, as Derrida would say, on signifying. In a film, a woman's presence will stop the action and then redirect the viewer's gaze toward men. At festivals, breasts serve the same purpose. The breasts aren't on stage: they are offstage, in the crowd, and they are more important as an entity than any single person or even any performer.

One of the things that Woodstock established was that rock concerts like it were more comfortable, more welcoming, and more intended for the male gender. Women's roles there, whether on stage or in the audience, are decorative: they serve to attract attention to the males who are the core market for promoters. They do what Mark Andrejevic has called "the work of being watched."

———

If you want to think about what the function of females at festivals is, a good exercise might be to think about what a festival *without* females would be like.

It's not difficult to find a festival lineup without women performers: that was practically the case at Heavy Montréal in 2014, which featured Metallica, Slayer, Lamb of God, Anthrax, Twisted Sister, the Offspring, and forty-five other bands, whose members were almost entirely male. Out of more than two hundred musicians pictured on the poster, five were women (three of them in a single band, the Japanese joke band Babymetal). And you could easily picture a similar bill at Coachella or Bonnaroo, with the addition of indie rock festival headliners like Kanye West and Kendrick Lamar, or Coldplay, Imagine Dragons, and Phoenix.

An all-male, or almost all-male, bill like that wouldn't faze anyone. At least, it hasn't, for many years. A different question entirely is what if the entire *audience* was male? A fairground full of forty thousand or fifty thousand guys in their early twenties would be uninviting, to say the least. Picture, if you will, forty thousand to fifty thousand young men all crammed together in some outdoor space, scantily clad due to the heat, riled up by the pounding sound of the music and by beer; they are jumping up and down in unison and chanting some three-word anthem.

The image conveyed is that of some historical fiction movie about a long-gone battle, *The 300* or *Troy*, perhaps, minus only the artificially worked-up hatred and the weapons. Or so one would hope. The fact is, artificially worked-up hatred could easily be instilled in such a crowd, and weapons can be made of practically anything.

Such an audience, forty-thousand-members strong, has not actually come to be, although many times the front areas of festival audiences, the area known as the mosh pit, has resembled this image, and the consequences of such gatherings can be dangerous, and dangerously gendered. Consider, for example, the aftermath of Woodstock '99. After that festival, held at the Griffiss Air Force Base (a known hazardous waste site) and drawing two hundred thousand people in the summer of 1999, an email describing some of the alleged sexual assaults the writer witnessed was widely distributed to the media (including myself). It said, in part, that the writer saw girls who "were forced into unclean porto-jons [sic] and A) punched in the face, pants pulled down, fingered vaginally/anally, punched again for crying ass spit on fuck in ass B) slammed faced into wall of stall, pants pulled down spit covered hand vaginal fisting, spit covered dick anal fuck, dropped to the floor."

This email was forwarded anonymously to the photographer Chris Habib and then was widely distributed to other journalists and to rock bands such as Sonic Youth. Perhaps because of its anonymity, it gained no traction in the mainstream press, although the accounts were corroborated to some extent by eight reported rapes and sexual assaults and forty-four arrests on charges ranging from disorderly conduct to sodomy, as well as two deaths. A total of 1,200 people were treated each day at the on-site medical facilities, and the Rome (NY) Memorial Hospital treated more than 120 attendees.

Only two rapes were subsequently prosecuted, but there is little doubt that more sexual assaults occurred. One Woodstock '99 volunteer named David Schneider told wire service reporters and the *Washington Post*, "I saw someone push this very skinny girl, maybe 90 or 100 pounds, then a couple of guys started taking her clothes off—not so much her top but her bottom. They pulled her pants down and were violating her and passing her back and forth. There were five guys that were raping this girl and having sex with her" (Wartofsky, "Police Investigate Reports" C-1).

Hearsay evidence like Schneider's is generally disallowed in conventional reporting; newspapers only follow up rapes that have been prosecuted. But whether one believes the bulk of the evidence or not, Woodstock '99 at the very least implies that festival spaces are more comfortable and inviting for men. Numerous mechanisms are in place that ought to keep women from wishing to attend, from the sanitary arrangements to the crush by the stage. Yet despite the inconvenience, women continue to attend festivals in large numbers, and their continued attendance is crucial to the continuance of festivals' success. Women, or rather, women's bodies, are objects of enormous importance to concert promoters, both as consumers and as draws: at festivals, their presence is necessary as a form of labor for which they are unpaid; or rather, which they pay in order to perform.

———

The gender problems that rock festivals caused were recognized almost instantly. In the early 1970s, women began organizing women-only concerts and events, and over the years, other attempts have been made to resituate women's roles both in the audience and onstage at rock festival events. The best-known example is the Michigan Womyn's Festival (or Michfest), which for forty years has been putting on a five-day concert at which only women are welcome to play.[2] Since 1976, the festival has drawn a largely lesbian crowd, ranging from three thousand to ten thousand or so attendees. At Michfest, the "women-only" stricture applies to more than just the performers: the festival uses female sound-technicians, lighting technicians, roadies, stagehands, and truckers—and it even requests that the shuttles that carry attendees from the airport assign their women drivers to the site.

Although not everyone who attends or plays Michfest is gay, the festival itself has always explicitly allied itself with lesbian and feminist causes and audiences. In 1991, an equally radical but entirely different female audience was forged in the punk rock circles of Washington state. That year, in August, a weeklong rock festival in Olympia, Washington, called the International Pop Underground Convention had a "girl night," officially titled "Love Rock Revolution Girl Style Now," at which only girls were allowed to play. It was intended to encourage girls to join bands and offset the male-oriented scene that dominated punk rock at the time, and it was a huge success, one that has left a lasting imprint on both the area and the music scene. In 2016, the Washington State History Museum hosted an exhibit entitled *A Revolution You Can Dance To*, documenting this "girl night," while some of the acts that performed at it, notably Bikini Kill, went on to become, if not household names, very much touchstones for a generation of female performers, inspiring them not only through music but through publishing ventures, activism, and grassroots organization. The gathering even produced a widely circulated manifesto that reads in part:

> BECAUSE we wanna make it easier for girls to see/hear each other's work so that we can share strategies and criticize-applaud each other.
> BECAUSE we must take over the means of production in order to create our own moanings.
> BECAUSE we are interested in creating non-hierarchical ways of being AND making music, friends, and scenes based on communication + understanding, instead of competition + good/bad categorizations.
> BECAUSE doing/reading/seeing/hearing cool things that validate and challenge us can help us gain the strength and sense of community that we need in order to figure out how bullshit like racism, able-bodieism, ageism, speciesism, classism, thinism, sexism, antisemitism and heterosexism figures in our own lives. BECAUSE we are angry at a society that tells us Girl = Dumb, Girl = Bad, Girl = Weak. (Hanna, "Riot Grrrl Manifesto")[3]

Like the Velvet Underground, about whom it is often said that its five hundred fans went on to form bands of their own, Revolution Girl Style and the Riot Grrrl Manifesto roused many of the women in that scene—Carrie Brownstein, Kathleen Hanna, and Miranda July, to name a few—to pursue projects that would in turn inspire other females to perform in new ways. Although the route was circuitous, the multi-platinum-selling British act the Spice Girls was clearly inspired by the movement to exploit its underlying aims for commercial purposes.

The International Pop Underground Convention was a small,

though potent force in changing women's roles both in audiences and onstage at concerts, but despite its high media profile and the long-term inroads it has made in music itself, it has done little to affect how mainstream rock audiences are treated. Indeed, safe and exclusively female spaces like Michfest and Riot Grrrl are or were subcultures, appealing only to small, relatively empowered, relatively educated, and relatively media-savvy persons. This changed slightly when, in 1997, the songwriter Sarah McLachlan spearheaded a festival tour of all-women artists aimed primarily at a female audience. Called Lilith Fair, it billed itself as "a celebration of women's music," and it was commercially successful for three years, between 1997 and 1999, grossing $16 million in sales in its first year of existence. In 1998 Lilith Fair enlisted the services of more than one hundred female-centric acts, including twenty-three rotating headliners and thirty second stagers, not to mention many more artists who earned their slots by winning contests. Each day, eleven bands performed, including McLachlan, Natalie Merchant, Sheryl Crow, the Indigo Girls, and Shawn Colvin. The third year, however, saw declining sales, which caused promoters to shelve the idea of a fourth year.

While it lasted, Lilith Fair did seem to fill a need. It provided a safe space for women to enjoy attending a rock festival without themselves becoming part of the spectacle. But although the tour had promise, its sincerely feminist underpinnings were sometimes undercut by its concomitant capitalist goals. At the time, the tour's booking agent, Marty Diamond, told me, "People said we could never have two women on the same bill back-to-back. I asked one guy, 'Why not?' He said, 'Because women don't buy merch.' I'm like, 'Yeah, they don't buy ugly black rock t shirts with a band's name printed on it.' We make really pretty merch, and they buy it. We have jewelry (designed by McLachlan), knapsacks—stuff people would want. We're really mindful of the audience, and how to get them to participate" (Arnold, "Fair Game"). It is unfortunate that the word "participate" here sounds like a euphemism for "spend." Indeed, Diamond made it sound like he was really only interested in creating a women's festival in order to exploit a more amiable marketplace.

Another thing Lilith Fair was criticized for was its reliance on a specific type of "soft," lyric- and feeling-driven music—that is, the kind of folkie, introspective fare often associated with women singer/ songwriters. And although this blithe musical characterization didn't describe every act at Lilith Fair, it was certainly true that the acts on stage put more emphasis on playing music than on displaying their bodies and that nudity, sexual antics, and pelvic thrusts were at a bare minimum. Also, despite the vast ratio of women to men in the audience, naked boobs were in short supply. Hence, Lilith Fair did not cater to the male gaze, and this may have contributed to its eventual demise.

Lilith Fair's tenure was plop in the middle of the grunge, or indie rock, era—post-Nirvana, pre-Napster, and absolutely at the height of the time when MTV ruled the music industry's coffers and playlists. Seen in retrospect, MTV had quite a large role to play in how women were configured—or objectified—in the world of rock. The fact that outdoor rock concerts continued to be the site of naked debauchery well after public nudity could by any stretch of the imagination be couched as a political gesture is probably due entirely to MTV. The cable network, which began broadcasting in 1981, initially showed music videos before branching out into live programming. In 1987, it began broadcasting "live" from Daytona Beach, Florida, during the week in early April that is generally designated Spring Break for college students—that is, it broadcast a show called *Spring Break* that was taped live at Daytona Beach during an earlier week in March. (The show itself was not live, it was broadcast later.) *Spring Break*'s use of the *idea* of "live taping'" (rather than the reality of it) apes that of Live Aid and shows that MTV had absorbed the idea of a live media event by creating a High Holy Day of its own. Moreover, its event could be repeated annually, giving it a more ritualized or ceremonial significance.

For seven straight years, the MTV *Spring Break* event was held in Daytona Beach, but in 1994 it was moved (briefly) to San Diego and later to Cancun and elsewhere, depending on which city would give the network the best breaks. In 1994, the year I attended every day of the taping, the event was attended by between ten thousand and thirty-five thousand kids per day, all of whom flocked to Marina Point to participate in events staged for MTV. The shoot took ten days and required four hundred crew members to produce a mere sixteen hours of programming, which was then put on repeat throughout the rest of the season. According to the executive producer of the event, Joel Silverman, it was worth it to MTV. "Locally when you touch 1,000 people personally, you're really building a solid fan base," he told me. "In 10 days we'll have touched 10,000 people personally. It's the least exclusive event at MTV: anyone can show up and be on it" (Arnold, "U-N-I-T-Y").

One of the most popular participatory aspects of *Spring Break* was its provision of free concerts to the thousands upon thousands of college students who attended it. At these shows, acts like Destiny's Child, Limp Bizkit, and Eminem performed for free in outdoor settings, accompanied by fun snippets of audience participation contests, many of which had a distinctly prurient, and utterly sexist, bent. These included fashion shows of skimpy beachwear, cleavage contests in which busty contestants rolled seductively in honey and feathers, games of onstage strip poker, kids swapping bathing suits in Volkswagen Beetles or making each other "outfits" using whipped cream, and, of course, the inevitable wet T-shirt trophy (Horn, "MTV Spring Break"). The contests objectified women's bodies, period.

Throughout the 1990s, *Spring Break* was one of MTVs most popular features, and it surely helped to prolong outdated countercultural notions of rock festivals as places of sexual freedom. At least, it offered sexual free-*ness*: attending a *Spring Break* concert or contest was gratis, whether one was on-site or in the living room watching it on TV. And by 1997, a direct-to-video venture, *Girls Gone Wild: Spring Break*, had begun to commercialize the concept. The *Girls Gone Wild* franchise also used the unpaid labor of girls met at *Spring Break* as amateur "talent" in soft-core porn acts, and it earned $20 million in its first two years, mostly through television marketing via infomercials.

MTV's *Spring Break* and *Girls Gone Wild* both helped shape what became normative crowd behavior among females in American festival settings in the late twentieth century. Indeed, for some college students, these mediated *Spring Break* concerts have replaced more utopian, free-form, countercultural concerts as places of transgression. As with earlier rock festivals, in these spaces they can enact "temporary" breaches of heterosexual and middle-class norms, in consequence-free spaces. In her article "The Staging of Agency in *Girls Gone Wild*," Karen Pitcher also points out the raced and classed nature of the bodies that one sees on both MTV's *Spring Break* and in the *Girls Gone Wild* videos: not only are they mostly white, but they are "appropriately disciplined in their careful ornamentation and self-care . . . typically free of excessive tattoos and funky piercings, almost all are exceptionally suntanned, wear makeup, dress in trendy if revealing clothes, and are usually free of body hair" (202).

What Pitcher is driving at is that these girls have been disciplined; they are made docile for public consumption by the power structure into which they have inserted themselves. Hence, the breasts on display at these rock concerts serve a double purpose. As spectacle, they attract attention. But, in addition, because they are on camera, being recorded and broadcast both on-site (on giant TV screens) and on television, they are also helping to inscribe the power relationship into being.

Of course, no direct line connects the idyllic shots of breasts at Woodstock to the iron mandate at Guns N' Roses concerts of the mid-1990s whereby girls caught on video by the video cameramen during intermission were enjoined to "show us your tits!" or risk being booed by an arena full of metal heads. And yet, maybe there is a direct line. The picture in *Rolling Stone* magazine that accompanies its coverage of the Aquarian Festival is of a topless girl, a fact that somehow exacerbates the final sentence in the review about the "one involuntary chick."

One would like to think that this cavalier dismissal was due to the unenlightened nature of the era, but twenty years later, the association of women, rape, and rock 'n' roll is still going strong. In 1987, for example, the original artwork chosen for the cover of the Guns N' Roses album *Appetite for Destruction* depicted a half-naked, splay-legged girl, panties around her ankles, who has seemingly just been raped by a robot. The band claimed—according to their label's head, Eddie Rosenblatt—that it was meant as a "symbolic social statement, with the robot representing the industrial system that's raping and polluting our environment" (Patrick Goldstein, "Geffen's Guns N' Roses"), but if you've heard the band sing "Turn around, bitch, I got a use for you, besides, you ain't got nothing better to do, and I'm bored" from the song "It's So Easy," their claim is not that convincing.

What this all seems to add up to is the sad conclusion that power and women are antithetical at rock festivals. Some would say this is because the festivals are owned by, worked at, and performed in mostly by men. At Woodstock, the gender proportion was only four women artists (Janis Joplin, Melanie, Joan Baez, and Grace Slick) out of hundreds of male musicians, and that proportion has held steady throughout the years. At the US Festival in 1984, the female-to-male ratio was six women to three hundred men, or 2 percent. At Live Aid in 1985, nine women appeared on stage in the course of seventy-five acts. At Coachella in 1999, less than 10 percent of three hundred performers were female. At Coachella in 2015, twenty-six women took the stage. That's out of 160 bands.

As disturbing as these figures seem to be, the number of women on stage needn't affect the numbers in the audience, however, and apparently they don't. According to a Nielsen[4] study in 2014, 51 percent of festivalgoers were female (Ulloa, "32 Million People"). The trouble is that attending a rock festival whilst female is becoming increasingly problematic. Woodstock '99 seemed like an aberration at the time, but accounts of violence done to women in rock concert audiences more recently are either on the rise or it just seems like they're on the rise because an increasing number of women write about rock concerts and are willing to broach the topic. Amy McCarthy's article "Punched, Groped, Beer Thrown in My Face" is a case in point: the experiences she describes are not new, but the wide circulation of stories like hers may be. McCarthy's article documents the rapes reported at numerous concerts and festivals, including Outside Lands, Stagecoach, Made in America, and Electric Zoo (to name just a few), and describes assaults at countless other shows of every rock genre. The article points out that venues aren't held responsible for these attacks, nor are the perpetrators punished, but the artists themselves can sometimes be called on to intervene from the stage. As an example, Staind's singer once stopped a concert to help a female fan who was being sexually assaulted in the pit in front of him.

Unfortunately, artists are often part of the problem, not the solution. Reports of sexual violence on the Vans Warped Tour—with bands accused of raping and violating underage fans over and over with no consequences—are unfortunately well-substantiated.

Meanwhile, a visual link between sex and rock music has been established that seems strangely unbreakable. And as time goes by, the link is becoming increasingly explicit. Today, naked, or nearly naked, breasts dot the pop landscape like so many pneumatic flesh mountains. They are in or on music videos, movies, ads for Macy's, children's anime, and Monster High dolls. They are an inescapable feature of modern life and certainly of rock festivals, and although there is nothing wrong with that—women's bodies themselves are not the problem here; it is their abuse that I complain of—it would be hard to argue that it is indicative of some kind of sexual equality, progress, or empowerment. If anything, the glossy, oiled perfection of each and every female body seems to have exerted some other, less wonderful, effect on viewers.

Indeed, while one hopes that women festivalgoers are able to forge their own forms of community and pleasure in all of these arenas, there could be a link between the festival's exploitation of women's bodies as a spectacle and the way the sight of women's bodies has been devalued in recent years. From pornography to politics, the price of a woman's nakedness seems to be literally *less valuable* than it was formerly. Just as they were at the Lighter Than Air Sky Rock Festival in Seattle, naked breasts are present at Lovevolution, at Coachella, and at Burning Man, but their meaning has changed. They've gone from a subversive gesture—*a bas la bourgeoisie!*—to a free sales pitch, made by unremunerated toilers laboring for concert promoters to get attendees' feet inside the gate. Rather than representing a moment of liberation, today's naked breasts symbolize a loss of freedom and power.

Partly, this is just another one of the consequences of the internet, which has drastically changed the economic scale of pornography by allowing images to be circulated for free. But by providing a commercial space in which to display the movement toward sexual openness, rock festivals may have done this first, before the internet was even invented.

CHAPTER 7

A Peculiar Euphoria: Raves, Crowds, and Freedom

*A comfortable, smooth, reasonable, democratic unfreedom prevails
in advanced industrial civilization, a token of technical progress.*
—HERBERT MARCUSE, *ONE-DIMENSIONAL MAN*

O NE EVENING IN 1994, a friend of mine who worked for *Rolling
Stone* called me up in a dither. She had arrived in San Francisco that afternoon on assignment to cover a Full Moon Rave
in Santa Cruz, and she couldn't for the life of her find out where
it was to be held.

The rave was of the kind that gave clues, rather than a map, to its
location. For example, a typical invitation—perhaps a flyer, given out
at a bar—would ask you to call a number that would then direct you
to the name of a store in Hunter's Point, where you then had to buy
something—perhaps a carton of eggs, indicated by an image on the
original flyer—and written on a single egg inside the carton would be
the longitude and latitude of the rave's location in Golden Gate Park.

Today, such devices seem laughably simplistic. If you were told to
find a store in Hunter's Point called Quikmart, you'd google its address, and if you were then given a location written in longitude and
latitude, you'd use an app on your smartphone to find it. In 1994, this

was not the case. You could spend hours driving around Hunter's Point looking for the right shop, and you'd be especially hampered if you were from out of town. This is why my friend was flummoxed. I was, too, but as it turned out, my downstairs neighbor was d-jaying the rave, so I just asked him where he was going.

In other words, we found out the old-fashioned way, through word of mouth.

As this story indicates, the clues to these dance parties ranged from obvious to obscure, but they were part of a larger project that elevated the experience of attending a rave to one of ideology rather than function. Just as grunge recouped ideas about punk rock and class status and inserted them into a more modern musical landscape, the intention of techno music was to meld the sonic output of electronic technologies with bodily pleasure, intellect with emotion. The "search" was part of this project, and it had other advantages as well, eliminating casual comers and creating imagined communities of like-minded individuals.

What's interesting about this is that the concept of *search*, combined with the concept of the *crowd*, is integral to what is possibly the 1990s' most entrenched technology and cultural shifter, the search engine. The search engine, which was developed throughout that decade, has changed the way most people think and even act. If, as Trevor Pinch and other SCOT (social construction of technology) theorists would have it, technology is socially constructed by users and not the other way around, then searching for raves is the perfect metaphor for its time. To do so, at least in San Francisco, was to participate in the zeitgeist and to experience the cutting edge of the postindustrial age and its byproduct, the new media economy.

But to *search* is different than to *seek*. Ravers, like hippies, were more likely to describe themselves as seekers after enlightenment and a form of mental freedom. To *search* for something is a more prosaic activity. A seeker is on a personal journey. A searcher—like John Wayne in the movie of the same title—sets out on a more public quest. A search engine (rather than a seek engine) looks through public information, and this act, like Wayne's hunt for his kidnapped niece, may have broad consequences.

Searching for music festivals, then, is different from seeking enlightenment, and it has a different outcome. As early as 2000, researchers were suggesting that the codes used to rank search results were (or perhaps one should say "are") inherently political, based on invisible rankings built into the system (Introna and Nissenbaum, "Shaping the Web"). As we have seen, music festivals have been used as spaces for political statements, gestures, and ideologies, but as with the politics of search, the biases and ideologies at festivals aren't always entirely apparent: instead, the power hierarchies they inscribe are invisible. On the internet, search crawlers ("spiders") crawl the web, displaying the "best"—that is, most popular, useful, or frequently asked for—results to users. This is a good allegory for music festivals. They too are spiders, crawling through culture, displaying results, popular acts, popular technologies, and advertisements to attendees, who then spread them to the culture at large.

Of the many technologies on display at raves (turntables, sound systems, MDMA, portable toilets), the most obvious display is that of the attendees: ravers, scantily clad in glittery costumes with wings, face paint, spangles, backpacks, and pacifiers, dancing ecstatically into the night. On the surface, raves seem to be advertisements not for people, or for music, but for a state of mind. Ravers would have it that this state of mind is the same as that of the hippies—peace, love, freedom, and oneness: the merging of society with the self. But it may be more complicated than that. The rise of techno, through the medium of the rave, is a giant endorsement for the post-industrial economy and all its affordances. If, as Marx once said, history repeats itself, the second time as farce, then ravers are reproducing the gestures of the counterculture, without a hint of irony—or of lessons learned.

———

Andreas Gursky is a German artist whose work addresses the human side of global commerce. His large-scale photographs depict crowds at concerts and sporting events, as well as in airports, automobile factories, parking lots, and trading floors. His work has been described as "crystallizing physical and social reality" (Siegel, "The Big Picture" 104), and as Alix Ohlin said in *Art Journal*, "In their determined, oblivious way, the people in his photographs make clear that there is no longer any nature uncharted by man. In place of nature we find the invasive landmarks of a global economy" ("Andreas Gursky" 22).

One feature of the global economy that Gursky documents in his work is the space occupied by the modern music festival. In his 1995 work *Union Rave*, he documents a singular moment in the history of EDM (electronic dance music), the latest contemporary space where mass behavior and individuality meet and melt. Ideologically, raves like the one photographed in *Union Rave* were at their purest in the mid-1990s: as with Woodstock, the crowds drawn to it and to raves like it would eventually be commodified and sold (specifically, in Germany, to a fitness club company called Mcfit). But the moment Gursky captures in *Union Rave* shows the era just prior to that—the transformative, transcendent, beatific moment before commercialization has taken hold. On the one hand, *Union Rave*, like so many of Gursky's other works, shows humanity at its least individuated. On the other, it is a literal depiction of the deconstructionist meaning of *jouissance*: that is, it is more than just "enjoyment"—it is the actual right to enjoy. People appear in the very act of taking pleasure in (or because of) surplus value, excess, property ownership, and the possession and display of wealth. The Union of *Union Rave* could refer to Europe, unified at last less than two years earlier. But the title may well be meant ironically.

Moreover, attendance at raves like the one Gursky documents are, like attendance at all music festivals, a good reminder of Canetti's opening gambit in *Crowds and Power*, in which he posits that it is only in a crowd that man becomes free of the fear of being touched. "The more fiercely people press together," he writes, "the more certain they feel that they do not fear each other" (16). This reversal of fear is, according to Canetti, one of the reasons why people seek to crowd. Only in a crowd, he claims, can people feel equal. "It is for this blessed moment," he asserts, "when no-one is greater or better than another, that people become a crowd" (18).

As we saw in the previous chapter, Canetti is wrong about many crowds. Today's crowds are often fearful places, and with good reason. Many crowds can be dangerous, and, at the very least, they are often unpleasant. To begin with, however, most raves were neither, and *Union Rave* epitomizes this idealized view of the crowd. It shows a mass of young people dancing at a German May Day rave. An invisible rhythm emanates from the still photo, wafting off the images of their physical bodies. Their arms are raised, and they are all focusing on some point upward and slightly to the left of the photographer, such that there is a visceral sense that they are reacting to something that has just occurred. The people in this photo are clearly having a good time, but although their faces convey intensity and contentment, they are not smiling. Still, despite the crowdedness, they feel they are united in a safe place—as is indicated by the fact that many of them have flung their arms in the air. Their torsos are exposed like targets, and they have no accessories, such as purses or backpacks. They are warm, for no one wears a jacket, so God only knows where they are keeping their wallets and their car keys. They are almost all young, perhaps under thirty. They are male and female, but all of them—every one of them—is white.

What Gursky's work makes clear is that, at least to themselves, ravers are an imagined community. They are, like Europe, whose union had only recently been sanctified by the Maastricht Treaty and the Schengen Agreement, *unified*. Yet despite the attendees' uniformity—of age, of class, of garb, of activity—there is a sense that they are acting privately, and therefore they do not really coalesce into the type of crowd that we typically associate with photos of the most famous moments of mass participation in the twentieth century—moments of anonymous masses bowing in Mecca, filling Red Square, or marching on Washington. The ravers in *Union Rave* predate both iPods and smartphones, but you can almost imagine them in silhouette, like the original iPod commercials, wearing headphones, holding what's now called a "silent rave." Together, they depict an updated, twenty-first-century version of those crowds of humanity, of the "mob porn" mentioned by Schnapp and Tiews as a hallmark of the twentieth century's explosion in population; a flip side, if you will, to the dehumanized masses that writers like Negri and Hardt and artists like Sebastião Salgado see as the victims of capitalism. And this is not surprising, given that the image of the mob has now been usurped by that of the smart mob. Today, the troll and the hacker are the most feared figures of the age: mutant individuals, sabotaging first the cyberworld and then reality and electing Donald Trump. In the warmer, less anonymous world of the *Union Rave*, these monsters do not yet exist.

Gursky's work does not comment on the aesthetic nature of the gathering; there are no visual clues as to what is occurring in front of the people in it or what type of music is being played. Theoretically, it could be a photo of people trying to escape from a loud noise or of people listening to a political rally, an opera, or a symphony. Yet the electronic nature of the music in *Union Rave* is implicit in the event that it depicts. Raves like May Day were unique to the 1990s, a twist on the rock festivals that came before, but with many of the same ideals and goals. They too were utopian in concept; they also strove to be free—and like rock festivals, they created a kind of "exclusive mass," welcoming only those who understood their rhetoric, puzzling and off-putting to those who did not. What is interesting about rave crowds is that they are instant communities, yet they bear none of the hallmarks of other communities, that is, no kinship ties or social rules of governance. Ravers are extremely self-conscious *about being a part of a crowd*. Their identity is explicitly stated, both to themselves and to others, but rather than attaching to individuality, identity is attached to the idea of becoming an anonymous crowd member. It differs from other types of rock fandoms, where to declare oneself a Dead Head or a fan of Bruce Springsteen is to announce one's values and beliefs. Raving is not about individuality; it's about group behavior. Its adherents identify not with a particular artist, but with the event itself. The rave's insistence on the crowd as the star of the show has influenced the way rock festivals present themselves to their audiences today. At most rock shows, the crowd, rather than the artist, is displayed on the giant video screens, so the crowd can observe *itself* as it reacts to the music. As media theorist and early cyberpunk advocate Douglas Rushkoff has said, "Unlike a rock concert, which unites its audience in mutual adoration for the sexy singers on stage, the rave unites its audience in mutual adoration for one another. The DJ providing the rhythm is more of an anonymous shaman than a performer, mixing records from a remote corner of the room. The stage is the dance floor, and the stars are the ravers themselves. The group celebrates itself" (*Cyberia* 356).

———

When it comes to rock festivals, raves represent an evolutionary as well as a chronological step. At present, more people attend, or have been to, raves and dance parties than have been to rock festivals, and there are, of course, many aesthetic and economic differences between the two (particularly in terms of space control and motivation). But they have the same genesis and, ostensibly, the same utopian aims. They are more similar than they are different. Moreover, if rock festivals like Newport and the US Festival reflected and refracted changes in sonic culture, helping audiences to experience and understand technological changes in music dissemination, then raves are the logical next frontier. The invention, or rather the popularization, of the web and internet parallels the growth of raves as well as of rock festivals, and nowhere as much as in the realm of EDM, or electronic dance music. Rock music—and the rock festival—are analog, and as such are played through wire and wood. EDM is digital, and it is played through plastic. There is a human element in both, but there is nonetheless a difference.

The genesis of rock festivals was in the folk world among non-amplified instruments. (The amplification, as we have seen, was highly problematic.) Even today, guitar-based popular music is tied to folk idioms, particularly in country music, where stringed instruments, twang, and lyrics about a stable, heteronormative past where men work and women dote dominate the lyrics. By contrast, techno music—house, jungle, and EDM in all its varieties—has evolved alongside the internet and our uses of it. This is in part because computers and their affordances (such as software, laptops, digitized music files, and so on) have made d-jaying so much simpler, but there are other factors at play as well. The popularization of EDM raises some questions about the evolution of rock crowds and power. Has the (for lack of a better word) *techno-y* sound of techno music acclimated audiences to their more technologically informed world? Is techno music's move away from narrative (songs with stories) toward code-driven and automated soundscapes a move away from humanity, or does the way techno music calls to bodies merely reiterate the human need to gather with others to listen together to music?

These are questions embedded in the evolution of technological music and the enormous free concerts, known as raves, that have helped to popularize it. But another question lurks inside anything to do with raves, and rave music, and that question has to do with drugs. Most people who have heard it would support the assumption that techno music sounds better if you're high. This assumption is supported by the factual evidence that raves *are* places where people gather to do drugs; indeed, certain types of drugs are an enhancement that is almost mandatory to enjoy these gatherings. The huge role of drugs at raves begs a final question about modern crowds, since drug use at festivals is symptomatic of a far larger point about technology, the economy, and modernity in the late twentieth and early twenty-first centuries. It's hard to put into words, but basically, it is simply this: what do drugs have to do with it?

Drug use has long been associated with the 1960s, cyberculture, counterculture, and rock festivals. Indeed, if one goes by the ubiquity of the mantra "sex & drugs & rock 'n' roll," drug use was a crucial ingredient. In the early 1960s, as John Markoff has shown in his book *What the Dormouse Said*, experimenting with psychedelic drugs was a key component in research centering on computers. Ken Kesey, who had taken LSD at Stanford University in 1959, later began what he called the Acid Tests, culminating in the Trips Festival; the same group of people who had introduced him to the drug were to use it at SRI (the Stanford Research Institute) in their pursuit of what the poet Richard Brautigan ironically called "machines of loving grace" ("Where mammals and computers live together/in mutual programming harmony").

By the time Woodstock came along, LSD would have seemed, from journalistic accounts, to have been a key component of the music festival experience. But as with nudity, it may not have been as rampant as the media made out. As Louis Menand points out in his critique of Joan Didion's *Slouching Towards Bethlehem*, despite sensationally negative press coverage about college kids on acid jumping out of windows, in 1967, only 1 percent of college students had tried LSD. Menand says, "The sensationalized press coverage of the period has left a permanent image of the late nineteen-sixties as a time when everyone was tripping or stoned. . . . [But] in 1969, only four percent of adults said they had smoked marijuana. Recreational drug use soared in the nineteen-seventies, but the press was no longer interested" ("The Radicalization of Joan Didion" 68). By contrast, in a study on drug use at raves done in 2007, 97 percent of the three hundred respondents had tried marijuana and 92 percent had used ecstasy (Hunt, Evans, and Kares, "Drug Use" 75).

Although Hunt et al.'s study targeted rave-goers rather than the general population, it is still clear from that statistic that something has changed radically in the interim. Alarmist articles about the dangers of drug use are a constant across those forty years. But there are two competing discourses about it. The official one characterizes drug use at raves and dance events as excessively risky behavior, in need of regulation. These events are, as one set of researchers studying date-rape drugs put it, "space-times fraught with sexual and pharmacological risks" (Moore and Valverde, "Maidens at Risk" 525). This narrative is the one that drives the law's quest to regulate dance parties as well as drugs: it is also, one need hardly add, an ancient story about parental control.

The other narrative—driven by participants—emphasizes the importance and pleasures of drug use, to which they often attribute spiritual, educational, and even transcendent qualities. Rushkoff, for example, uses utopian rhetoric to describe the experience of taking MDMA, or ecstasy (often referred to within the scene as "e"), writing:

> The peak of the E-xperience is when the drug and dance ritual brings the revelers into a state of collective consciousness. Descriptions of these extended moments of group awareness often fall into cliché, but they are profound, life-changing events for those who have experienced them. The dancers achieve what can only be called "group organism" . . . . The mass spectacle results in a fleeting but undeniable rush of collective awareness. Dancers move about freely on the floor, making eye contact that feels as though one were looking in the mirror: a single being with thousands of pairs of eyes, using people who formerly thought of themselves as individuals to examine itself. (*Cyberia* 356)

Rushkoff's reveries are completely typical. In the following passage, Hillegonda Rietveld, a professor at South Bank University and director of its program in sonic industry, describes a similar, but different rave:

> The amplified dance music carries me into another plane of experience, its regular beat comforting me while a world of musical textures, rhythms and visual impressions whirls around me. I forget

about how I arrived here, about my usual daily life, myself. My
body seems to have shed its burdens of human existence, its limitations reduced: free at last, free at last. Time is now and always,
fragments of seconds, breaking to a blur of party weekends, then
smoothening out into a transcendental sense of forever. Bodies of
fellow dancers brushing, strangers have gone, we are all friends,
in it together, we are as one. ("Entranced" 45)

Ecstatic prose like this is typical of the hyperbole surrounding
dance music or "techno," a term first used by Alvin Toffler in his book
The Third Wave (1980). The first techno band, Kraftwerk, was Teu-
tonic in origin; but the form became Americanized in the late 1970s,
when its use of machine-made beats was adapted by funk-steeped
d-jays in Detroit with whom, theorists like to argue, it struck a chord
because it "allowed the city to rethink its post-industrial future in
terms of information age technology" (Rietveld, "Entranced" 48). As
the documentary *High Tech Soul* puts it, Detroit was the perfect place
for techno to thrive, because one of the few resources it had was
space—"and not just empty space; space full of the artifacts of American industrial culture" (Bredow, *High Tech Soul*).

The result was house music—which, as the Detroit techno musician Derrick May notes in *High Tech Soul*, sounded "like Kraftwerk
and George Clinton were stuck in an elevator with only a sequencer
to keep them company." In the early 1980s, the deep implications
of techno music as the sound of a new economy were very much in
the zeitgeist, flowering into the mainstream with a single rapture-
inducing performance by Michael Jackson (whose life-history was
also governed by the death of an old industry, steel) imitating a
cyborg in the dance known as the moonwalk.

As a genre, house music was somewhat subcultural, the preferred
music of partygoers rather than radio listeners. Although one could
purchase tapes of it, it was essentially a live form, made by d-jays in
the moment, encouraging use of the idiomatic phrase, "you had to be
there." Since those days, it has spawned a number of music types that
are sometimes referred to as EDM, or electronic dance music. EDM
is like hip-hop, an umbrella term used to describe a host of different
types of music with one common factor, a dance beat generated by an

electronic timekeeper. "Real" drummers may generate or play along-side this beat, but EDM music (house, acid, trance, ambient, trap, etc.) uses a plethora of electronic noises to generate the tempo. In re-cent years, tunes, lyrics, and singers have been added to make EDM more radio-friendly, but d-jays like Calvin Harris, Steve Aoki, David Guetta, and Mark Ronson (to name just a few) are not musicians per se; rather, they preside over musical collaborations that can re-sult in more conventional record sales (that is, in downloads or cross-platforms and the other economic transactions that have character-ized the new music industry since digitization). The stars of EDM thus correlate to the post-industrial changes in work and production that Toffler predicted, and, unsurprisingly, the aesthetics of such music has its own rules and values. Unlike rock, it is not judged on lyrics, a meaningful narrative, or the timbre, persona, and perceived authen-ticity of the artist and vocalist.

That said, practically speaking, EDM *does* what all music does, that is, it translates emotion and even logic into a bodily feeling. When ex-perienced in a festival setting, EDM may in fact do this better than rock bands can. Since EDM is essentially a modern affordance, it's worth considering if the *sound* of it is, as Rietveld suggests, the "inter-face between complex technology and humans" ("Entranced" 55), and, as such, whether it connotes both the dread and the bliss of the twenty-first century, the obsolescence of the male body, and other post-industrial woes. Sonically, this may be so. But at the same time, as these festivals draw ever-larger crowds into ever-larger spaces, in part by providing a multiplicity of musical genres (much of it techno) that plays 24/7 for days on end, they are also enacting ideas that Fredric Jameson put forth about postmodernism. Such festivals em-body pastiche, the disappearance of the individual subject, and the loss of historicity that he claims are the chief indicators of the post-modern era.

Postmodernism, Jameson says, signified

the end, for example, of style, in the sense of the unique and the personal, the end of the distinctive individual brush stroke (as sym-bolized by the emergent primacy of mechanical reproduction). As for expression and feelings or emotions, the liberation, in contem-

porary society, from the older anomie of the centered subject may
also mean not merely a liberation from anxiety but a liberation
from every other kind of feeling as well, since there is no longer
a self present to do the feeling. This is not to say that the cultural
products of the postmodern era are utterly devoid of feeling, but
rather that such feelings—which it may be better and more accurate, following J.-F. Lyotard, to call "intensities"—are now free-
floating and impersonal and tend to be dominated by a peculiar
kind of euphoria. (Quoted in Natoli and Hutcheon, *A Postmodern
Reader* 319)

Here, Jameson presages the embrace of a mechanized musical aesthetic that is tolerable only when listened to together.

By the 1990s, raves had become widespread in large cities, especially New York and San Francisco, but they also occurred in rural
parts of Wisconsin (Matos, *The Underground Is Massive*). Drug use
was rampant at all of them. According to Julie Holland, a medical
researcher at Mount Sinai Hospital, who happened to frequent raves
in New York City in the mid-1990s, MDMA was used by about 80
percent of those in attendance. The drug was officially deemed illegal in 1985 and, by 2003, was subject to explicit legislation, namely
an act of Congress introduced by Senator Joe Biden that was called
the RAVE act. (It stands for Reducing Americans' Vulnerability to Ecstasy.) The act, which subjected rave promoters and venue owners to
fines and prison time for use of MDMA on their watch or property,
fell through, but the similar Illicit Drug Anti-Proliferation Act passed
in a different form the next year as part of the AMBER Alert Bill.
According to Michaelangelo Matos's exhaustive history of the rave
scene, although drugs were (and are) prevalent at such parties, even
the police don't see them as preceding the events. Rather, says one
Chicago-area police sergeant quoted by Matos, "The promoters don't
push the drugs. What they push is the music and the experience. They
put together a package. But then others come along and sell" (Matos,
The Underground Is Massive 313). The word "push" here is key, since
raves explicitly borrow the rhetoric of rock festivals and counterculture that suggests drug use is a necessary part of the experience.

Certainly much of the rhetoric surrounding these events echoes

the 1960s ideology of "freeing the mind" and "opening the heart."
But by the 1980s, illicit drug usage and sales had become a grey economy that was deeply intertwined with rock music. Music festivals in
particular were a site of consumption and distribution, and there is a
clear link between raves, Dead Heads, and the grey economy of LSD
sales that dogged the community and the concerts given by that particular band. According to Matos, when Jerry Garcia died in 1995,
many Dead Heads—and LSD dealers—transferred their activities to
raves.

Jesse Jarnow, a WFMU d-jay, *Rolling Stone* reporter, jam band expert, and the author of *Heads: A Biography of Psychedelic America*,
calls the connection between drug dealing and festivals "hip economics," a term he borrowed from the late Jerry Garcia. The term, he
says, "describes the way drug sales so often fund cultural entities, à la
LSD chemist Owsley Stanley supporting the Dead in their early days.
And the model absolutely extends into the ecstasy age. Even before
the rave explosion, there were lots of people who used ecstasy sales
to fund their operations when ecstasy was still legal" (Jarnow, personal interview).

"Hip economics" is the notion that ties together music festivals
with other extrafinancial transactions (like, at the Dead's shows,
concert-tape trading, sales of acid and weed, and other minor businesses like hair wraps and burritos). It is also one that can help festivals manifest as what Hakim Bey called a "temporary autonomous
zone," that is, "an uprising which does not engage directly with the
State, a guerilla operation which liberates an area (of land, of time,
of imagination) and then dissolves itself to re-form elsewhere/else-
when, *before* the State can crush it" (Bey, *TAZ* 99). Bey specifically
likens these zones to festivals, borrowing Stephen Pearl Andrews's
image of anarchy as "a *dinner party*, in which all structure of authority
dissolves in conviviality and celebration." Says Bey: "Participants in
insurrection (i.e., in the creation of a T.A.Z.) invariably note its festive
aspects, even in the midst of armed struggle, danger, and risk. The
uprising is like a saturnalia which has slipped loose (or been forced
to vanish) from its intercalary interval and is now at liberty to pop up
anywhere or when" (*TAZ* 103). Originally, raves and dance parties did
exactly this, occurring at irregular intervals in mystery spots. And as

Jarnow suggests, considering such festivals as this type of temporary autonomous zone goes a long way toward describing both their popularity and their role in the culture.

Considered thus, from a shamanistic, that is, ideological standpoint, it is possible that raves were once the purist distillation of rock festivals' utopian promises, providing attendees with truly life-changing experiences. The real discourses being circulated may be slightly different, however. From an economic perspective, for example, raves have morphed into EDM festivals, and these are an extremely profitable site of commerce. Beyond Wonderland, Electric Daisy Carnival, TomorrowWorld, the Ultra Music Festival, and hundreds of other festivals draw huge crowds to cities and spaces across the country every summer. Most (if not all) rock festivals now have an EDM component, and in 2015, tickets for Coachella, Bonnaroo, and Burning Man topped $400 *each*, with the entire experience, including shelter, transportation, and food, generally costing several thousand dollars for each attendee. Burning Man is especially notable, since it exemplifies the festival ethos as a site of conspicuous consumption and global degradation, from the cost of tickets, vehicles, gas, food, and water to the gross overpopulation of the festival's site in a desert: additionally, attendance at it is practically mandatory for a certain element of the tech sector in San Francisco. Burning Man is a rich man's playground, and as such it mimics other such locations—green golf courses in arid Texas, for example—with CEOs helicoptering in and enormous, temporary temples, complete with chefs and hot tubs, being built on the Playa. It is the T.A.Z. to end all T.A.Z.'s.

Granted, Burning Man is not strictly a rave or a rock festival; it merely incorporates elements of those types of events on the vast Nevada desert plain on which it is held every Labor Day weekend.[1] The communications scholar Fred Turner credits Burning Man with helping to shape how Google, surely the largest and most influential technology company of the twenty-first century, not only conceived of itself and its role in society, but also how it has organized itself as a company. According to his article on the subject, Burning Man serves as a key cultural infrastructure for companies like Google, and he goes on to show how Burning Man, and attendance at it, has "help(ed) to shape and legitimate the collaborative manufacturing processes driving the Bay Area's new media industries" ("Burning Man at Google" 73). Just as, Turner notes, "100 years ago, churches translated Max Weber's protestant ethic into a lived experience for congregations of industrial workers, so today Burning Man transforms the ideals and social structures of bohemian art worlds, their very particular ways of being 'creative,' into psychological, social and material resources for the workers of a new, supremely fluid world of post-industrial information work" (75).

Turner's insights about Burning Man rest on the ways that business is being conducted differently in the twenty-first century, but others have noted the festival's influence on festivals, as festivals. For example, according to the British scholar Roxy Robinson, Burning Man's ethos has shifted how the British festival industry conceives of events. Burning Man's original conception involved a new definition of audience/citizenship, one that (according to itself) required attendees to help build the infrastructure and provide the entertainment, as well as adhere to a broad repertoire of principles including, according to their own guidelines, civic responsibility, communal effort, de-commodification, radical self-reliance, radical inclusion, radical self-expression, and gifting. While Burning Man itself seems to have recently moved beyond some of these ideals and to a different place, Robinson notes how new British festivals like Secret Garden Party and Boomtown Fair are "delivering audience members from the role of spectators" (*Music Festivals* 18), in part by providing them with new modes of consumption—of the type sometimes called "prosumption"—that include moments of autonomy. This, she argues, is partially a result of Burning Man's widely distributed ethos of "no spectators," and that statement alone can be directly attributed to raves and their history.

———

If, as was suggested earlier in this book, changes in sound are harbingers of ideological shifts, then is the actual *sound* of techno music and EDM symbolic of the shift from an industrial to a postindustrial society? I think it is fair to say yes. Yes, it is. Does this music's insertion into raves and dance parties, where many humans, their consciousness heightened by designer drugs, congregate in crowds in order to feel a passionate sense of community and spiritual togetherness then connote a way back into humanness? Sure. Probably. Do raves and dance parties then constitute the new rock crowds, with a power to display new technologies (such as search engines) and transform old ideologies into nice narratives about them? Yes again. Is Burning Man—the most successful, ambitious, and truly powerful crowd site ever to amass on a yearly basis—somehow emblematic of where all this energy has been deposited? A qualified yes to that too. But rather than end with these answers, a little pressure should be put on what all this—and especially the last statement—means on the ground.

To begin with a fanciful allegory: search engines mine and organize data dumps, and what is an EDM festival—what is Burning Man—if not exactly the physical embodiment of that idea? Each person at Burning Man—or Electric Daisy Carnival, or Beyond Wonderland, or wherever—has in his or her brain an enormous capacity for information. It is information, however, that is both singular and disorganized. When placed together in these landscapes and set to a beat, the brains begin to function together, creating, as attendees often say, "one enormous organism," a mass of humanity with a single thought. In this sense, perhaps, a rave is a way of organizing information, of bringing it into line. It is not rhythmic; it is algorhythmic: that is, it is a set of calculations that can perform automated reasoning.

Herein is the trouble not only with raves but with rock crowds. They are suggestible, energetic, and susceptible to groupthink. This is what Turner means when he suggests that, at Burning Man, "the festival is not only a ritual space but a potential factory" ("Burning Man at Google" 91). And the lesson it may be giving us, in terms of rock crowds and power, is that there are virtually no limits to the size and scope of such endeavors. Even with the global population reaching seven billion, America, and the planet, abounds with empty spaces that could be utilized for this purpose. All that is needed is infrastructure, and Burning Man has shown that there is a willing free labor force that will create—and dismantle—this kind of pop-up city.

In September 2015, after Burners had returned from the desert, Quizno's sandwich chain released an internet-only ad mocking the festival. Framed as a trailer for a dystopian movie "like *The Maze Runner* and *Scorch Trials* only with less clothing," the voice-over narration intoned solemn statements like, "It's safe to say that Coachella was a complete success. We don't know why . . . but millennials are willing to fork over tons of cash to attend overcrowded festivals in the middle of the desert," and, "Indio was one thing. But you won't last a day on the Playa without subtle exposure to corporate influence!" After goofing on some of Burning Man's more piquant features—a unicorn tank, a human car wash, and a gazing workshop—the trailer peaks with the hero yelling, "They lied to us! They said it was an anti-establishment society based on radical self-expression, but it's become a place for rich people to check off their bucket list," at which the Voice of God narration intones, "The course of the festival will determine the course of humanity."

Since the ad itself is in aid of a corporate entity, it is easy to dismiss its crass attempt to co-opt Burning Man's cultural capital. But even so, it is surely proof that the underlying aims of festivals like Burning Man and Coachella have reached mainstream consciousness.

In the same week in 2015 that saw Burning Man's twenty-fifth erection (and destruction) in the Nevada desert, pictures were widely circulated of a Syrian refugee camp in Jordan called Zaatari that, from the air, looked remarkably similar to Burning Man's temporary metropolis, Black Rock City. Zaatari houses some seventy-five thousand refugees, a number roughly comparable to the number of tickets sold to Burning Man (although sadly, Burning Man provides 1,000 portable toilets for residents; Zaatari only provides 380). The sites are entirely different in function and purpose: no one would dare suggest that the residents of a refugee camp would be better off if techno music was being blasted into it all day and night, or that Burning Man would provide the same kind of spiritual solace and release if its attendees were made to live there indefinitely. And yet, there is a link, for if nothing else, enormous rock festivals and gatherings like Burning Man may be refining the ability of organizations to create better-run and more comfortable tent cities on the vast scale now needed. This year at Roskilde, one of Europe's largest annual rock festivals, a company called Rockwool tested its product, stone wool, for use as an especially cheap and weather-resistant shelter-building material and as a urine-absorbent wall-making material, specifically for use at refugee camps. The company, based in Denmark, sees the festival grounds as the perfect "living lab" in which to test its products on the more than eighty thousand people in attendance. According to Dorte Gram, the company's innovation manager, their goal at Roskilde is to use the festival "as a platform for shouting out to the world that stone wool can insulate from fire, heat, cold and noise—and suggest organizations to come play with us, because we think it can benefit refugees around the world" (Gram, personal interview).

Rockwool's impulse to fuse corporate ends with humanitarian and ecological ideals hearkens directly back to Woodstock, where humanitarian aid was needed, where new ideas about ecology were circulated, and which, as an isolated social project, could indeed have been called a "living lab." The explicitly stated fusion of these kinds of goals at festivals like Roskilde and Burning Man certainly emphasizes the ways that rock festivals are becoming something of a nostalgic form, especially since their music, their practitioners, and their fans age—and nostalgia, and rock festivals, as the Quiznos ad proves, are fairly easy to mock. But to do so may not be entirely fair to the genre. In 2015, a friend who had just returned from the Playa defended Burning Man to me thus: "While I saw all the usual douchery and creepiness you'd expect from a gathering of 70,000, it was also strangely hopeful," he commented. "[The experience] reminded me of the line in Ian Frazier's *The Rez* when someone accuses him of being a 'wanna-be Indian.'—'What's wrong with wanting to be something?'"[2]

CHAPTER 8

Hardly Strictly Utopian, Hardly Strictly Bluegrass

In the context of the whole history of rock 'n' roll, there have really been only brief moments when the possibility of mass freedom seemed fulfilled. Those are the moments from which rock has drawn its utopian reputation, and a good deal of its moral and cultural capital.
—ELLEN WILLIS, *STARS DON'T STAND STILL IN THE SKY: MUSIC AND MYTH*

TWO MONTHS AFTER WOODSTOCK, in October 1969, some sixty people, including the writer Ken Kesey, Woodstock promoter Michael Lang, activist Paul Krassner, singer Mimi Fariña, and Grateful Dead manager Rock Scully, met at a hot springs and commune in New Mexico to discuss what one participant called "the architecture of mass gatherings" (Hopkins, "Sympowowsium"). The stated purpose of this "sympowowsium" was to design the 1970s Woodstock, or what they referred to as "the Mind Blower," or "the Big One." What they envisioned was a festival that would draw one million or more people to a site on rural land that would be accessed by "pilgrims" in the form of young people, all going "back to the land."

The Big One was, of course, a fantasy. As the weekend progressed through talks about this imaginary festival being "the new life style's

State Fair" and "speeding up the evolutionary process," many ideas were bandied about, including buying some festival land with festival profits[1] and turning it into a permanent commune, making festivalgoers walk the final ten miles to the site, and the invention of something the symposium goers called "Festi-Cola," a healthy soft drink. (This was apparently unimaginable in the days before Vitamin Water and Hanson's soda.) Alas, according to the *Rolling Stone* writer Jerry Hopkins, who covered the Sympowowsium in the December 27 issue of the magazine, the talks broke down over funding, because the potential organizers were terribly reluctant to consider charging festivalgoers a ticket fee. Instead, they suggested a variety of unfeasible alternatives, such as charging for toilet use, getting corporate backing, and finally, tapping into "enlightened inheritances."

Despite the immediate failure of a number of festivals that occurred directly after Woodstock in the summer of 1970—the legendarily disastrous Isle of Wight Festival in England and the Powder Ridge Rock Festival in Middlefield, Connecticut, which played host to forty thousand attendees despite being canceled beforehand, to name the best known—the ensuing decades would see the rise of the rock festival as an increasingly successful form of live event. It just wasn't in the form that the Sympowowsiasts imagined. Instead, festivals like Watkins Glen (1973) and Texxas Jam (Texas World Music Festival, 1978) were exactly the opposite of what they had proposed. Although toilet use would be free, the festivals would cost money to attend. They were sponsored by corporations. Rather than having anything to do with nature, they mostly took place in concrete stadiums and—as the framers must have guessed would be the case, given these three circumstances—they had less and less cultural resonance. It would take until 2001 for the truly utopian festival that Kesey and others had envisioned to come into being, but when it did, it was sponsored, just as they had originally suggested, by an "enlightened inheritance," that of the Wells Fargo heir and venture capitalist Warren Hellman. From 2001 until his death in 2011, Hellman used part of the fortune he had both inherited and amassed as a venture capitalist investor in Levi Strauss, NASDAQ, Young and Rubicon, DoubleClick, and Axel Springer to fund an annual free music festival in San Francisco that he named "Hardly Strictly Bluegrass." After Hellman died in 2011, the festival continued thanks to his posthumous endowment.

Hardly Strictly Bluegrass is an annual music festival that in every way *is* the Big One, almost exactly as described by Kesey and Company. No corporate sponsors. No entrance fee. No charge for toilets. There's even healthy soda available, although that is no longer the non sequitur it was in 1969. The first year, the festival featured one stage and six bands; today it spreads across five stages and three days, showcases ninety acts, and costs upward of a million dollars to finance. By 2009, it was drawing a reported 750,000 people to Golden Gate Park across its three-day duration, and it did so while fulfilling Woodstock's most controversial promise in that it is, at long last, *truly free*. To date it has been peaceful, safe, and well-organized, with plenty of food, toilets, and amenities like valet bike parking and shuttle bus service for the disabled. It serves a diverse community, has an educational component, and, much like the New Orleans Jazz Fest, celebrates America's musical heritage by featuring many older vernacular American artists like Hazel Dickens and Ralph Stanley between star turns of more famous and popular performers like Elvis Costello, John Cougar Mellencamp, Willie Nelson, Dolly Parton, and Robert Plant.

———

Since its inauguration in 2001, Hardly Strictly Bluegrass has become a San Francisco tradition, a destination festival, and the highlight of many people's autumns. Year after year, it has benefited from spectacular weather and awesome musical lineups, creating days and days of live music heaven and serving as a weirdly concrete end-point in Golden Gate Park's historic link to the counterculture. It helps that the festival always happens on the same weekend, the first one of October, during Fleet Week, which usually has the best weather of the year. In the post-9/11 years, the festival was a nostalgic reverie about what was good about America. During the Obama years, it was a celebration of it. But by 2017, during the Trump presidency, it had gone from being a heartwarming escape from consumer culture to something far more essential.

This was made crystal clear when the festival was scheduled, as usual, for the first weekend in October, and thus fell a mere four days after the massacre of 58 festival attendees and the wounding of 851 others in a horrific mass shooting at the Route 91 Harvest country music festival in Las Vegas. Hardly Strictly Bluegrass's mandate en-

tirely precludes having any kind of restrictions on attendance—no
tickets, no gates, no searches, no prohibitions. Of course, the organizers were careful to make gestures toward increased safety mea-
sures in the press, but the reality on the ground was that there was no
way to implement them, and this, in the end, turned out to be what
made that year's festival, if anything, the best one to date. After all,
the mass shooting in Las Vegas is not part of the story of rock festivals as much as it is about the rise in gun violence, racism, fascism,
poverty, fear, and inequality, aspects of America that have roots in
events of the 1960s, the civil rights movement, the counterculture,
and the subsequent rise of the counter-movement toward the right.
It says much more about the place that America had become at that
juncture than it does about crowds. I'd go one step further and say
that the massacre in Las Vegas actually meant that the stated reason
for the Hardly Strictly Bluegrass Festival is more important now than
it ever was before. Not only is Hardly Strictly Bluegrass meant to be
utopian, but it was, according to Hellman, who was the festival's moving force and its ultimate bankroller, "about thanking America" (Hellman, personal interview).

The fall of 2017 may not have seemed like a great time to "thank"
America. But it wasn't in 2001, either, when Hellman launched the
festival. That first iteration was in October 2001, less than four weeks
after 9/11, and that fact is key to what makes Hardly Strictly Bluegrass a site of intense meaning even now. Simply put, the festival re-
imagines America and American history. By redefining the enormous
range of music it showcases as "hardly" strictly bluegrass, Hellman's
festival allows concertgoers to connect to a vision of America as a
warm, beneficent, and inspirational global force.

In 2001, this felt transformational. And in 2017, applying this sonic
balm to wounded American pride was, if possible, even more important. When I interviewed him in 2009, Hellman said:

[Watching the festival] you stand up there and you think . . . how
do I put this without sounding stupid or maudlin or both?—this
is the GOOD side of America. This music, it makes you feel good
that this is so central to the United States. Whether it's bluegrass
or roots music or old time music coming out of the backwoods of
other parts of the States, or black music coming from Africa, only

restated, or repotted in the United States . . . [listening to this music is] as close to being patriotic as I can imagine being.

Hellman's words are especially poignant today, when reasons to be patriotic are so desperately needed: with Donald Trump as president, and a threatening nuclear standoff with North Korea, the buzz of the Blue Angels flying overhead is infinitely more ominous than it has been in years past. Can a festival be utopian when we live in an actual dystopia? Apparently, it can, for despite the dark wood we have, like Dante before us, found ourselves plunged into at this juncture, the 2017 iteration of Hardly Strictly Bluegrass still shone with the same kind of starry-eyed belief in live music as a space for spiritual healing that Warren Hellman was so attached to, that he was so eager for it to be.

That week was also notable because it had brought the untimely death of rock star Tom Petty, whose music, in its way, epitomized the very best and most venerable aspects of southern rock 'n' roll music. Rather than dwell on terrorism, musicians chose to honor Petty, and throughout all three days, band after band paid tribute to him with covers of his music, playing "American Girl" and "Free Fallin'," "Wildflowers" and "Runnin' Down a Dream," "I Won't Back Down" and "Refugee," to name just a few. Over and over, shards of the memory of Petty's chiming Rickenbacker guitar and gorgeous harmonies punctured the sky, audiences stood and sang along, and people rejoiced rather than mourned. And the same could be said about Hellman, whose patriotism was what gives this festival both its awe-inspiring credibility and its rhetorical power. Not only is it free, not only does it lack corporate sponsorship, but it is actually *about* something.

Hellman's commitment to keeping the festival, which is so uniquely San Franciscan and so strongly linked to history, in San Francisco was in some ways hard to justify. Some people might question whether his bequest was the best use of this vast amount of money, but Hellman himself believed that it was. When I spoke to him, several years before his death, he said that he saw the festival as a deeply moving community unifier that confers all kinds of benefits on San Francisco. In his lifetime, Hellman donated to many projects, including the San Francisco Free Clinic and the Bay Area News Project. What links Hardly Strictly Bluegrass, which seems at first glance like nothing but an enormous outdoor rock party, to these more solemn-minded and worthy philanthropic projects was Hellman's belief in the public sphere as a communal good and his desire to maintain Golden Gate Park itself as a utopian space.

According to Hellman, the impetus for the festival began in 1998, when he helped fund a project to build a parking garage under the De Young Museum and California Academy of Sciences (two landmarks in the center of Golden Gate Park). It was a move, he says, that he initiated expressly to keep the museums in the park open and eventually to close the park to traffic on weekends. He saw this as a way to keep the park itself sacrosanct. Unfortunately, he recalled, the result was eight years of legal wrangling and $5 million in legal fees, all paid out of his own pocket. The Bluegrass Festival followed on that project (it began in the midst of it) as another way to help revitalize park usage. Like the museum garage project, Hellman said he saw the festival's core value as historical preservation—and not just of space, but also of music, history, and patriotism (Lelchuk, "Controversial Garage"). Preserving spaces in California is the overriding legacy that Hellman said he would like to be remembered for.

For Hellman, that particular goal, and the value it embraces, was hereditary in nature. Although he spent years on the East Coast as president of Lehman Brothers, Hellman grew up in San Francisco: he attended Lowell High School (when it was located on the edge of Golden Gate Park) and UC Berkeley (though his tenure there predated not only the Summer of Love but the free speech movement). His impulse to philanthropy was, he said, "bred in the bone": his great-grandfather Isaias Hellman amassed an enormous fortune and funded many major social institutions in California, including the Los Angeles water system, the *Los Angeles Times*, and the University of Southern California, and his descendants have used part of the original Hellman fortune to support a variety of California-centric cultural causes (the San Francisco Ballet, for instance, is much indebted to them). In her biography of Isaias Hellman, Hellman's cousin Frances Dinkelspiel points out that the family as a whole is entrenched in California as an idea and as an ideology: one reason why the older Hellman was so generous to California, she says, is that he (and fellow entrepreneurs like the Haas family, Adolf Sutro, and Levi Strauss) found California to be free of the kind of anti-Semitism they were fleeing in Europe and that had dogged them on the East Coast. For them, California was about the freedom to be accepted and integrated into society, so they became community leaders, and they gave back to the community that embraced them.

In her book, Dinkelspiel avows that Isaias Hellman was "the major investor and promoter of at least eight industries that shaped California: banking, transportation, education, land development, water, electricity, oil and wine" (*Towers of Gold* 3). As she puts it, "he played a critical role in the creation of one of America's most astounding economic miracles" (6). It seems fitting that, just as the younger Hellman's great-grandfather was instrumental in creating the wealth of California, he himself was willing in his lifetime to spend equal amounts of money to ensure that California retains its ideals. Rather than pledging allegiance to America, at bottom, he was patriotic to California, to California history, and to the city of San Francisco as the home of golden dreams and social freedom. Hardly Strictly Bluegrass reflects that.

Hellman passed away just after the festival's tenth year, but Hardly Strictly Bluegrass has changed very little. It is still held the first weekend of October. The weather during the festival is still spectacular. And the Blue Angels still buzz the six stages, which still host about one hundred acts performing to upward of a half-million fans over the course of the three-day weekend. The only major changes that have occurred at this festival in fifteen years are technological. When Hardly Strictly Bluegrass began, neither iPhones nor iPods nor social media existed. Now the ghost of Instagram stalks every glade, as selfies are taken by every single tree and meadow.

In a similar vein, when the festival began, all cell phone service around the park would cease and finding your friends on the five-mile-long fairground was practically impossible. Today, the Google Maps "find your friends" app makes meeting up with people easy. Also, Uber and Lyft now seriously relieve some of the parking problems that used to plague the festival, as does the Nextbus app.

Other noticeable changes over the years: the legalization of weed has cut down on the amount of pot brownies being sold; there is a preponderance of gluten-free and vegan options at food booths; and there are fewer dogs.

Musically, however, the festival is much the same as it has always been; that is, a crazy melee of bands and artists from five continents performing across the park, bumping up against one another in ways that are both challenging and rewarding, mixing up folk, blues, and world beat music in some kind of cosmic iPod shuffle in the sky. On the Friday afternoon in 2017, at one point, one was within hearing distance of the Bo-Keys, a soul supergroup featuring Don Bryant and Percy Wiggins from Memphis, Tennessee; Seun Kuti and Egypt 80 from Nigeria; and First Aid Kit, a band from Sweden.

Just prior to that set, the English singer Billy Bragg had played the Banjo Stage with an act that embodied every single value embedded in Hardly Strictly Bluegrass's original manifesto. As the keeper of Woody Guthrie's archive and a longtime political activist whose songs are pointedly left-wing, he seemed self-charged with keeping the atmosphere tied to the ideology of the 1960s. "I was pleased to hear the word socialism used in your last election," Bragg opined at one point, after mentioning Jeremy Corbyn. "You know what social-ism would look like? If anyone asks you? Tell them it would look like a free concert in a park, a concert open to everyone, with acts of every kind . . . it would look exactly like this."

Bragg went on to sing Dylan's "The Times They Are a-Changin'," with a few pointed lyrical changes, including swipes at Donald Trump and the addition of the Bob Roberts–inspired word ". . . back," as well as a finale of his own number "There Is Power in a Union" that he per-formed to furious applause.

Bragg's set was very much in keeping with other Hardly Strictly Bluegrass moments, many of which have been explicitly connected to politics, and, to a lesser degree, to Golden Gate Park's rich history as a site of protest. In 2005, Dolly Parton played "Where Have All the Flowers Gone" as a tribute to soldiers newly deployed to Iraq. In 2009 Steve Earle, Tom Morello, and many others sang Woody Guthrie's "This Land Is Your Land" as a statement about immigration reform, while in 2016, the fields rang out with anti-Republican sentiments.

As Bragg's comment indicates, in many ways, Hardly Strictly Blue-grass is the perfect festival, the fulfillment of every promise ever held out by the rock festival paradigm. Each year, it provides a truly uto-pian moment. But it also begs the question of why, in a country where both the accumulation of wealth and its spending are valorized beyond all other things, a musical experience that is *free* is still so very persuasive. Moreover, as Bragg noted, the values that are on display and that are revered at this and other similar events could all be described as explicitly socialistic—even when, as in this case, the festival is funded by a single wealthy capitalist. Or maybe this dichotomy isn't so strange, since the idea of "free music" makes so much more sense in an age when music has ceased to be a literal, material commodity. Hardly Strictly Bluegrass makes visible the idea of a gift economy.

In short, despite its nostalgic nature, Hardly Strictly Bluegrass is the ultimate expression of the networked information society, a giant advertisement for the pleasurable side of the postindustrial economy, and San Francisco is the perfect setting for it. Every October, when one enters the gates, one walks straight into an old hippie's fantasy world come true; a place where music is free and people are rich, kind, and gentle. It invariably makes one think, hey: what's so funny about peace, love, and understanding?

Hardly Strictly Bluegrass also needs to be considered in relation to the era it evolved in. Although it would have been welcomed at any time, Hardly Strictly Bluegrass arrived in San Francisco during the boom years (2000 to 2007). It is only impervious to economic strife because Hellman was, like so many ultrarich, impervious to shifts in the economy: thus, the festival's existence is a reminder that the American economy is selectively bad, felling only those whose wealth is derived from old, industrial patterns and not those, like Hellman, whose wealth is derived from the flow of knowledge and money. This may not be exactly what the Sympowowsium had in mind—or even what Hellman had in mind. But Hardly Strictly Bluegrass illustrates these ideals better than any other single festival since Woodstock.

Attending Hardly Strictly Bluegrass is the highlight of many San Francisco music lovers' year. According to the tourist bureau, it attracts millions of dollars to San Francisco, and it may even affect more intangible economic indicators like housing prices. Every year I've been to it—sixteen years and counting—the weather has been that fantastic blue-and-gold fall weather that San Francisco is known for. At the same time, the festival has an almost unbelievable record for lack of violence or incident.

And Hardly Strictly Bluegrass isn't just pleasurable; it is charitable. On the Friday of its commencement, the festival provides some kind of free concert for San Francisco's Unified School District sixthgraders, which includes free lunches for the entire school district's middle school students in attendance (as well as the buses to bring them there). At the 2009 iteration of the event, I helped escort an elementary school class to a morning concert featuring MC Hammer, a local rap star who, in 1990, produced one of the all-time best-selling rap LPs: *Please Hammer, Don't Hurt 'Em*, featuring the much-covered and sampled single, "U Can't Touch This." His music is a staple of hiphop sampling, but it has nothing to do with bluegrass; if anything, it is the opposite. It is, however, extremely appropriate and entertaining music for ten thousand schoolchildren, who know the song from Radio Disney. Performing with a dance troupe of breathtakingly expert breakers, Hammer was able to command the entire field area, and near the end of his performance, students were able to get on stage and dance to "U Can't Touch This" with him.

After MC Hammer, 2009's concert officially began on the afternoon of October 2 with a performance by Tom Morello, formerly the guitarist for the hard rock band Rage Against the Machine, and in many ways his act crystallized the imagined narrative contradictions that cleave to Hardly Strictly Bluegrass. Morello is a Harvard graduate whose father was at one time Kenya's ambassador to the United Nations. In Rage Against the Machine, Morello was one of the premiere grunge guitarists, but by 2009 he was reimagining himself as a radical solo acoustic folk singer, a reinvention that links ideas about racial inclusion, socialism, and youth culture to Hardly Strictly Bluegrass's wider concepts.

Rage was strictly an agitprop band whose hit single "Killing in the Name" featured the memorable chorus "Fuck you, I won't do what you tell me!" and other anticapitalist rants. As a solo artist, Morello clearly sees himself continuing this battle in a new musical idiom—folk music that appeals to a different, older (but equally white) demographic. To this end, Morello finished up his set that year with Woody Guthrie's song "This Land Is Your Land," joined on stage by country stars Steve Earle and Allison Moorer and rapper Boots Riley of the Oakland hip-hop act the Coup. Morello made a point of singing what he called "the censored verses that they didn't let you sing in third grade":

As I went walking, I saw a sign there
And on that sign it said "Private Property"
But on the other side, it didn't say nothin'
That side was made for you and me.

This song, with the addition of these lyrics, was sung many times over the course of the weekend, as it became a sort of de facto anthem or theme song for the 2009 festival. (Earle claims to have sung it six times in one day, adding, "I happen to be one of those people who believe music can change the world.")[2] The song, and the underscored additional lyrics, could be said to embody many of the narratives that Hardly Strictly Bluegrass wished concertgoers to take away from the concert: Hellman had said he would like to think that Woody Guthrie could be seen as a kind of overarching historical presence. Yet this in itself is slightly peculiar, since the battles that Guthrie waged for unionism and socialism are not battles that are actively being waged on a wide scale in America today: if anything, both issues (unionism and socialism) are considered negatives by the vast majority of Americans. I can only suggest that the free use made of Guthrie's name and music was a euphemism for some other value or purpose that could just faintly be glimpsed through the thick metaphor provided by the sight and sound of Morello, a black heavy-metal guitarist, playing the iconic music of a white American folk musician. The dissonance of this sight argued that, just as Morello fuses communist ideology with capitalist principles, Hardly Strictly Bluegrass is working to fuse similarly opposing forces. How? By mythologizing the American past; by melding together a number of disharmonious strands and then dubbing them "hardly strictly bluegrass."

Weirdly, however, this disjunction sort of works, a fact reflected in part by the lineups themselves. In 2009, the bill included nearly one hundred acts.[3]

This list, as do the lists of acts for all subsequent years' festivals, indicates the wide variety of musical genres included, from traditional bluegrass—Scruggs, Dickens, and Stanley were all progenitors with

Hardly Strictly Bluegrass schedule, 2009.

careers dating to the mid-twentieth century—to new practitioners and adapters like Old Crow Medicine Show and Fire Ants. The list also included African pop (Malo and Amadou and Mariam), old hippies (Kaukonen, Havens), and other American vernacular forms (Toussaint, Booker T.). Across the last decade, there has been a smattering of punk and post-punk acts included on the bills, including X, the Bob Mould Band, Conor Oberst, Jello Biafra (of the Dead Kennedys) and Henry Rollins (of Black Flag), Paul Weller (of the Jam), the Dropkick Murphys, and the Mekons. There has been some, though not much, rap. And there is always a huge helping of the kind of Austin-area "alternative" country music mentioned in the chapter on the US Festival—led by Robert Earl Keen and the Flatlanders—and a number of pure pop acts (Marshall Crenshaw, Neko Case, Nick Lowe, etc.). Thus, Hardly Strictly Bluegrass bills always provide an overview of all types of "folk" music, if "folk" is defined as "folks listen to it."

To a person who has attended countless outdoor rock festivals, both in Golden Gate Park and elsewhere, the two most striking aspects of this concert are the preponderance of dogs and the preponderance of food. At children's soccer games in Golden Gate Park, dogs are banned, but they aren't banned here, and there are hundreds, if not thousands of them wandering through the crowds (mostly restrained by their masters). The choice of food is astonishing. A partial list of the food available at booths includes funnel cakes, fish tacos, crab garlic fries, gourmet donuts, cookies and ice cream, pretzels, Dove bars, kettle corn, curry, sausages (all types), coffee drinks, smoothies, beignets, acai-berry blends, flatbread pizza, knishes, steak, pork, turkey, corn, Thai food, Chinese food, sushi, crawfish *étouffée*, and sweet potato pie cobbler. It is difficult to get a burger or a hot dog here, unless they are redefined as "Cajun sausage" or "sliders."

When Hardly Strictly Bluegrass got started in 2001, the emphasis on gourmet, regional food was fairly unique. In fact, it was prescient, predating the food truck craze by a decade and providing a great location for many of San Francisco's favorite trucks to develop and thrive. Today, what seems most unique and pertinent about the food at Hardly Strictly Bluegrass is not its regionality, but what is *not* available for sale: candy, chips, soda pop of any kind, and beer. Alcohol, although not forbidden, is not for sale. (It is very much present in hip flasks and coolers.) Drunkenness is not much in evidence at Hardly Strictly Bluegrass, as the drug of choice is clearly marijuana: quite a number of people are visibly stoned. Moreover, here and there one comes across individual businesspeople selling "really delicious brownies," or in one case, "really delicious Rice Krispies squares," sold by a girl in a fairy costume, with wings: that these wares cost ten dollars is an indication that they are perhaps not made entirely of Rice Krispies.

Food aside, however, compared to most commercial festivals, Hardly Strictly Bluegrass has an extremely minimal amount of merchandise on offer. There are commemorative T-shirts for sale, but they aren't aggressively marketed, and these are the only official merchandise around. Various locations in the park also feature booths that make commemorative pennies—machines roll over a penny stamping it with an image of a guitar and the phrase "Hardly Strictly Bluegrass" written in old-fashioned script—for free. The only other things for purchase are all sold by private entrepreneurs (like the drug dealers). These include homemade Grateful Dead T-shirts, homemade bumper stickers that say "co-exist" and "peace" on them, and chunky hippie-style jewelry and clothing (like knit caps and crystal bracelets). And drugs, of course; the drug-whisperers sidle up to people on the paths to mutter out their wares. These entrepreneurs tend to circle the perimeters of the concert, and they are probably doing well, but the San Francisco businesspeople who are really benefiting from the concert today are the Uber and taxi drivers, who cruise up and down Fulton and Lincoln Avenues carrying people who can't fit onto the buses. Surge pricing does apply.

In 2009 the *San Francisco Chronicle* reported that 750,000 people attended this concert, and that estimate has held steady over the ensuing years. Other concerts—the Tibetan Freedom Concert, Outside Lands, and various others held in the same location—generally attract up to sixty thousand people to the single stage at Polo Fields, but three-quarters of a million people implies that *five times* that number are coming to Hardly Strictly Bluegrass each day.

As that number indicates, attending Hardly Strictly Bluegrass is not for the faint of heart: musically it is an embarrassment of riches and finding your own path through its wares can become a very personal endeavor. Moreover, there is something uncannily postmodern about an event that allows a person interested in the aftereffects of Woodstock to watch Richie Havens essentially recreate his performance there, forty years on. (Havens's performance, which in 2009 took place early on Saturday, October 7, was awash with nostalgia.) But the highlights of any Hardly Strictly Bluegrass weekend can be far more moving than this example would imply. Indeed, the sight of Mavis Staples, of Wattstax fame, singing "I'll Take You There" in a sunlit glade was very much like going to church. In 2005, I saw Dolly Parton sing "Where Have All the Flowers Gone" as a nod to our troops in Iraq, and, like Jesus, I wept.

Dolly Parton is probably the quintessential American artist to have taken the stage there, and every year, Hardly Strictly Bluegrass features numerous authentic bluegrass groups and performers like her. Other acts at the festival, however, have a highly contrived relationship not only to bluegrass, but to American vernacular folk music itself. It happens over and over again throughout the fairgrounds, in sets by artists as disparate as Marianne Faithfull and Patti Smith, the early English punks the Mekons and Elvis Costello, the Czech gypsies Gogol Bordello, the Mexican guitarists Rodrigo y Gabriela, and American indie rockers like Big Star, Cheap Trick, Bob Mould, and Conor Oberst. So all-encompassing is the festival's overarching narrative that it is able to easily accommodate African pop stars like Amadou and Mariam and young jam bands like Dr. Dog.

The one form that Hardly Strictly Bluegrass can't accommodate is techno—that is, music made primarily on synthesizers that is played and amplified by disk jockeys who cannot be configured as artists, musicians, or "folks." In 2015, the festival inaugurated a number of "silent raves" on its grounds—that is, d-jayed events listened to through headphones, so that the music itself is essentially invisible. But for the most part, the mechanized sound of techno is sent to other locations—downtown San Francisco, for example, where in 2009 on the same weekend as Hardly Strictly Bluegrass, a rave (or self-described "electronic dance festival") called Lovevolution drew ten thousand people to a ticketed event in Civic Center Plaza, some sans underpants.

——

Magically turning every act it books into an authentic purveyor of Americana music is Hardly Strictly Bluegrass's perfect party trick. Its other most persuasive strategy is its lack of commodification. The grounds of Lovevolution contained a whole marketplace labeled as such, selling all kinds of merchandise, and the same is true at all commercial concerts (Outside Lands, Lollapalooza, even the Virgin FreeFest). And while there is little doubt that those attending these more commercial concerts understand the relationship between the concert experience and the fact that these concerts are underwritten by corporate sponsors, advertisers, and merchandisers, what is less obvious is the way the *absence* of these commercial elements at Hardly Strictly Bluegrass affects the audience so profoundly. Other than food—which works in its own right to emphasize the concert's elaborate discourse of Americana and which could be deemed a necessity—Hardly Strictly Bluegrass's lack of merchandise, advertising, sponsors, and political detritus is, in fact, exactly what makes it both unique and utopian. Indeed, I would go so far as to say that it is this lack that explains the absence of violence and the idyllic sense of peace that descends over Golden Gate Park for all three days.

If this is the case, however, it requires some explanation, since it posits that rock festival audiences (and organizers) envision a *utopian idyll* as a place that extols American values while simultaneously subduing or eliminating the role of that most American of values, the marketplace. I believe this is because Hardly Strictly Bluegrass is very much an American reading of American experience, a story we tell about ourselves. The story we tell—or perhaps the story we *experience*, vicariously, through the music presented—is about rural poverty and our relationship to it. This rock festival has at its core a *story* about the American economy and our feelings about our economic history. In this story, the nostalgic past is full of rural poor who nonetheless create great art in the form of folk music; by participating in this music—by attending and listening—the audience *feels* as if it has taken part in both the poverty and the escape from it. Hence, whatever their socioeconomic reality (and most of the festivalgoers are middle or upper-middle class), the audience enjoys the same feeling of benevolence and catharsis that in fact *should* belong solely to Warren Hellman.

That Hellman felt those things—benevolence and catharsis—is unquestionable (though when I spoke to him before his death in 2011 he joked that he was "sick of being thanked"). He was very clear that he would never allow anyone to buy or sponsor Hardly Strictly Bluegrass, although he told me he had gotten many, many offers to do so. ("I don't even feel comfortable allowing nonprofits in," he asserted.) He added that "it's important that the festival be pure." And in order for that to be, he insisted, it has to be anticorporate. "I don't want anyone else getting involved in Hardly Strictly because they might want to have influence. I want to not have influence, and I don't want someone else who does, either."

In short, Hellman's festival is a gift, and as Marcel Mauss argued in *The Gift*, gifts are never "free"; instead, they impose on the receiver an obligation: reciprocity. Here, it isn't gratitude that is at stake, though: it's acceptance. At the most basic level, the fact that Hellman—who was extolled every year throughout the concert for making it possible (as Wozniak was at the US Festival before him)—was rich enough to provide this largesse is proof to many that "the system works." At a more nuanced level, however, the festival works ideologically by making the qualities of what I call "the digital diaspora" visible. The term "digital diaspora" describes the last decade's sudden ejection of music from its industrial economic base to the internet, where it leads a more nomadic existence. Prior to the advent of the MP3 (or digital music file) in the late 1990s, music was tethered to a highly industrial system of dissemination. It is not my intention here to re-hash the major points of the debate over the legal issues surrounding digital downloading. But those who believe that music should be paid for are missing the larger point of the technological advance that has made its shareability possible—a point that Hardly Strictly Bluegrass materializes by its very existence. In fanciful terms, the concert grounds, with its many stages and wide array of music all available for free, creates an embodied version of the inside of your MP3 player (on shuffle). Music lovers are able to walk around and hear what they like for free. Speaking more materially, the way that the festival encourages music to be experienced allows festivalgoers to see that the value of music is no longer a commodity fetish—the LP, the CD, the cassette. The value is in the music itself: its history, its performance, its ability to bring communities together, and that nameless, magical quality that is in its actual *notes*.

These aspects of music may have gotten somewhat lost in the fifty-odd years since companies like Warner Brothers, Capital, CBS, Atlantic, Disney, and RCA[4] controlled and dominated the dissemination of most branches of popular music (via their synergistic practices with popular radio stations, now almost all owned by Clear Channel and a few other conglomerates). By freeing music from the commodity market—detaching it from its bondage to a small, flat, round object—the digital file has destroyed almost every accompanying fetish that made participating in the market such a fascinating feature of twentieth-century life.

Put another way: prior to the year 2000, popular music was a crucial part of identity formation. Its idioms—punk, metal, country, rap, jazz, and so on—have served as cultural signposts, heralds of "distinction," as Bourdieu would put it, that described and delineated the social context of everyday life. (Lower-class whites were attracted to music by Metallica; upper-class college kids preferred Radiohead, etc.) But, because of the digital diaspora, *this is no longer the case*. Thus, one reading of Hardly Strictly Bluegrass is that it reinstates folk music into popular culture while also inserting popular culture into folk music, as it did in 2017 when one of the largest-drawing headlining acts on the last day of the festival was the almost cartoon-like ur-pop metal act from the 1970s, Cheap Trick. In fact, what Hardly Strictly Bluegrass may be doing when it includes such acts is reversing some of the more negative effects of pop music's forced migration to cyberspace. By adding aura to folk music, the festival is recouping the displaced status of the Folk.

There is another level of economic theory that must be considered here. Marcel Mauss's theories of a gift economy were based on paradigms of Polynesian islands. But a new form of the gift economy has emerged in postindustrial society via the internet. Chris Anderson's controversial 2003 article "Free! Why $0.00 Is the Future of Business," in *Wired*, showed how the diminishing costs of processing power, digital storage space, and bandwidth has created a web economy in which many if not most things *must* be priced at . . . free. And free, Anderson reminds us, is an entirely different market from "almost free." This can be seen in bas-relief in the music world, where micropayments of 99 cents per download or concert tickets that cost 99.7 cents (or another price based on a radio station's call numbers) are far less inspiring than concerts or music that is shared for free.

Anderson's insights into the free realm of the digital world are particularly informative when applied to music and the digital diaspora. In some senses, music has always been free, or at least has *felt* free, to listeners accessing it on the radio. Radio played music for listeners for free, although it was paid for by a third party: advertisers. But this model is becoming unsustainable because listeners prefer the ad-free world of the iPod or streamed music.

In other words, now that music can be shared online at no cost, radio's apparent freeness has become literal. For the free festival mode to work, it must deliver something of value to its sponsor. When he was alive, Hellman didn't seem to need anything more than thanks: he was astute enough to see the value accrued in sustaining San Francisco and Golden Gate Park as beautiful, natural, and deeply historic. But other free festivals, with other sponsors, will need to glean similarly symbolic values from their captive audience. In the most straightforward cases, as, for example, at the Virgin FreeFest in Washington, DC, or Alice's Now and Zen festival in Golden Gate Park, concertgoers accrue corporate goodwill.

One of the things Anderson's article highlights is the way that the gift economy of the internet mimics some of the tactics of the media, specifically radio and television, which traditionally have not directly charged audiences to participate in their market. What's different about digital music is that now, in order for a gift economy music model to generate money for a third party—as it did in the days of record companies and advertising—the music needs to persuade the listener of its value on a moral, rather than on a business, basis. Anderson points out:

> Just because products are free doesn't mean that someone, somewhere, isn't making huge gobs of money. Google is the prime example of this. The monetary benefits of craigslist are enormous as well, but they're distributed among its tens of thousands of users rather than funneled straight to Craig Newmark Inc. To follow the money, you have to shift from a basic view of a market as a matching of two parties—buyers and sellers—to a broader sense of an ecosystem with many parties, only some of which exchange cash.

In the digital economy, the third party attempting to make money off a digital music file may in fact be the artist who wrote the music, rather than some vast impersonal corporation. Yet this does not obviate the problem that today *no one need pay for music* in order to hear it. Thus, finding ways for the third party to participate in (and fund) the process has been the sticking point in the modern music paradigm.[5]

Significantly, peer-to-peer file sharing (the process by which music is distributed online) became a widespread practice in the year 2000, the same year that Hellman initiated Hardly Strictly Bluegrass. Since then, making music for commercial purposes has become all but impossible for most musicians and artists. Only performers who are able to turn their music into a tangible commodity—like the winners of *American Idol*, who are able to cash in on that brand name; the kids of Radio Disney, who star in television series and then lend their names to backpacks, notebooks, lunchboxes, and other actual commodities; or the multiplatform artists like singer/actress/fashion designer Beyoncé Knowles—are now able to turn pop songs into cash. Music, as music, now holds a quasi-refugee status, wandering from iPod to iPod, from field to shining field.

With its steadfast emphasis on rural America, poverty, nostalgia, and the moral superiority of folk music driving home its argument, Hardly Strictly Bluegrass makes these issues more visible to festival attendees. By adding moral value to the music it promotes, by giving this music away for free, and by making that which is absent—commercial pop, electronic, alcohol, soda, nudity, cell phone service, and every type of commodity fetish—obvious, Hardly Strictly Bluegrass forces attendees to think about both the new and the old economic paradigms.

To put it in a nutshell, in the world of Hardly Strictly Bluegrass, music is free and music is valuable. Just as Woodstock reconciled deeply conflicted Americans to capitalism, Wattstax celebrated civil rights, and the US Festival invited participants to partake in computers, Hardly Strictly Bluegrass works to reconcile the conundrums of postindustrial society. Indeed, by dramatizing the most attractive aspects of globalization, by legitimating and reanimating American culture, and by rehistoricizing the twentieth century's relationship to music, Hardly Strictly Bluegrass seems to fulfill the promises of postindustrialization. Rather than conforming to late capitalism and what Jameson has termed "the waning of affect" that comes with that process, Hardly Strictly Bluegrass argues that the digital diaspora has done the opposite, legitimating and reanimating folk music—and by association America—on both a moral and an aesthetic plane.

And yet, there are limitations to this conclusion. Hellman was just one of a long line of quirky, rich philanthropists who have generously given to northern California's cultural institutions. Other northern California philanthropists include the aforementioned Steve Wozniak, George Lucas, David Packard (who built the Monterey Bay Aquarium), Salesforce head Marc Benioff, Facebook inventor Mark Zuckerberg, Oracle founder Larry Ellison, and Google founders Sergey Brin and Larry Page. The visibility of these men and many of their projects may reinforce the idea that California's economy is perpetually thriving, and Hardly Strictly Bluegrass serves a similar purpose. Even as it provides the population of San Francisco with a free commodity—music—it also provides a visible reassurance that the state itself is still an enormously exciting and successful venture.

To its credit, however, Hardly Strictly Bluegrass goes a lot further than Ellison's support of the America's Cup or Benioff's support of local hospitals. In theory, at least, Hardly Strictly Bluegrass illustrates that a free festival that conforms exactly to the utopian idyll postulated by Woodstock has possible implications for the future. These include toying with (or performing) the possibilities of socialism, making the digital diaspora more visible, and, most compellingly, reinvigorating even the more doubtful promises of the postindustrial society. Because this last argument—and, in fact, the festival itself—relies on the largesse of a single individual venture capitalist, this seems like a rather precarious conclusion to draw; nonetheless, I'm going to draw it. Every year at Hardly Strictly Bluegrass, Warren Hellman, like Steve Wozniak before him, becomes a silent symbol of personal success . . . and hence a symbol of the success of capitalism itself.

Conclusion: Small Is Beautiful

WHILE I WAS WRITING THIS BOOK, the whole world changed. One result is that the spirit of the rock festival may have begun to move away from those vast crowded fields to far smaller venues. This was what I thought, anyway, after attending one such festival, Burger Boogaloo, in Oakland, California.

Burger Boogaloo doesn't depend on the rhetoric of nature, and you don't have to drive to it, because it's right next to a BART station. I did drive to it, though, and the result was that I had to park my car in a very empty space next to a very seedy Carl's Junior on a very sketchy corner in Oakland and leave it there for six hours. Of course, I know this is not an advisable move, but I didn't quite know where I was going, so I pulled the trigger and parked. And I immediately knew I was where I wanted to be when I saw a couple walking down the street who were clearly heading for the same location.

The woman in the couple was wearing a polka dot miniskirt, hot pink biker shorts, and white Doc Marten boots, and she had a cotton-candy-colored beehive hairdo. The man was sporting tons of tattoos, a baseball hat, and a black T-shirt with a zombie on it, and strapped to his chest was a baby carrier stuffed with a little-bitty rockabilly baby.

Somehow, the three of them epitomized all things Burger Boogaloo: unified, defiant, fun, happy, and strangely untouched by the ravages of our era. They looked like they'd stepped out of one of those fun 1980s indie movies, like *Repo Man* or *Liquid Sky*. They were very awesome, especially the baby.

Burger Boogaloo is a three-year-old music festival sponsored by Burger Records, a cassette-only punk-rock label that only releases music in that old-fashioned format, thus avoiding competition from other labels. According to their website (which describes the company as "a rock 'n' roll philanthropic quasi-religious borderline cultish propaganda spreading group"), Burger has sold over one hundred thousand cassettes to date. This, given the current state of the music business and the world in general, is the musical equivalent of publishing handmade chapbooks of poetry individually reproduced on typewriters into a market of people who no longer know how to read. That Burger Records has succeeded at it is worthy of a giant sigh of relief; it also lessens the surprise that they've been able to insert themselves so successfully into a new festival aesthetic.

This festival takes place in Mosswood Park in downtown Oakland, the kind of very urban park that, even in the midst of a punk-rock extravaganza, still has a pick-up basketball game on its courts. It's surrounded by beautiful oak trees (not for nothing is Oakland called Oakland) and Kaiser Permanente, in an area of the town we used to call "pill hill." It's a particularly weird place for a music festival, but (a) music festivals are becoming weirder, and (b) Burger Boogaloo is a weird music festival. On the day of the show, I didn't have a ticket, but I figured I could pick one up outside, and indeed I could: before I'd walked very far down MacArthur, a nice scalper guy offered me a cheap-ish VIP wristband.

"But how do I know it's genuine?" I asked.

"Oh, I'll walk you in and you can pay me inside the venue," he said.

Done. He put it on my wrist, we walked in together—chatting about the glory of Iggy Pop's set the day before, exactly as if we knew one another—and then I paid him. It was unbelievably civilized, and it was easily the nicest illegal ticket transaction I have ever been involved in. It made me want to start a website: www.ratemyscalper .com.

As that transaction indicated, festivals have changed—as has Oakland itself, both for better and for worse. Some bits of it—Mosswood Park, for example—are nicer than they used to be. Others, not so much. At one juncture on my drive to the concert, I found myself on Market Street or Telegraph going under an underpass, and it was the underpass from hell. It looked like a homeless encampment in a dystopian movie like *District 9*. Later, I asked my Oaklish friend what that was.

"Oh, that was Mortville," she said.

"Mortville?"

"Yeah, you know . . . like in the John Waters film *Desperate Living*— it's like a shantytown where people go when life has mortified them."

"When life has mortified you." Hmmm. Many of us, not just those poor people under the freeway, feel mortified a lot these days, and for that reason, we may need utopian rock festival experiences more than we ever did. The experiences we crave now may look a little bit different; they are informed in part by all the ways that the internet and social media and the iPod shuffle have changed our interior lives, especially musically. But in other ways, they are the same. Many of the bands playing at Burger Boogaloo were ones I had seen in other festival contexts. But the overall experience felt more humane—you know, like playing a cassette does, compared to downloading a file.

Still, some things are perennial. When I arrived at Burger Boogaloo in midafternoon, the band Shannon and the Clams were performing on the "Gone Shrimpin'" second stage, and it was packed. People wearing witches' hats were sitting in the plethora of oak trees, looking down on other people, who were moshing in the tiny pit, and the band was rocking out. Before I even had a moment to gather my thoughts, however, I ran into my friend, who had a very broken arm. She was wandering around the park not sitting down, because she couldn't get up again if she did. So we wandered around together, and we soon discovered that, probably much like Coachella or Bonnaroo, Burger Boogaloo was full of swag. Within a few minutes, I had a free T-shirt advertising a vodka company, two peach-flavored chapsticks, a bandana, a pin, and several cans of soda-flavored cold coffee from Stumptown, a Portland-based coffee shop that must be coming to Oakland, because it was promoting itself there.

We also went to many a merchandise booth and saw a lot of very cool stuff, most of which said "FUCK YOU" on it. The merch booths, all operated by local artisans and vendors, included an anarchist book collective and a bunch of tables selling items with the Burger aesthetic. They underlined the fact that Burger Boogaloo, and festivals like it, now overtly celebrate a certain kind of capitalism; not capitalist realism, à la Mark Fisher, but merely like what Michel de Certeau discusses in *The Practice of Everyday Life*, that is, the tactics and strategies that make life under capitalism possible for those who wish to elude it: not how to live without capitalism, but how to live within it.

———

When I began writing this book, I had some core questions about rock crowds. I began it with the supposition that rock festivals link old symbolic narratives about rock, freedom, America, and capitalism with new ones about technology, power, media coverage, and data. I wanted to know what rhetoric and mechanisms were used to persuade audiences of these ideals and who was being left out of those fields and fields of discourse.

In a nutshell, here are my answers. First: rock crowds became symbols of freedom, power, and human agency when the widely circulated film and concert depictions of the Woodstock Festival tied visual narratives about the idyllic aspects of nature and the American West to the idea of seeing music in a patently crowded, non-idyllic, setting: a natural landscape turned temporarily urban. Second: as Wattstax, the US Festival, and the Hardly Strictly Bluegrass Festival indicate, the real ideologies that are circulating at rock festivals are, simply put, those that bolster the notion of America as a natural place of freedom, sometimes in the face of much evidence to the contrary. Third: the rhetoric that festivals use to persuade their audiences to attend them rest on four specific practices and beliefs, namely, automobility (the ability to leave urban areas, in cars, at will), nature (because the settings of these festivals invoke the experience of nature, even as they destroy it), the legalization of drugs (especially marijuana, although utopian beliefs about ecstasy and speed are also in evidence at raves), and the sexualization of black and female bodies (always and forever a core component of American popular music). Finally: I concluded, the rock crowd is essentially normed to the white male psyche, and as long as this is the case, it has some serious liabilities to contend with.

Burger Boogaloo didn't conform to any of these appeals, which is great. That said, as with earlier forms, Burger continues to circulate ideas about America, capitalism, democracy, and the free market, and I believe that it, and other festivals large and small, are going to continue to do so for a little while longer, even as rock crowds and festivals change to a more networked, less embodied, smaller, more intimate, more "free" form. I know this is the case because the popularity of such festivals has increased tenfold since I began writing this book. In 2011, when I finished my research, rock festivals were pretty popular, but the form has grown exponentially since then. In Europe, there are well over twenty festivals each summer that draw from two hundred thousand to five hundred thousand attendees, implying a minimum audience of five million and probably closer to ten million. Summerfest, an annual festival held in Milwaukee in July, now draws over a million people over the course of eleven days. Donauinselfest, in Austria, draws over two million people in three days to hear a mostly Austrian lineup of music. The international music festival Mawazine, in Morocco, drew 2.5 million people in 2013.

These numbers suggest that attending rock festivals is now many people's formative shared experience, replacing older crowd formations, which gathered people together for reasons of protest, pleasure, entertainment, or solace. Today, we can see that rock festival narratives about nature and the American West have been some (though not all) of the most compelling appeals that have drawn audiences into their midst across a full half-century. Narratives about sex and drugs have undergone radical changes as social mores and laws have changed, but the success of *nature* as an appealing rhetorical strategy is constant. Festivals may be subject to the vagaries of politics, economics, and technological change, but those appeals are still working, and frankly, that's a little bit surprising. After all, since the year 2000, America has undergone a sea change in societal self-esteem: a horrific terrorist attack, a global economic downturn, a loss of national confidence, the extreme polarization of political parties, and a small but loud turn toward a radical libertarianism cannot but have had an effect on the mood of all large social gatherings. One way or another, we are all living in Mortville now, and it has to have taken a toll. Moreover, anecdotally, large celebratory crowds have become more violent every year. Flash mobs in Philadelphia have made downtown streets temporarily uninhabitable, post-sports-victory celebrations in Michigan have led to huge amounts of property damage, and the once-peaceful Bay to Breakers foot race in San Francisco is now a drunken debauch that is best avoided by families, athletes, and other nondrinkers. Such gatherings have all been increasingly marred by violence; in the summer of 2010, a rush to enter a Love Parade in Duisburg, Germany, resulted in twenty-one deaths, while the mass shooting in Las Vegas in 2017 put a very succinct period on that increase.

Until very recently, because of Woodstock's indelible rhetoric, rock festivals, even larger ones like Bonnaroo and Coachella, still seem less affected by violence than many other crowd sites. This in itself speaks to their usefulness as exhibitors of social movements, to the great pleasure they provide, and ultimately, to their power. It also speaks to the single emotion that dominates them: nostalgia. They are now an old-fashioned form of entertainment, overtaken by digitally enhanced and disseminated technological interventions, like the flash mob and the twitter feed. Nostalgia is what powers rock crowds, and nostalgia is a powerful weapon.

This was borne home once and for all when, in October 2016, the Empire Polo Fields in Indio, California—site of the Coachella Festival—welcomed what may well be the last, best niche market left in rock by holding a festival specifically aimed at the elderly. The average age of the artists performing on the bill was seventy-two: the audience hovered around that age as well. To cater to their needs, the promoter, Goldenvoice, hired three thousand toilets and provided comfortable camping opportunities, seats, and food options that ranged from the usual to four-course meals with wine pairings cooked by well-known chefs. Tickets, as befit an older, wealthier audience, were pricey, ranging from $199 for the "cheap" seats to $1,599 for better ones. The festival's 75,000 tickets sold out in hours.

Technically entitled Desert Trip, Oldchella (as it was popularly called) leads to certain inevitable conclusions about the era of rock festivals—about rock festivals and identity, rock festivals and youth culture, rock festivals and ideology, rock style and the counterculture, and where all these ideas are today. It also reinforces some of the observations herein. Many if not most Oldchella participants came of age in the 1960s, perhaps attending ur-fests like Woodstock, Wattstax, and Glastonbury. Do these fans acknowledge themselves now as a market, rather than a movement? Do they believe that the Indio fairgrounds will unite them in song? What does it mean when rock stars and fans age together on the field?

Oldchella spread across three nights and two weekends, and reports from the field were that, musically speaking, it was fantastic. Paul McCartney, the Rolling Stones, and Neil Young all played sets that neared three hours; Bob Dylan, Roger Waters, and the Who also brought the goods, although when Paul McCartney was joined on stage by the twenty-eight-year-old superstar Rhianna, CBC noted that few people there seemed to know who she was—including the official Desert Trip Facebook and Twitter pages, which ignored her.

Another thing that was nearly ignored was politics. On the Sunday night of the first weekend, just after the leaked revelation about Donald Trump's attitude toward sexually assaulting women and the second presidential debate, Roger Waters let his famous giant inflatable pig, a holdover from Pink Floyd's Animals and Wall tours, float over the audience with the words "Ignorant, lying, racist, sexist PIG—Fuck Trump and his wall" written on it. The message may or may not have been appreciated by an audience that was not necessarily on board with the sentiment. As the reporter Jill Mapes wrote in *Pitchfork* at the time:

> Not everyone was pleased with the performance, including one man in a "Golf Is Life" shirt that I met later on, who told me he bolted after the Bush poem. It makes sense: The clusters of gated communities and country clubs surrounding Indio's Empire Polo Club, which played host to Desert Trip, would not exist without conservative money, and Trump signs were not hard to spot around town all weekend. But the first Waters walkouts were less widespread than you might expect, at least within the reserved seats on the field, which cost $1,599 for the entire weekend. (More of a mass exodus, plus screams of "anti-Semite," arrived after Waters launched into an extended anti-Israel/free Palestine diatribe, however.) All weekend long I found myself eyeing ordinary-looking folks my parents' age and wondering, *Is it even possible to dig Dylan and vote for Trump?*

Mapes got her definitive answer a few weeks later, when Trump was elected president. The answer was yes. The fact is, the endorsement of Hillary Clinton by numerous enormously popular rock stars, including Bruce Springsteen, Beyoncé, Madonna, and many others, was meaningless to many voters. Today, rock's power, whatever it once was, is now at best illusive and at worst counterproductive.

As that event foreshadowed, by 2017, the zeitgeist of America had changed radically, and one of the ways you could see the shift was in some of the narratives surrounding rock festivals. Rather than providing safe spaces to celebrate false utopias and nature, today's festivals provide proxy-spectacles for social and cultural capital, which in themselves are proxies for power and access. And even worse: rock festivals have emerged as places of terror. To begin with, the collapse of the normative narratives was relatively benign (except for those caught up in attending them). It could be seen, for example, in the ridiculous story of the Fyre Festival, in the Bahamas. This was a festival that cost five figures to attend, and for that money you were supposed to get luxury beach lodgings, special food, and all-access passes, but the luxuries melted into thin air on contact with the Bahamas, leaving ticket-buyers stranded on the beach without lodging or food, having been fleeced of $12,500.

At first, it was fun to think about: all these rich people stuck on an island in little tents eating prefab cheese sandwiches, having preloaded all their money onto wristbands that didn't work in town, and so on. But it got depressing real fast. If you look even cursorily at the festival's monetization plan, it exhibited the sort of greedy stupidity that characterized the 2016 election as well: rather than focusing on music or even on ideology, this festival, like today's political culture, focused on the creation of brand, wealth, and ultimately, the homogenization of experience.

In short, the Fyre Festival's failure is symptomatic of the vast misunderstanding that undergirds all civic life right now. It reminds me of what someone once called "the slutty allure" of a second-order simulacrum. Trump Presidency = Fyre Festival = Boom.

This was bad enough. But as the year 2017 progressed, the zeitgeist of the planet degenerated in ways that made rock crowds into something far more dangerous. Although, of course, festivals have always had dangerous edges to them—spectators might fight or girls might get groped—they have now become, like everywhere else where crowds gather, targets of anger and madness that outsiders can violate with ease. The Bataclan. The Manchester Arena. Apparently, these were sites that ISIS and its affiliates may have seen as bastions of Western debauchery. Then, in October 2017, a lone gunman in Las Vegas, from his room high above the Strip, sprayed an outdoor country rock festival called Route 91 with bullets, killing 58 people and wounding 851 others.

The "Violent Incident" at Las Vegas, as Facebook called it in its newsfeed, was an American massacre akin in scale to Wounded Knee or the Battle of the Little Bighorn. It marked a turning point not—alas—in American ideas about weaponry or our political will to change that, but in civilian notions about mass gatherings. That shooter (who doesn't deserve to be named) may not have allied with the specific notions of ISIS, but his actions showed that he thought of rock crowds as symbols similarly worth exploding. Was it because he wanted to disrupt the traditions of festivity? Of community? Of listening to music together?

If so, he did a good job, because every incident like this makes the prospect of joining a rock crowd less appealing. And that is a terrible shame, because, as Canetti said, it is "only in a crowd that we lose our fear of being touched." Indeed, it is in crowds that we often experience our most profound and memorable moments. Sports crowds, religious crowds, and yes, pop concert crowds: crowds are where we become humanity, rather than merely human. The threatened destruction of a crowd isn't a random gesture; it's an assault on one of the most deep-seated and powerful impulses we have, sociality.

———

In the course of completing this study of rock crowds and power, I have spent a large amount of time theorizing about them and comparatively little time actually experiencing them. But throughout this book's writing, I have tried not to lose sight of my original impetus for it, which is the many nights I have spent in the company of America doing just that—not only the night in Ohio when Ministry's audience destroyed the bleachers of the Riverfront Amphitheater, but the other nights as well—in Berkeley with Rancid, in Denmark with Nirvana, in Berlin with Fugazi, in Istanbul and the Czech Republic with Pearl Jam, in Dallas and Atlanta and Knoxville and Seattle and San Diego and Phoenix and San Jose alongside Metallica, Green Day, Rage Against the Machine, the Red Hot Chili Peppers, the Beastie Boys, the Breeders, Alice in Chains, the Flaming Lips, Guns N' Roses, U2, the Pixies, Soundgarden, the Butthole Surfers, Jane's Addiction, and so, so, so many others, when it was my job to witness and chronicle the spectacle. At the time, I believed that what I was chronicling was a ritual of American culture, but writing this book has given me the opportunity to think about what was going on in those fields and gardens in a more far-reaching way. And what I discovered was that what was going on in those spaces was partially symbolic, but at the same time it may be of real consequence in culture and society.

I believe that rock festivals matter: that they signify. I think that they have consubstantiated generations in ways that can be harnessed to reframe the way their attendees think about themselves and their goals and desires. Festivals can not only shape a person's identity, but they can shape how each identity thinks, at least partially, about the world and their role in it. But so what? Why might these insights matter for future concertgoers, future concert conveners, or future cultural historians? I see several important takeaways from this study of rock crowds and power. First, the longevity of the appeal of discourses about nature suggests that such narrative devices are viable for future large festivals or other gatherings; it also hints at the deep feelings that nature, and its possible destruction, calls out to in the American psyche. At the same time, the vexed way that festivals use these feelings calls into question the efficacy of this strategy for affecting lasting change around these issues. While rock festivals have configured a generation that cares about nature—and sex and drugs—they have also created a space where this interest can be deposited, and reimagined, in ways that are not necessarily productive. In other words, the disjunction between the material reality of participating in a rock festival and the utopian ideologies such festivals uphold says a lot about the ability of the human mind to draw a veil over anything that it does not wish to acknowledge.

Second, the role of race at rock festivals begs the question of how and why such festivals could become more inclusive spaces where Paul Gilroy's concept of "listening together" might occur, spaces that might be more reflective of the discourse of equality that undergirds most Americans' conception of democracy, which these festivals certainly portray themselves as fulfilling. Having acknowledged the mechanisms and limitations that have already been instantiated in these spaces, I can only suggest that the organizers of rock festivals need to move away from discourses about drugs, nature, and black sexuality or at least become more aware of the purpose and effect of these appeals.

I have already explored one model of a festival—the We Are One concert on the Washington Mall—that downplayed these rhetorics with enormous success. Because that festival did *not* immerse itself in any rhetoric about nature, because it was accessible by public transport, and because the performers all wore unrevealing, bulky winter coats, conversations about race and gender were allowed to go forth in ways that did not alienate a multicultural audience. In fact, race and race relations were the central topic of this concert. The speakers invoked and embodied multiracial discourses, and the music that was played was clearly meant to invoke American musical history. But without the other distracting and, to many, unappealing narratives about black and female sexuality, America as a pristine forest, and the legalization of drugs, the discourse about race became direct, welcoming, and unthreatening; it was a possible way of, to quote Hazel Markus and Paula Moya, "doing difference differently." At the We Are One concert on the Mall, race became depolemicized; it was simply a conversation that was waiting to be had. And I think that can happen elsewhere.

The success of We Are One also shows the dangers of the exclusionary practices that these festivals have come to use automatically, the haze of disingenuous rhetoric that surrounds them, and the possibility that these gatherings may foreclose meaningful discourse around subjects like the legalization of drugs, ecological disaster, and political discourse in general. By tying ideals about freedom and democracy to music and to corporate branding, such festivals can exploit the naiveté of a music-loving population. It seems possible that these giant rock festivals may even be undermining meaningful understanding about historical and cultural moments—as when Bonnaroo's "radiate positivity" ad campaign recently used a Martin Luther King Jr. quote to describe not racial equality but how much fun millennials will have on their fairgrounds.

Rock festivals can certainly be spaces of positivity and liberation, and although they may not effect change, they can further conversations about it, as we saw with Rockwool's use of a festival to experiment with housing for refugees. Even so, my final observation here is a negative one. I'd like to suggest that these popular, enjoyable, shared cultural experiences of collective effervescence, these community-built events where identification serves as a mechanism to consubstantiate an entire generation's experience, have had a dampening effect on public gatherings in the late twentieth century. The startling and violent riots in Chicago in 1968 and the World Trade Organization protests in 2000 point to a larger, invisible truth: in America today, large, peaceful, but most importantly, *effective* protest crowds—and by that I mean, crowds populated largely by middle-class white people with a single, unified aim—have become almost nonexistent. Instead, the issues that such crowds care about have been channeled into ones preselected by rock festivals; that is, ecology, legalization of drugs, and other issues that connect to the natural world and to deep-seated feelings about America as a place of freedom and democracy and as a natural idyll. As important as these issues are, and as heartfelt as the appeals made around them can be, they are not issues that can effect political or social change in America in meaningful ways.

Almost as a corollary, most racialized crowds—that is, the ones who have *not* been attending festivals in large numbers—are at sites of political protest. Since 1963, the year that Martin Luther King Jr. gathered one million people on the Washington Mall to hear his "I Have a Dream" speech, the most committed and effective crowd gatherings have all been nonmusically centered ones with racial issues at the core. The Million Man March and the 2006 marches for immigration reform, to name just two, represent crowds with a political goal in mind that goes beyond nature and freedom, crowds who have formed explicitly to effect political change. Most recently, the Black Lives Matter movement has marshaled large crowds to protest police brutality and other social wrongs, and many attendees have been white. So was the months-long protest at Standing Rock in North Dakota to protest the building of the Dakota Access Pipeline. At that site, protesters battled very real and very dangerous forces, facing down pepper spray and the government and the oil companies, which posed a material threat to a very specific piece of land. Yet un-interested onlookers, seeing photos on the internet or reading articles titled "Neil Young Celebrates 71st Birthday Performing at Standing Rock Protest Site" in *Rolling Stone*, might be forgiven for thinking that the gathering was merely an outgrowth of some giant rock festival. According to some reports, the protest was for a time being "colonized" by white people who "bring guitars and drums, use up valuable donated resources, and seem to be there for the cultural experience" (Richardson, "Complaints Grow"). "This is not Burning Man or a festival," read one widely circulated Twitter letter hashtagged DAPL. "Do not bring your party at the expense of these peoples fighting for life or death."

The confusion between the Standing Rock protest site and a rock festival was understandable. For the last forty years, the largest majority-white gatherings have been at rock festivals where seemingly political discourses may be circulated but that don't even pretend to invoke lasting policy or political change. They are places of innocence. Thus, my final observation is simply this: over the past sixty years, sports gatherings, community celebrations, and, most especially, rock festivals and raves have trained largely white crowds to gather peacefully, but they have trained them in ways that allow them to believe they are effecting change merely by gathering to listen to music. At these loci, the consubstantiation of these attendees' identities is so strong that, to them, no other change need then take place.

As stated earlier in this book, this somewhat pessimistic conclusion is not meant to downplay the real pleasures involved in attending a music festival. No one knows, or rather, no one *should* know, better than I the unholy pleasure involved in participating in an embodied mass gathering. This is what I wrote, over twenty years ago, about standing amidst a crowd of 160,000 Danes watching their victory in the finals of the European Football Championships while simultaneously awaiting Nirvana, then the most popular band on the planet, to take the stage at the Roskilde Music Festival:

> It was eleven p.m. and not yet twilight in Denmark when the
> whistle blew in Sweden with Denmark still ahead. And then all the

Americans sitting backstage at the orange tent in Roskilde rushed up onstage to watch the revels. Somehow almost everyone on that field had contrived to make a flag out of a shard of a T-shirt, perhaps they'd brought them with them, hidden among their stuff for just this contingency. Anyway, they were waving these Danish flags like mad, making the humongous meadow seem like a scene out of the Crusades or something. Beneath us lay a sea of faces, many of them painted bright red with lipstick, a white cross drawn on their cheeks, and their mouths, wide open, were bright red too. Someone handed us each a plastic cup and poured us champagne . . . and then the crowd, which was loud, became louder. What's louder than loudest? The world's amps turned to eleven.

Everything was noise and confusion, an antic swarm of humanity rending up the nearly-night. And looking out at that endless field of faces, I imagined a giant tower of speakers that could blast across the whole wide hemisphere, reaching every heart and mind in the entire western world. I felt much too small to be holding so much love in my own safekeeping. And as I watched Nirvana burst their guts into the universe that night, I felt a violent shudder of victory so complete it made Denmark's come from nowhere victory over Germany pale by comparison. It felt as if someone had opened up all our mouths and poured pure goddamn gold down our throats. (*Route 666* 204–5)

Pure goddamn gold. I end with that passage, because I think it captures something about attending a rock festival that the rest of this book has had to leave out. Rock festivals are places of disjunction and deception, commodified spaces with arguments of their own to make. They are white. They are polluted. They are not exactly what they seem. But they are also spaces of primal pleasure; they are places where we experience some of the most intense emotional moments of our lives. As Pierre Nora said, such events allow us to "participate emotionally in history." When I traveled with Nirvana and watched them command those fervent fields and fields of faces, there was no question that I felt like I was witnessing a cataclysmic moment in the story of the world. In fact, I wasn't. And my gradual realization that a rock festival is only a place where we can *pretend* to be historic is the notion that fuels this text.

At the same time, I don't want to plead complete disillusionment with the form. A rock festival is an imagined community, whose rules and regulations have nothing whatsoever to do with reality. When we enter one, we check our values, our beliefs, and our ideologies—what Althusser called "our imagined relationship to the real conditions of our existence"—at the gate, and we do so for a reason: because the real conditions of life lived under capitalism are frustrating and sad, and we have an innate sense that our imagined relationship to them is deeply flawed. By suspending those conditions, rock festivals hold out new and frankly more attractive ways of thinking about the basic paradigms we live under. For instance, they allow us to believe that nature isn't being despoiled, when it is. They allow us to believe that race is invisible, when it isn't, that drug use will free our minds, when it won't, and that the free market itself is some kind of moral force with actual ethical underpinnings.

In other words, rock festivals allow us to change not just how we think about our culture, but how we *feel* about it. Some of those changes may be useful, others less so, but either way, rock festivals serve as a reminder that live music is a set of lived social relations. Like all other social relations, they create systems of meaning that can have enormous longevity. Picture again the image of the crowds at Luisa Tetrazzini's Christmas Eve concert on the steps of the *San Francisco Chronicle* in 1910. In many ways that picture is mired in a distant and inaccessible past, and yet, nestled inside that event are the seeds of all the others mentioned here, from Nazi rallies to Newport, from Woodstock to Wattstax, from a May Day rave somewhere outside of Berlin in 1996 all the way to South Dakota. Connecting them all are intricate layers of invisible networks—ones that extend from there to here, and from here far into the future.

Notes

1. This was written before the events of October 1, 2017, at the Route 91 Harvest country music festival in Las Vegas: the effects of that incident on rock festivals and their audiences are part of a separate American narrative and will be reserved for the end of this book.

2. The success of the European rock festival versus those in America has much to do with geography and car culture and will be discussed elsewhere in this book.

CHAPTER 1

1. The *San Francisco Chronicle* does report, however, that her voice, "unaided by artificial means," was heard miles away from the *Chronicle* at the corner of Haight and Webster, when a businessman identified as Ray Stone held his telephone out the window of his office on Geary Street and had his family listen in ("Augmented Crowds"). Sixty years later, a friend of mine successfully asked the bartender to unhook the phone at CBGBs so she could hear all of Television's set there.

CHAPTER 2

1. The damage caused the cancellation of that week's scheduled Natalie Cole concert.

2. It is not my intention here to rehash the events leading up to Woodstock, which are widely known.

3. These two examples have counterparts all across America.

4. For a more detailed look at this specific festival's context and narratives, Elijah Wald's book *Dylan Goes Electric! Newport, Seeger, Dylan, and the Night That Split the Sixties* (2015) is essential reading.

5. Consider, for example, the stage announcements at Woodstock about being wary of the brown acid.

6. The deaths of fifty-eight concertgoers at the Route 91 Harvest country music festival in Las Vegas in 2017 are aberrant, one hopes: they have little to do with rock crowds and everything to do with gun violence in America.

7. Dylan himself alludes to this possibility in his contemporaneous song "Ballad of a Thin Man" (1965): "There's something happening here and you don't know what it is, do you, Mr. Jones?"

8. On the tape of this concert, however, the boos are quite audible.

9. During this period, filmmaker Robert Drew did several groundbreaking, intimate, cinema verité documentaries for network television, including *Crisis: Behind a Presidential Commitment* and *Primary*. D. A. Pennebaker, who went on to make *Don't Look Back* about this particular Dylan tour, was his cameraman on both projects.

10. In rock, everything happens twice, and just as Marx says, "The first time as tragedy, the second as farce." This scenario repeated itself in a milder form in the early 1980s with the band R.E.M. Their second album, *Murmur*, which fans lovingly dubbed "Mumble," was a paean to indecipherability that only the cultural elite could "read." As the band grew more articulate, their early fans grew restive.

11. From a personal conversation.

CHAPTER 3

1. A corollary to this can be seen in the way we regard social media and the ill effects it has had on politics: on the one hand, we love our social networks, but on the other, we know them to be a sort of original sin.

2. Rick Carroll, personal interview.

3. Surely the destruction of that last event by the advent of a parade of death eaters ought to be a lesson to us all.

4. Personal email.

CHAPTER 4

1. In his history of Apple computers, *Revolution in the Valley*, the writer Andy Hertzfeld claims that UNUSON's name stood for "Unite Nations Using Singing Over Network," but nowhere else is this version confirmed; more typically it is said to stand for "Unite Us In Song."

2. It was also a feature at the first festival in 1982, but on a far smaller scale, consisting of only a short broadcast of a travelogue about Russia and short snippets of a concert beamed from Moscow and a few snippets of Eddie Money's set beamed back. The second incarnation of the festival in 1983 is the focus here because the broadcast of the event is viewable on videotape.

CHAPTER 5

1. According to a recent story in the *San Francisco Chronicle*, less than 1 percent of all visitors to Yosemite are African American. According to Shelton Johnson, one of the park's few African American forest rangers, the "rejection of the natural world by the black community is a scar left over from slavery" (*Chronicle*, August 9, 2009).

2. Hazel Markus and Paula Moya, *Doing Race*, 328.

3. Although this may reflect demographic accuracy, it seems odd given that the music of acts like 50 Cent speaks exclusively about the African American experience.

4. In order to thwart scalping, Ticketmaster is about to inaugurate a "ticketless" purchase plan whereby one swipes one's credit card at the concert gate to get in. This will mean that only credit card holders can go to concerts, preventing an even larger number of lower-income people from attending concerts.

5. Quite a bit of hip-hop music does not celebrate violence, violence against women, or crime. But sadly, this is the less popular branch of the form.

6. Stuart's acknowledgment of racial power dynamics is revelatory. Among other things, he insisted on using as many black camera people as possible on the shoot: forty-five out of a total of forty-eight were black,

all recruited from local colleges and programs, many of them from south-central Los Angeles (Saul, "What You See Is What You Get'").

7. The gritty urban nature of the opening may remind viewers that the film works as a response to *Woodstock*, then less than two years old and still wildly successful.

8. According to Ward, he also had a recording contract with Stax.

9. Perhaps the most interesting aspect of these shots is simply that they exist: had YouTube existed in the 1960s and 1970s, we might have seen a similar record of Woodstock, Wattstax, and other concerts.

10. The Obama family can be seen singing along on the HBO special. Moreover, the commentators on the NPR broadcast point out that this particular song seems to have energized the president and his family.

CHAPTER 6

1. Unfortunately, the event ended up $5,000 in the hole.

2. The 2015 festival, its fortieth, was its last.

3. The Riot Grrrl Manifesto originally appeared in 1991 in the Bikini Kill fanzine #2. It is generally credited to Kathleen Hanna.

4. Nielsen study: http://www.nielsen.com/us/en/insights/news/2015/for-music-fans-the-summer-is-all-a-stage.html.

CHAPTER 7

1. According to Burning Man originator John Law, one of the festival's influences was the pop-up performance space known as Mojave Exodus, in 1984, an event that featured the German noise band Einstürzende Neubauten and the fire-and-explosives conceptual art of Mark Pauline, but today's events have more in common with Germany's Love Parade.

2. Von Busack.

CHAPTER 8

1. This has been done by the organizers of Bonnaroo.

2. Private conversation.

3. Knox, an Australian aborigine, was denied a visa at the last minute and couldn't appear.

4. These are some of the bigger names, but from the 1960s onward, six main companies dominated the record business, and these have since been reduced to four.

5. The classic experiment in moral pricing occurred when Radiohead released its record *In Rainbows* digitally for free in 2007. Downloaders were instructed to pay whatever they felt like, which turned out to be an average of six dollars per download. Lest this be seen as a factor of their popularity, I should add that the band Wonderlick released its second LP under similar circumstances, with the average price working out to $25 per download.

Bibliography

Abbott, Paige. "Some Like It Rock." *San Jose Mercury News*, May 24, 1969.

Adorno, Theodor. *Current of Music: Elements of a Radio Theory*. Germany: Suhrkamp, 2006.

Adorno, Theodor W., and J. M. Bernstein. *The Culture Industry: Selected Essays on Mass Culture*. London: Routledge, 2001.

Agnew, Jean-Christophe. *Worlds Apart: The Market and the Theater in Anglo-American Thought, 1550–1750*. Cambridge: Cambridge University Press, 1986.

Allen, Michael. "I Just Want to Be a Cosmic Cowboy: Hippies, Cowboy Code and the Culture of a Counterculture." *Western Historical Quarterly* 36, no. 3 (Autumn 2005).

Anderson, Chris. "Free! Why $0.00 Is the Future of Business." *Wired*, February 25, 2008. http://www.wired.com/techbiz/it/magazine/16-03/ff_free.

Andrejevic, Mark. *Reality TV: The Work of Being Watched*. Lanham, MD: Rowman & Littlefield, 2004.

Arnold, Gina. "Fair Game." *Los Angeles New Times*, June 18, 1997.

———. "Pop Perfect." *Metro*, June 14, 2001.

———. *Route 666: The Road to Nirvana*. New York: St. Martin's, 1993.

————. "U-N-I-T-Y." *San Diego Reader*, March 31, 1994.

Attali, Jacques. *Noise: The Political Economy of Music*. Minneapolis: University of Minnesota Press, 1985.

"Augmented Crowds in Best of Humor Fill the Thoroughfares: No Untoward Incident Mars the Diva's Singing in the Open Air on Christmas Eve." *San Francisco Chronicle*, December 25, 1910.

Auslander, Philip. *Liveness: Performance in a Mediatized Culture*. London: Routledge, 2008.

Balaji, Murali. *The Professor and the Pupil: The Politics of W.E.B. Du Bois and Paul Robeson*. New York: Nation, 2007.

Barsam, Richard Meran. *Nonfiction Film: A Critical History*. New York: Dutton, 1973.

"Battlefield Earth." Advertisement. *Los Angeles Times*, September 4, 1982, C24.

Baudelaire, Charles. "Crowds." In *The Flowers of Evil & Paris Spleen: Selected Poems*. Mineola, NY: Dover, 2010.

Beck, Marilyn. "Hollywood Hotline." *Pasadena Star News*, December 4, 1972.

Benjamin, Walter. *Charles Baudelaire: A Lyric Poet in the Era of High Capitalism*. London: Verso, 1997.

Berry, William Earl. "How Wattstax Festival Renews Black Unity." *Jet*, September 14, 1972.

Bey, Hakim. *TAZ: The Temporary Autonomous Zone, Ontological Anarchy, Poetic Terrorism*. New York: Autonomedia, 2003.

"Bluegrass Music: The Roots." Ibma.org. http://www.ibma.org/about.blue grass/history/index.asp.

Boyd, Joe. *White Bicycles: Making Music in the 1960s*. London: Serpent's Tail, 2007.

Boyum, Joy Gould. "A Bit More Than Just Music at a Black Concert." *Wall Street Journal*, February 26, 1973, 12.

Brand, Stewart. "Point the Institution: Verbal Snapshots from the Last Quarter Century." *Whole Earth Review*, May 1985.

Brant, Marley. *Join Together: Forty Years of the Rock Music Festival*. New York: Backbeat, 2008.

Braudel, Fernand. *The Wheels of Commerce, Volume II: Civilization and Capitalism, 15th–18th Century*. Translated by Sian Reynolds. New York: Harper & Row, 1982.

Braunstein, Peter, and Michael William Doyle. *Imagine Nation: The American Counterculture of the 1960s and '70s*. New York: Routledge, 2002.

Brautigan, Richard. "Machines of Loving Grace." In *All Watched Over by Machines of Loving Grace*. San Francisco: Communication, 1967.

Brecht, Bertolt. "The Radio as Communications Apparatus: A Lecture on the Function of Radio." In *Brecht on Film and Radio*, edited by Marc Silberman. Grand Rapids, MI: Methuen, 2001.

Bredow, Derrick, director. *High Tech Soul*. 2006.

Brightman, Carol. *Sweet Chaos: The Grateful Dead's American Adventure*. New York: C. Potter, 1998.

Burke, Kenneth. *Language as Symbolic Action*. Saratoga Springs, NY: Empire State College, State University of New York Press, 1973.

C, Jay. "Pauline Kael vs. Gimme Shelter." Thedocumentaryblog.com. July 10, 2007. http://www.thedocumentaryblog.com/index.php/2007/09 /10/pauline-kael-vs-gimme-shelter/.

Campbell, Joseph. "Joseph Campbell on the Grateful Dead." Democratic underground.com. May 28, 2005. http://www.democraticunderground .com/discuss/duboard.php?az=view_all&address=105x7772949>.

Canetti, Elias. *Crowds and Power*. Translated by Carol Stewart. New York: Farrar, Straus and Giroux, 1984.

Carroll, Rick. "Along with Entertainment, There Was Plenty of Action– Mostly at 'Be In.'" *San Jose Mercury News*, May 26, 1969.

Castells, Manuel. *The Rise of the Network Society*. Vol. 1. Malden, MA: Blackwell, 1996.

"CIA Funds Rock Festival." *Berkeley Tribe*, November 7, 1969.

Clinton, Bill. *My Life*. New York: Knopf, 2004.

Considine, Bob. "There's Good News Today." *Phairos-Tribune and Press*, October 15, 1972, 4.

Cooper, Arthur. "Watts Happening." *Newsweek*, February 26, 1973, 88.

The Crowd. Directed by King Vidor. 1928. DVD.

Dayan, Daniel, and Elihu Katz. *Media Events: The Live Broadcasting of History*. Cambridge, MA: Harvard University Press, 1992.

"Deafening Spell Woven by the King of Rock." *San Jose Mercury News*, May 26, 1969.

Debord, Guy. *The Society of the Spectacle*. Translated by Donald Nicholson-Smith. New York: Zone, 2006.

Dickens, Charles. *A Tale of Two Cities*. New York: Toby, 2003.

Dickson, Samuel. *Tales of San Francisco*. Stanford University Press, 1968.

Dinkelspiel, Frances. *Towers of Gold: How One Jewish Immigrant Named Isaias Hellman Created California*. New York: St. Martin's, 2008.

Dowdy, Michael. "Live Hip Hop, Collective Agency, and 'Acting in Concert.'" *Popular Music and Society* 30, no. 1 (2007): 75–91.

The Dramatics. "Whatcha See Is Whatcha Get." *Soul Hits of the Seventies.* 1971. CD.

Du Bois, W. E. B. *The Souls of Black Folk.* New York: Modern Library, 2003.

Durkheim, Émile, and Karen E. Fields. *The Elementary Forms of Religious Life.* New York: Free, 1995.

Dylan, Bob. "Visions of Johanna." *No Direction Home: The Soundtrack.* Columbia/Legacy, 2005. CD.

Easy Rider. Directed by Dennis Hopper. Columbia Pictures, 1969. DVD.

Ede, Lisa, and Andrea Lunsford. "Audience Addressed/Audience Invoked: The Role of Audience in Composition Theory and Pedagogy." *College Composition and Communication* 35, no. 2 (1984): 155–71.

Egan, Jennifer. *A Visit from the Goon Squad.* New York: Alfred A. Knopf, 2010.

Ehrenreich, Barbara. *Dancing in the Streets: A History of Collective Joy.* New York: Henry Holt, 2007.

Ehrlich, Paul. *The Population Bomb.* San Francisco: Sierra Club Books, 1968.

Electric Apricot: The Quest for Festeroo. Dir. Les Claypool. 2008.

Ellis, Peter. Telephone interview. April 3, 2010.

Epstein, Andrew. "A High Tech Lark in the Park." *Los Angeles Times,* August 18, 1982, sec. G: 1.

———. "Major Music Fest-Computer Fair Set." *Los Angeles Times,* July 20, 1982, sec. G: 2.

Fast, Howard. *Being Red.* Boston: Houghton Mifflin, 1990.

"Festival Survives Rocky Moments." *San Jose Mercury News,* May 25, 1969.

Finding Nemo. Directed by Andrew Stanton and Lee Unkrich. 2003; Emeryville, CA: Pixar Animation Studios, 2003. DVD.

"For Music Fans, Summer Is All a Stage." *Nielsen Reports,* April 4, 2014. www.nielsen.com.

Franzen, Jonathan. *Freedom.* New York: Farrar, Straus and Giroux, 2010.

"Free Food, Rock Bands at 'Be-In.'" *Spartan Daily,* May 22, 1969.

Freud, Sigmund. "Group Psychology and the Analysis of the Ego." In *The Standard Edition of the Complete Psychological Works of Sigmund Freud,* translated by James Strachey. Vol. 18. London: Hogarth, 1955.

Frith, Simon. "'The Magic That Can Set You Free': The Ideology of Folk and the Myth of the Rock Community." *Popular Music* 1 (1981): 159.

Geertz, Clifford. "Deep Play: Notes on the Balinese Cockfight." *Daedalus* 134, no. 4 (2005): 56–86.

George, Nelson. *The Death of Rhythm and Blues.* New York: Penguin, 2003.

Gibson, Emily F. "Annual Watts Summer Festival Has Come and Gone." *Los Angeles Sentinel*, August 31, 1972, A7.

Gilroy, Paul. "Between the Blues and Blues Dance: Some Soundscapes of the Black Atlantic." In *The Auditory Culture Reader*, edited by Michael Bull and Les Back. Oxford: Berg, 2003.

———. "Sounds Authentic: Black Music, Ethnicity, and the Challenge of a 'Changing' Same." *Black Music Research Journal* 11, no. 2 (1991): 111–36.

Gimme Shelter. Directed by David Maysles and Albert Maysles. 1970; New York: Maysles Films, Cinema 5, 1970. DVD.

Gold, Rebecca. *A Wizard Called Woz*. Minneapolis, MN: Lerner, 1994.

Goldstein, Patrick. "Geffen's Guns N' Roses Fires Volley at PMRC." *Los Angeles Times*, August 16, 1987.

Goldstein, Stanley. "*The Wild One* and *Gimme Shelter*." National Film Board Registry. Library of Congress, November 10, 1998. http://www .loc.gov/film/goldstein.html.

Gram, Dorte. Personal interview. April 2015.

Grossberg, Lawrence. "Rock, Politics and Territorialization." In *We Gotta Get Out of This Place: Popular Conservatism and Postmodern Culture*. New York: Routledge, 1992.

Grushkin, Paul. *The Art of Rock: Posters from Presley to Punk*. New York: Abbeville, 1987.

Guns N' Roses. "It's So Easy." *Appetite for Destruction*. Geffen Records. 1987.

Gursky, Andreas. *Union Rave*. 1996. De Young Museum, San Francisco.

Guthrie, Woody. "This Land Is Your Land." February 23, 1940.

Haggerty, Sandra. "Black Tragedy Becomes Celebration." *Tucson Daily Citizen*, January 18, 1973, 19.

Hanna, Kathleen. "Riot Grrrl Manifesto." From *Bikini Kill #2*, 1991. http:// onewarart.org/riot_grrrl_manifesto.htm.

Hardt, Michael, and Antonio Negri. *Multitude: War and Democracy in the Age of Empire*. New York: Penguin, 2004.

Harris, Kathryn. "'Woz' Risking Millions on US Festival." *Los Angeles Times*, May 27, 1983, Orange County ed., 5A.

Harvey, Carlos. CFO, US Festival. Archivist, Woz.org. Personal interview. May 6, 2009.

Heavy Metal Parking Lot. Directed by Jeff Krulik. 1986. DVD.

Heise, Ursula. "The Virtual Crowd." In *The ISLE Reader: Ecocriticism, 1993–2003*, edited by Michael P. Branch and Scott Slovic. Athens: University of Georgia Press, 2003.

Hellman, Warren. Personal interview. October 10, 2009.

Hertzfeld, Andy. *Revolution in the Valley: The Insanely Great Story of How the Mac Was Made*. Sebastopol, CA: O' Reilly Media, 2005.

Hilburn, Robert. "Graham's Really Big on US Festival's 'Big Idea.'" *Los Angeles Times*, August 24, 1982, G1.

———. "US Fest Ends with a Whimper." *Los Angeles Times*, June 6, 1983, H1.

———. "US Success: Meticulous Plans." *Los Angeles Times*, September 7, 1982, G1.

Hopkins, Jerry. "Crashers, Cops, Producers Spoil Newport '69." *Rolling Stone*, July 26, 1969.

———. "Festival Shucks." *Rolling Stone*, June 28, 1969.

———. "Sympowowsium." *Rolling Stone*, December 27, 1969.

Horn, Leslie. "MTV Spring Break Used to Rule." Deadspin.com. March 19, 2015.

Hunt, Dennis. "Pryor Highlight of Wattstax Collage." *Los Angeles Times*, February 21, 1973, 80.

Hunt, Geoffrey P., Kristin Evans, and Faith Kares. "Drug Use and Meanings of Risk and Pleasure." *Journal of Youth Studies* 10, no. 1 (2007): 73–96.

Hunter, David. "Steve Wozniak Throws a Party." *Softalk*, October 1982. Usfestivals.com. Woz.org. www.usfestivals.com.

Introna, Lucas D., and Helen Nissenbaum. "Shaping the Web: Why the Politics of Search Engines Matters." *The Information Society* 16, no. 3 (2000): 169–85.

Jarnow, Jesse. Personal interview. September 2014.

"John Stallone, Synanon." Telephone interview. April 18, 2009.

Jordan, Teresa, James Hepworth, and Evelyn White. "Black Women in the Wilderness." In *The Stories That Shape Us: Contemporary Women Write about the West: An Anthology*. New York: Norton, 1995.

Kael, Pauline. "Gimme Shelter." *The New Yorker*, December 19, 1970.

Keister, Edwin. "Woodstock and Beyond . . . Why?" *Today's Health* 48, no. 7 (1970).

Kershaw, Andy. "Bob Dylan: How I Found the Man Who Shouted Judas." *Independent*, September 23, 2005. http://www.independent.co.uk/arts -entertainment/music/features/bob-dylan-how-i-found-the-man-who -shouted-judas-507883.html.

Kesey, Ken. *Sometimes a Great Notion*. New York: Penguin, 2006.

"KFAT Memories." May 25, 2009. www.kfat.com/kfat.html.

"Killing in the Name." *Rage Against the Machine*. New York: Epic Associated, 1992. CD.

Kirk, Andrew G. *Counterculture Green: The Whole Earth Catalog and American Environmentalism*. Lawrence: University of Kansas Press, 2007.

Kitwana, Bakari. "The Cotton Club." *Village Voice*, June 2, 2005.

Knight, Arthur. "Facing Reality." *Saturday Review*, March 10, 1973, 71.

Krier, Beth Ann. "A U.S.-Moscow Hot Line for the Fun of It." *Los Angeles Times*, May 30, 1983, Orange County ed., C1.

Landau, Jon. *It's Too Late to Stop Now: A Rock 'n' Roll Journal*. New York: Straight Arrow, 1973.

Le Bon, Gustave. *The Crowd: A Study of the Popular Mind*. Grand Rapids, MI: Filiquarian, 2006.

LeDoux, Chris. "The Cowboy and the Hippie." *Gold Buckle Dreams*. American Cowboy Songs, 1987. CD.

Lefebvre, Henri. *The Production of Space*. Translated by Donald Nicholson-Smith. Malden, MA: Blackwell, 2008.

Lelchuk, Ilene. "Controversial Garage for Park Opens." *San Francisco Chronicle*, October 14, 2005.

Lent, Ron. "Fisticuffs, Dancing at San Jose 'Be-In.'" *Spartan Daily*, May 27, 1969.

"Local Be-In Crimes Included Theft, Assault, Rape, Drugs." *San Jose Mercury News*, May 29, 1969.

Lombardi, John. "Atlantic City: Pop! Goes the Boardwalk." *Rolling Stone*, September 6, 1969, 8.

London, Michael. "Clashing Opinions on US Festival." *Los Angeles Times*, May 28, 1983, E1.

———. "Fear and Loathing at the US Fest." *Los Angeles Times*, June 5, 1983, T2.

"Lonely Boy." Performed by Paul Anka; directed by Wolf Koenig and Roman Kroitor. 1963; Montreal: National Film Board of Canada, 1962. DVD.

Lott, Eric. *Love and Theft: Blackface Minstrelsy and the American Working Class*. New York: Oxford University Press, 1993.

Mann, Geoff. "Why Does Country Music Sound White? Race and the Voice of Nostalgia." *Ethnic and Racial Studies* 31, no. 1 (August 24, 2007): 73–100.

Manovich, Lev. *The Language of New Media*. Cambridge, MA: MIT Press, 2002.

Mapes, Jillian. "Surviving Oldchella: Scenes from the Ultimate Classic Rock Rager." Pitchfork.com. October 11, 2016. https://pitchfork.com/features/festival-report/9960-surviving-oldchella-scenes-from-the-ultimate-classic-rock-rager/.

Marcus, Greil. *Like a Rolling Stone: Bob Dylan at the Crossroads*. New York: Public Affairs, 2006.

Marcuse, Herbert. *One-Dimensional Man: Studies in the Ideology of Advanced Industrial Society*. London: Routledge, 1991.

Markus, Hazel, and Paula M. L. Moya. *Doing Race: 21 Essays for the 21st Century*. New York: W.W. Norton, 2010.

Matos, Michaelangelo. *The Underground Is Massive: How Electronic Dance Music Conquered America*. New York: Harper Collins, 2015.

McCarthy, Amy. "Punched, Groped, Beer Thrown in My Face." *Salon*, May 16, 2015.

McLean, Don. *American Pie*. New York: United Artists, 1971. CD.

McLuhan, Marshall. *Understanding Media: The Extensions of Man*. New York: Signet Books, 1964.

McNair, Brian. *Porno? Chic! How Pornography Changed the World and Made It a Better Place*. Abingdon, UK: Routledge, 2013.

Melton, Barry. "Fixin' to Die Rag." Performed by Country Joe and the Fish. *Woodstock Music from the Original Soundtrack and More*. Los Angeles: Rhino, 2009. CD.

Menand, Louis. "The Radicalization of Joan Didion." *The New Yorker*, April 24, 2015.

Mitchell, Joni. "Woodstock." Performed by Crosby, Stills, and Nash. *Woodstock Music from the Original Soundtrack and More*. Los Angeles: Rhino, 2009. CD.

"Money Plays Right Tune for Festival." *San Jose Mercury News*, May 24, 1969.

Monterey Pop. Directed by D. A. Pennebaker. 1968; San Francisco: Leacock Pennebaker, 1967. DVD.

Moore, Dawn, and Mariana Valverde. "Maidens at Risk: 'Date Rape Drugs' and the Formation of Hybrid Risk Knowledges." *Economy and Society* 29, no. 4 (2000): 514–31.

Morain, Dan. "Mountain Town Waits Nervously for Rockers." *Los Angeles Times*, September 1, 1982, Orange County ed., A6.

———. "US Festival: Will Biggest Be the Best?" *Los Angeles Times*, May 22, 1982, T57.

Morain, Dan, and Robert Hilburn. "Promoter of US Festival Claims Long-Shot Victory." *Los Angeles Times*, September 6, 1982, 1.

Moritz, Michael. *The Little Kingdom: The Private Story of Apple Computer*. New York: William Morrow, 1984.

Natoli, Joseph, and Linda Hutcheon. *A Postmodern Reader*. Albany, NY: SUNY Press, 1993.

Nolte, Carl. "Luisa Tetrazzini's Gift Ends S.F. Era on High Note." *San Francisco Chronicle*, December 24, 2010. www.sfgate.com/news/article/Luisa-Tetrazzini-s-gift-ends-S-F-era-on-high-note-2452300.php.

Nye, Joseph. "China's Soft Power Deficit." *Wall Street Journal*, May 8, 2012.

Ohlin, Alix. "Andreas Gursky and the Contemporary Sublime." *Art Journal* 61, no. 4 (2002): 22–35.

Orwell, George. "Shooting an Elephant." In *Shooting an Elephant and Other Essays*. New York: Harcourt, Brace, 1950.

Pinch, Trevor. "Giving Birth to New Users." In *How Users Matter: The Co-Construction of Users and Technologies*, edited by Nelly Oudshoorn and Trevor Pinch. Cambridge, MA: MIT Press, 2003.

Pitcher, Karen. "The Staging of Agency in *Girls Gone Wild*." *Critical Studies in Media Communication* 33, no. 3 (2006).

Poe, Edgar Allan. "The Man of the Crowd." In *Edgar Allen Poe: Complete Tales and Poems*. Edison, NJ: Castle Books, 2002.

Quiznos. "Burn Trials: Out of the Maze and onto the Playa." Quiznos Toaster. September 8, 2015. www.youtube.com/watch?v=CBVBHRD5lNU.

Regis, Helen A., and Shana Walton. "Producing the Folk at the New Orleans Jazz and Heritage Festival." *Journal of American Folklore* 121, no. 482 (2008): 400–440.

Reich, Charles A. *The Greening of America: How the Youth Revolution Is Trying to Make America Livable*. New York: Random House, 1970.

Rheingold, Howard. *Smart Mobs: The Next Social Revolution*. Cambridge, MA: Perseus, 2003.

Richardson, Valerie. "Complaints Grow over Whites Turning Dakota Access Protest into Hippie Festival." *Washington Times*, November 28, 2016.

Rietveld, H. "Entranced: Embodied Spirituality on the Post-Industrial Dance Floor." *International Journal of Critical Psychology* 8 (2003): 47–67.

Robinson, Roxy. *Music Festivals and the Politics of Participation*. Abingdon, UK: Routledge, 2016.

"Rock Festival Gets the Ax." *San Jose Mercury News*, May 28, 1969.

Rogers, Nicholas. *Crowds, Culture, and Politics in Georgian Britain*. Oxford: Clarendon, 1998.

Rosenfield. "Bluegrass and Serendipity." *Bluegrass Unlimited*, November 1967.

Roszak, Theodore. *The Making of a Counter Culture: Reflections on the Technocratic Society and Its Youthful Opposition*. London: Faber and Faber, 1970.

Rushkoff, Douglas. *Cyberia: Life in the Trenches of Cyberspace*. Manchester, UK: Clinamen, 2002.

Salkin, Jeffrey K. "Sixty Years since the Peekskill Riots." Forward.com. September 2, 2009. http://forward.com/culture/113279/sixty-years -since-the-peekskill-riots/www.forward.com.

Samuels, David. "Rock Is Dead: Sex, Drugs and Raw Sewage at Woodstock 99." *Harpers*, November 1999.

"San Jose Rocks—Gently." *San Jose Mercury News*, May 24, 1969.

Saul, Scott. "'What You See Is What You Get': *Wattstax*, Richard Pryor, and the Secret History of the Black Aesthetic." Post45.com. August 12, 2014. www.post-45.Yale.edu.

Schnapp, Jeffrey T., and Matthew Tiews. *Crowds*. Stanford, CA: Stanford University Press, 2006.

Seiler, Cotten. *Republic of Drivers: A Cultural History of Automobility in America*. Chicago: University of Chicago Press, 2008.

———. "'So That We as a Race Might Have Something Authentic to Travel By': African American Automobility and Cold-War Liberalism." *American Quarterly* 58, no. 4 (2006): 1091–17.

Selvin, Joel. *Summer of Love: The Inside Story of LSD, Rock and Roll, Free Love and High Times in the Wild West*. New York: Plume, 1995.

Shelton, Robert. "Beneath the Festival's Razzle-Dazzle." *New York Times*, August 1, 1965.

Showalter, Daniel F. "Remembering the Dangers of Rock and Roll: Toward a Historical Narrative of the Rock Festival." *Critical Studies in Media Communication* 17, no. 1 (2000).

Siegel, Katy. "The Big Picture." *Art Forum*, January 2001.

Solomon, Charles. "Laser Animation to Be Showcased." *Los Angeles Times*, May 27, 1983, Orange County ed., D9.

Sontag, Susan. "Simone Weil." *New York Review of Books*, February 1, 1963.

Sragow, Michael. "Gimme Shelter: The True Story." Salon.com. August 10, 2000. http://www.salon.com/entertainment/col/srag/2000/08/10 /gimme_shelter.

Star, Susan L., and James Greisemer. "'Translation' and Boundary Objects: Amateurs and Professionals at Berkeley's Museum of Vertebrate Zoology." *Social Studies of Science* 19 (1989): 383–420.

Stoever, Jennifer. "Experience Music Project Pop Conference." In "'Lollapalooza Every Day, Every Year': Music, Multiculturalism, and Whiteness in the 1990s." 2006. Unpublished.

Surowiecki, James. *The Wisdom of Crowds*. New York: Anchor, 2005.

Taking Woodstock. Directed by Ang Lee. 2009; Los Angeles: Focus Features, 2009. DVD.

Thompson, Victor. "Racialized Mass Incarceration." In *Doing Race: 21 Essays for the 21st Century*, edited by Hazel Markus and Paula M. L. Moya. New York: W.W. Norton, 2010.

Tiber, Elliot, and Tom Monte. *Taking Woodstock*. Garden City Park, NY: Square One, 2007.

Triumph of the Will. Directed by Leni Riefenstahl. 1936; Chicago: International Historic Films, Inc., 2011. DVD.

Turner, Fred. "Burning Man at Google: A Cultural Infrastructure for New Media Production." *New Media and Society* 11, no. 73 (2009).

———. *From Counterculture to Cyberculture: Stewart Brand, the Whole Earth Network, and the Rise of Digital Utopianism*. Chicago: University of Chicago Press, 2006.

Ulloa, Nina. "32 Million People in the U.S. Attend Festivals." Digitalmusic news.com. April 14, 2015.

US '83: Today, Tomorrow, Together (music concert festival program). Lake Forest, CA: Richard Boyle, Stephen Wozniak, 1983.

US Festival. Footage, private collection. Woz.org.

US Festival. UNUSON. February 2, 2009. Woz.org.

"US Festival Will Feature Music and Computers." *Silicon Gulch Gazette*, July 1982.

Vanderbilt, Thomas. *Survival City: Adventures among the Ruins of Atomic America*. New York: Princeton Architectural, 2002.

Wald, Elijah. *Dylan Goes Electric! Newport, Seeger, Dylan, and the Night That Split the Sixties*. New York: Harper Collins, 2015.

Walsh, Joe. "Life's Been Good." *But Seriously Folks*. 1978. CD.

Ward, Brian. *Just My Soul Responding: Rhythm and Blues, Black Consciousness, and Race Relations*. Berkeley: University of California Press, 1998.

Wartofsky, Alona. "Police Investigate Reports of Rapes at Woodstock." *Washington Post*, July 29, 1999, 1.

Watts, Laurie, James Hickman, and Paul Geffert. *Today, Tomorrow, Together: US 83 Program*. 1983.

"Wattstax." Advertisement. *Los Angeles Times*, February 1, 1973, 12.

Wattstax. Directed by Mel Stuart. Los Angeles: Columbia Pictures, 1973. DVD.

"Wattstax: You Can't Judge a Movie by Its Color." Advertisement. *Wisconsin State Journal*, April 1, 1973.

Weiss, Jeff. "Paid Dues: Hip Hop Festival in San Bernadino." *Los Angeles Times*, March 30, 2009.

White, Evelyn C. "Black Women and the Wilderness." In *The Stories That Shape Us: Contemporary Women Write about the West: An Anthology*, edited by Teresa Jordan and James Hepworth. New York: Norton, 1995.

Wickham, Harvey. "Melody That Went Up to the Stars Marked the Greatest Moment in Tetrazzini's Life." *San Francisco Chronicle*, December 25, 1910.

Wilderness Act of 1964. Public Law 88-577.

Williams, Lance. "Wattstax: Giving Something Back to Community." *Los Angeles Times*, August 20, 1972, X1, X16.

Williams, Linda. *Porn Studies*. Durham, NC: Duke University Press, 2004.

Willis, Ellen. "Crowds and Freedom." In *Stars Don't Stand Still in the Sky: Music and Myth*, 152–59. New York: New York University Press, 1999.

Winner, Langdon. *The Whale and the Reactor: A Search for Limits in an Age of High Technology*. Chicago: University of Chicago Press, 1989.

Wolfe, Tom. *Radical Chic & Mau-Mauing the Flak Catchers*. New York: Farrar, Straus and Giroux, 1987.

Woodstock: 3 Days of Peace & Music. Directed by Michael Wadleigh and Martin Scorsese. 1970; Burbank, CA: Warner Bros., 1994. DVD.

Wozniak, Steve, and Gina Smith. *iWoz*. New York: Norton, 2006.

York, Maddie. "Glastonbury's Rubbish: Going against the Green Ethos Ruins It for Everybody." *The Guardian*, July 1, 2015.

Zimmerman, Nadya. "Consuming Nature: The Grateful Dead's Performance of an Anti-Commercial Counterculture." *American Music* 24, no. 2 (Summer 2006): 194–216. http://www.jstor.org/stable/25046013.

Index

Adler, Lou, 38–42
Adorno, Theodor, 21
All Tomorrow's Parties, 13
Altamont, 17, 24, 47, 55–56, 84
Althusser, Louis, 90
American Bandstand, 23
"American Pie" (song), 104–105
Anderson, Chris, 158–159
Anka, Paul, 20–21
Apple, 60, 62, 71–72, 79, 181n4
Aquarian Family Festival, 43–50
Attali, Jacques, 17, 27

Balaji, Murali, 81–82
Baez, Joan, 111
Baudelaire, Charles, 6
Beatles, 21
Bey, Hakim, 135
Bikini Kill, 115
Bonnaroo, 6, 13, 36, 173, 182n1

Boyd, Joe, 26, 54
Bragg, Billy, 148
Brand, Stewart, 10, 66
Brautigan, Richard, 130
Brecht, Bertolt, 63, 64
Burgerama and Burger Boogaloo, 5,
  163–167
Burning Man, 13, 14, 136–140, 182n1
Butthole Surfers, 32

Campbell, Joseph, 13
Canetti, Elias, 3, 89, 126, 171
Carroll, Rick, 180n2
Carson, Rachel, 109
Casady, Jack, 39
Chance the Rapper, 97
Chicago Democratic Convention, 32
Coachella, 6, 13, 36, 120, 168–169
Cobain, Kurt, 33
Corbyn, Jeremy, 148

Cornell, Chris, 19
CTC, 60

Day on the Green, 57–58
De Anza College, 66
Deep Throat, 109
Denver Mile High Music Festival, 42
Desert Trip, 169–170
Didion, Joan, 130
Doctorow, E. L., 82
Don't Look Back, 36, 180n9
Drew, Robert, 40–41, 180n9
Dylan, Bob, 23–34; goes electric, 149, 180n4

Ed Sullivan Show, 23
Ehrenreich, Barbara, 110
Ehrlich, Paul, 12, 53
Einstürzende Neubauten, 32, 182n1
Electric Zoo, 120
Ellis, Peter, 67, 76, 80
Endless Summer, 40

Fast, Howard, 82
Fast Times at Ridgemont High, 61
Festival Express (film), 47
Finding Nemo, 16–17
Freedomland, 20–21
Freud, Sigmund, vii
Fyre Festival, 170

Garcia, Jerry, 135
Geldof, Bob, 59
George, Nelson, 88
Gerwe, Peter, 68, 76
Gilroy, Paul, 11–12, 82, 102, 172
Gimme Shelter (film), 53, 54, 55, 56
Girls Gone Wild, 118–119
Glastonbury, 6, 15
Glen Helen Regional Park, 61

Graham, Bill, 58, 71
Gram, Dorte, 140
Grateful Dead, 5, 26, 135
Great White, 26
Guns N' Roses, 119
Gursky, Andreas, 125–127
Guthrie, Woody, 3, 70, 150–151

Hanna, Kathleen, 182n3
Hardly Strictly Bluegrass, 143
Havens, Richie, 53
Hayes, Isaac, 91–93
Heavy Metal Montreal, 112
Heavy Metal Parking Lot, 59
Hellman, Warren, 142, 144–145, 151, 156, 158, 159, 160, 161
Hells Angels, 48, 84
Hendrix, Jimi, 37, 41, 82
Hilburn, Robert, 75, 78
Hitler, Adolf, 24
Holly, Buddy, 23
Hubbard, L. Ron, 70
Huggy Bear, 32
Human Be-In, 25
Hunter, Meredith, 84
Hurricane Katrina, 89, 98, 104
Hüsker Dü, 32

International Pop Underground 5, 114–115
Isle of Wight, 13, 142

Jackson 5, 21
Jackson, Jesse, 88, 96
Jackson, Michael, 132
Jagger, Mick, 17, 57, 76
Jameson, Fredric, 133
Jarnow, Jesse, 135
Jefferson Airplane, 17
Jobs, Steve, 75
Joplin, Janis, 37

K Records, 32
Kesey, Ken, 37, 130, 142
KFAT, 64, 74

Lang, Michael, 36, 50
Law, Don, 58
Law, John, 182n1
Le Bon, Gustave, 13
Lehman Brothers, 146
"Like A Rolling Stone," 28
Lilith Fair, 116–117
Live Aid, 13, 21, 59, 76, 83
Live Earth, 21, 83
Lollapalooza, 4, 6, 19, 21, 99–101
Lonely Boy (film), 20–21
Love Parade, 28, 182n1

Macworld, 60, 79
Made in America, 120
Magnaball, 13
Magnificent Coloring Day, 97, 101
Mamas and the Papas, 38
Mapes, Jill, 169–170
Marcus, Greil, 27
Markoff, John, 130
Markus, Hazel, 173
Marx, Karl, 125
Matos, Michaelangelo, 134
Mauss, Marcel, 156
May, Derrick, 132
Maysles Brothers, 55, 79
MC Hammer, 150
McCartney, Paul, 38
McLachlan, Sarah, 116
McLean, Don, 104
McLuhan, Marshall, 24–25, 31
Menand, Louis, 13
Metallica, 4
Michigan Womyn's Festival (Mich-
    fest), 114, 116
Ministry, 19

Mitchell, Joni, 52
Mojave Exodus, 182n1
Monterey Pop, 7, 22, 36
Morello, Tom, 150–151
Moritz, Michael, 73, 77
Mötley Crüe, 4
Motown, 22
Moya, Paula, 173
MTV Spring Break, 117–118
Mulvey, Laura, 110–111

New Orleans Jazz and Heritage Fes-
    tival, 86, 97–101, 143
Newport Folk Festival, 7, 13, 16, 24,
    26–27, 32–34, 42
Newport Pop Festival, 42–43
Nirvana, 176
Nixon, Richard, 91
Noise Pop, 5
Nora, Pierre, 176
North by Northeast, 5
Northern California Folk-Rock Festi-
    val, 44–47, 49
Nuremberg Rallies, 24
Nye, Joseph, 3

Oakland Coliseum, 57
Obama, Barack, 101, 104, 143, 182n10
Outside Lands, 13, 120

Paid Dues, 97
Parton, Dolly, 143, 148
Pauline, Mark, 182n1
Pauling, Linus, 48
Peekskill, New York, 81–83
Pennebaker, D. A., 36, 40–42
Petty, Tom, 145
Phish, 5
Playboy, 109
Presley, Elvis, 23
Pryor, Richard, 91

Radiohead, 183n5
Rage Against the Machine, 150
Redding, Otis, 37
Reed College, 66
Regis, Helen and Shana Walton, 98–99
Reich, Charles, 109
Riefenstahl, Leni, 24
Rietveld, Hillegonda, 131–132
Riley, Boots, 86
Riot Grrrl, 115–116, 182n3
Robeson, Paul, 82–83
Robinson, Roxy, 137
Rock in Rio, 13
Rock the Bells, 97
Rockwool, 139
Rolling Stones, 21, 57
Roskilde, 28, 139–140, 175
Roszak, Theodore, 33
Route 91 Harvest Festival, Las Vegas, 143–144, 171, 179n1, 180n6
Rushkoff, Douglas, 128, 131

San Francisco Chronicle, 9, 10, 12
San Jose State University, 43
Santana, 57, 111
Scientology, 70
SDS (Students for a Democratic Society), 37
Seeger, Pete, 32
Selvin, Joel, 47
"Shaft," 91
Shakira, 103
Sky River Rock Festival and Lighter Than Air Fair, 25, 107–108
Sleaford Mods, 32
Sontag, Susan, 32
Soundgarden, 19
Spice Girls, 115
Stagecoach, 120

Standing Rock, 175
Stax Records, 88, 182n8
Stoever, Jennifer, 99
Strummer, Joe, 70–71
Stuart, Mel, 90, 181n6
Surowiecki, James, 16
Sziget, 6

Taking Woodstock, 53
Tetrazzini, Luisa, 9, 177
The Association, 37
The Clash, 70, 71, 78
The Dramatics, 90
The English Beat, 80
The Who, 37
Thomas, Rufus, 92
Ticketmaster, 181n4
Till, Emmett, 85
Toffler, Alvin, 132
Trips Festival, 7, 130
Triumph of the Will, 24
Trump, Donald, 127, 143, 145, 148, 170
Turner, Fred, 53, 62, 66, 84, 137

U2, 4, 9, 10
Union Rave, 126–128
UNUSON, 61, 181n1
US Festival, 59–80, 120
Usher, 103

Vans Warped Tour, 120–121

Wadleigh, Michael, 51, 79
Wald, Elijah, 180n4
Walsh, Joe, 78
Watkins Glen, 5, 142
Watts riots, 28
Watts Summer Festival, 88
Wattstax, 84, 87, 88
Wattstax (film), 90–94

We Are One, 101–105, 173
White, Evelyn C., 85
Whole Earth Catalog, 66, 79, 109
Wild West Fest, 47
Williams, Linda, 110
Willie Wonka and the Chocolate Factory, 90
Wilson, Brian, 41
Wolfe, Tom, 37
Wonder, Stevie, 103
Wonderland, 13
Wonderlick, 183n5

Woodstock, 5, 13, 14, 15, 20, 21, 22, 24, 26, 36, 42, 83–84, 99, 102, 108, 113, 120, 141–142, 168, 180n2, 180n5
"Woodstock" (song), 52
Woodstock: 3 Days of Peace and Music, 36, 50, 54, 90, 108
Wozniak, Steve, 59, 61, 64–80

Yoyo A Go Go, 5

Zaatari refugee camp, 139

THE NEW AMERICAN CANON

Half a Million Strong: Crowds and Power from Woodstock to Coachella
by Gina Arnold

*Violet America: Regional Cosmopolitanism in U.S. Fiction
since the Great Depression*
by Jason Arthur

The Meanings of J. Robert Oppenheimer
by Lindsey Michael Banco

*Workshops of Empire: Stegner, Engle, and American Creative Writing
during the Cold War*
by Eric Bennett

Places in the Making: A Cultural Geography of American Poetry
by Jim Cocola

The Legacy of David Foster Wallace
edited by Samuel Cohen and Lee Konstantinou

Race Sounds: The Art of Listening in African American Literature
by Nicole Brittingham Furlonge

Postmodern/Postwar—and After: Rethinking American Literature
edited by Jason Gladstone, Andrew Hoberek, and Daniel Worden

*After the Program Era: The Past, Present, and Future of
Creative Writing in the University*
edited by Loren Glass

Hope Isn't Stupid: Utopian Affects in Contemporary American Literature
by Sean Austin Grattan

*It's Just the Normal Noises: Marcus, Guralnick, "No Depression,"
and the Mystery of Americana Music*
by Timothy Gray

*American Unexceptionalism: The Everyman and the
Suburban Novel after 9/11*
by Kathy Knapp

*Visible Dissent: Latin American Writers, Small U.S. Presses,
and Progressive Social Change*
by Teresa V. Longo

Pynchon's California
edited by Scott McClintock and John Miller

Richard Ford and the Ends of Realism
by Ian McGuire

Reading Capitalist Realism
edited by Alison Shonkwiler and Leigh Claire La Berge

*How to Revise a True War Story: Tim O'Brien's Process
of Textual Production*
by John K. Young